W9-BVJ-610

THE NAZI
TITANIC

THE NAZI
TITANIC

The Incredible Untold Story
of a Doomed Ship in World War II

Robert P. Watson

Da Capo Press
A Member of the Perseus Books Group

Copyright © 2016 by Robert P. Watson

All rights reserved. No part of this publication may be reproduced, stored in a
retrieval system, or transmitted, in any form or by any means, electronic, mechanical,
photocopying, recording, or otherwise, without the prior written permission of the
publisher. Printed in the United States of America. For information, address
Da Capo Press, 44 Farnsworth Street, 3rd Floor, Boston, MA 02210.

Designed by Janelle Fine
Set in 11 point Palatino LT Std by The Perseus Books Group

Cataloging-in-Publication data for this book is available from the Library of Congress.
First Da Capo Press edition 2016
ISBN: 978-0-306-82489-0 (hardcover)
ISBN: 978-0-306-82490-6 (e-book)

Published by Da Capo Press
A Member of the Perseus Books Group
www.dacapopress.com

Da Capo Press books are available at special discounts for bulk purchases in the U.S.
by corporations, institutions, and other organizations. For more information, please
contact the Special Markets Department at the Perseus Books Group, 2300 Chestnut
Street, Suite 200, Philadelphia, PA 19103, or call (800) 810-4145, ext. 5000, or e-mail
special.markets@perseusbooks.com.

10 9 8 7 6 5 4 3 2 1

Dedicated to all of those
aboard the Cap Arcona *that fateful day*

CONTENTS

PREFACE

THIS WAS, IN MANY WAYS, the most difficult book I have ever written. At the same time, it was also the most rewarding. I don't believe I have ever read a story that I have found, simultaneously, as irresistible and intriguing yet as deeply disturbing and emotional as this one. While the process of researching history can be tedious at times, the excitement of uncovering stories of interesting people and important events more than makes up for the hours spent in the endeavor. This is true even if there is not a happy ending, which is, sadly, too often the case.

This book would not have been possible without the support and assistance of others. Judith Alsdorf and Jared Wellman, librarians at Lynn University, assisted me in tracking down some hard-to-find articles, books, and documents. Carsten Jordan, head of corporate communications for Hamburg-Süd in Germany, provided me access to old documents from the time the company operated the *Cap Arcona*. Kerst Lehmann, Selina Keipert, and Stefan Wolf translated several documents written in German. George Goldstein, MD, was helpful in watching and listening to numerous oral history interviews with survivors of the *Cap Arcona*. Nancy Katz offered many constructive ideas on the original draft of the book. Also, my friends Steve and Judy West, Joan and Morrie Berger, Judy Hyman, Dan Isaacson, Arnie Mallot, Ed and Harriet Sol, Bob Terpstra, and

Mike and Audrey Dann were wonderful sounding boards as I put together ideas for the book.

The world is fortunate to have several remarkable repositories of information and documentation on the Holocaust and World War II. In no particular order, I acknowledge a few of the many individuals and organizations who helped with my research requests. Thanks to Simon Offord, Geoff Spender, Suzanne Bardgett, and Ian Carter of the Imperial War Museum in London; Megan Lewis, Jane Miller, Judith Cohen, and Peter Black of the United States Holocaust Memorial Museum; Lindsay Zarwell at the Steven Spielberg Film and Video Archive; Silva Sevlian and Danielle Gomez of the University of Southern California Shoah Foundation; Stephen D. Smith, executive director of the USC Shoah Foundation and UNESCO chair on genocide education; Yedida Kanfer at the Jewish Family and Children's Services Holocaust Center and Tauber Holocaust Library in San Francisco; Irena Steinfeld at Yad Vashem in Israel; and Stephen Tyas and Roger Nixon for sending me materials that saved me from a flight to London.

I owe a very special acknowledgment to a few other individuals who made many contributions to the book. I would like to recognize my literary agent, Laney Katz Becker with Lippincott Massie McQuilkin, and thank her for demonstrating complete confidence in my manuscript and providing me with invaluable advice and guidance throughout the process. I was also very fortunate to have Robert Pigeon of Da Capo Press as my editor. The opportunity to work with such an accomplished editor and knowledgeable and passionate historian was both a delight and an honor. Thanks also to Amber Morris, Annette Wenda, Justin Lovell, Sean Maher, Lissa Warren, Kevin Hanover, and the entire team at Da Capo Press and the Perseus Books Group for all the help in editing and marketing the book. A special thanks to my friend Deborah Oppenheimer and the entire Oppenheimer family. Debbie's remarkable documentary about the Kindertransport titled *Into the Arms of Strangers* won the Academy Award in 2001, and both Debbie and her film greatly inspired me. She also offered countless ideas on how to tell this story and generously passed along to me some important research contacts, all of whom proved most valuable.

To my wife Claudia for her support and invaluable assistance with this project. To my children Alessandro and Isabella for always being my inspiration.

The task of writing about this ill-fated ship and horrific event also reminded me of the importance of routinely dusting off the lessons of history and war and sharing them with each generation, lest they be forgotten and the mistakes and tragedies of the past be repeated. Oh, that we may finally learn from them! It is my hope that this book helps to shine light on this shocking series of events and serves as a testament to the survivors and victims of that terrible day. I dedicate the book to their memory.

ROBERT P. WATSON
Boca Raton, Florida

Introduction

HISTORY'S SECRETS

THE STORY OF THE *Cap Arcona* found me, not the other way around. The original plan was to write a book on the final week of World War II in Europe, from Adolf Hitler's suicide in his bunker on April 30, 1945, to Victory in Europe (VE) Day roughly one week later. By all accounts, these final days of the war and the Holocaust were marked by a complicated mix of heroism and relief as well as by tragedy and absolute chaos. This seemed to be a worthy topic for a book.

Nevertheless, upon discovering that the British government had sealed some of the war records from that final week of fighting, my interest was piqued. Subsequently, I stumbled upon the shocking details that constitute the end of the story you are about to read. It was a story I had never heard and one I could not resist. Needless to say, I never wrote the "other" book.

This is often how the process of historical discovery works. The stories of history often remain hidden for many years, as the process of historical discovery sometimes works in strange and frustratingly slow ways. Indeed, there is more we do not know than we do know about the past. Most of what happened in the past was never recorded, and the vast majority of documents, letters, and books that were produced at a particular time are lost to us today, whether by fire, decomposition, neglect, or intentional destruction. Apropos to the story in this book, it must be remembered that, while many survivors of the Holocaust sat down in subsequent years to record their stories, at least six million voices will never be heard. The same can be said for the sixty to seventy-five million people lost in World War II.

Yet World War II and the Holocaust were, respectively, history's bloodiest war and most costly example of genocide. As a result, many scholars have devoted their careers to telling these stories, as have the concentration camp survivors and other survivors and combat veterans who shared their painful memories with the next generation through published memoirs, candid talks with loved ones over the dinner table, and taped oral history interviews. The countless injustices of those two momentous events are among the most comprehensively studied and documented of any crisis or war in human history. It is thus tempting to think that we know everything there is to know about them. But this is not the case. Even events as thoroughly documented as these still have their secrets.

The story of the celebrated but ill-fated ship *Cap Arcona* has rarely been told. It does not appear in textbooks and has all but been ignored by journalists, scholars, and the news media. Even Hollywood, which has made many movies about World War II and a few memorable films on the Holocaust, has yet to feature the events surrounding this ship on the big screen.

Likewise, numerous museums, memorials, and other appropriate commemorations of these events exist around the world. Therefore, one would think such would be the case for the *Cap Arcona*, that the ship would be commemorated by grand memorials, statues, musical ballads, and theatrical performances. Yet this is not the case. The events surrounding the *Cap Arcona*'s remarkable saga have yet to be staged in a dramatic production, nor have they inspired touching lyrics or a somber musical score. Rather, the most intriguing and infamous ship in history is remembered through only a handful of obscure studies published in Germany several years ago, a couple of short documentaries, memoirs by two of the lucky few who lived through the ordeal to tell the tale, and a handful of other forgotten sources.

Today, just a single understated marker, hidden among the seaside hotels and fishermen's homes of Germany's Baltic coast, can be found at the site of the disaster. Only one small museum located nearby in Neustadt and opened in the year 1990 tells the story to the smattering of tourists who, from time to time, walk through its doors. Such are the lonely testaments to an extraordinary ship.

Every passing year brings with it fewer eyewitnesses to, and survivors of, the incident in question. Dwindling numbers of survivors and their family members gather on the anniversary of the tragedy to remember those lost. Even those living today near the site of the event along Germany's northern shoreline know little about the ghastly attack that killed thousands and are surprised to find that anyone else knows about their community's secret and dark past.

Case in point: A few years ago at one of the memorial services held at the site of the disaster, a reporter in attendance was approached by a resident of the nearby town. The local man was surprised that anyone would come to such an inconspicuous gathering, so he asked the reporter, "So your family is German?" When the reporter responded in the negative, the townsman questioned him further: "Oh, then you are Jewish?" The reply was again no. Finally, in a puzzled tone, the local resident wondered, "How could you possibly know about this?"

SHIPWRECKS AND MARITIME DISASTERS have always held a curious and dark place in human memory. They evoke an array of emotions and morbid fascination, perhaps all the while reminding us of our limited power over the sea. For some, they temper our natural drive to explore; for others, they entice our appetite for discovery and adventure. Yet few, if any, ordeals at sea are as tragic and shocking as that of the *Cap Arcona*. Even though the *Cap Arcona* has all but been forgotten, the German ocean liner was quite possibly the most intriguing ship ever to set sail.

There is another reason the story of the *Cap Arcona* remains enigmatic. At the conclusion of World War II, the British government sealed many documents pertaining to the ship. They were to be sealed until the year 2045—a full century after the end of the conflict, leading the late Benjamin Jacobs, one of the few people to have survived the ship's final voyage, to dub the incident "the 100-year secret."

What follows is one of the least well-known sagas of the Third Reich's terrifying reign. It is an adventure that starts with the ambitions of a German shipping company.

Opening Act

GERMANY'S *TITANIC*

Chapter 1

A BOLD IDEA

THE GERMANS LOVED THEIR SHIPS. And for good reason. Throughout the closing years of the nineteenth century and the opening of the twentieth, German shipyards produced some of the finest vessels afloat. They were a source of great national pride. So too was Germany's shipping industry a powerful engine driving the country's economy. However, all that changed with the outbreak of World War I on July 28, 1914. Merchant, luxury, and cargo ships were mothballed, scavenged for parts, or conscripted for wartime use. Others were sunk by enemy fire, irrespective of whether they were sailing under a military or commercial flag.

The total defeat of Germany at the end of World War I in 1918 plunged the country's economy into deep depression. Currency was not worth the paper on which it was printed, and severe food shortages plagued communities from Berlin to Bavaria to the Black Forest. The nation also mourned roughly seven million killed, wounded, missing in action, or taken prisoner. These hardships were made all the more bitter for the vanquished by the terms dictated by the victors at the Treaty of Versailles in France, which required the belligerent nation to demilitarize, deindustrialize, and pay steep reparations.

One of the industries particularly hard hit by the war and post-war agreements was shipping. During the four-year war, Germany's shipbuilders saw orders for new ships and payments on existing work orders subordinated to the war effort. After the war, orders for new ships and shipping services remained virtually nonexistent, despite the fact that Germany had lost many ships during the conflict. Those German ships that survived the war were seized by the Allies as war reparations and to replenish their own losses. The prospects for any German shipping company in 1918 were, at best, bleak.

One of Germany's most successful shipping companies prior to the war was the Hamburg–South America Steamship Company, popularly known as Hamburg-Süd. Founded on November 4, 1871, the company served the growing market of Germans eager to travel to South America. In the prewar years, the company provided regular monthly service to Argentina and Brazil.

The company did more than simply sail to the Southern Hemisphere. In the decades that followed its establishment, Hamburg-Süd emerged as a leader in the South American trade and transport business, with three ships sailing to South America. At the outbreak of the conflict in 1914, the company was operating more than fifty ships, constituting roughly 325,000 gross registered tons (GRT), and was a major force in international shipping. With the onset of "the war to end all wars," however, everything changed. Hamburg-Süd's fleet immediately came under attack in response to Germany's aggression in Europe.

One of Hamburg-Süd's finest ships, the *Cap Trafalgar*, was launched on March 1, 1914, and sailed on its maiden voyage just days later, on March 10. It was an impressive vessel. At more than six hundred feet in length, the 18,710-GRT behemoth was capable of seventeen knots and was adorned with what was then state-of-the-art technology and amenities. But none of that mattered when hostilities commenced in July of that same year.

In response to the declaration of war, the government of Kaiser Wilhelm II and Hamburg-Süd armed ships such as the *Cap Trafalgar*.

However, its armaments were light, consisting of only two small cannons and six machine guns. In an effort to further ensure its safe passage, one of the ship's funnels was removed, and it was repainted to disguise it as a British liner. It did not work.

In September 1914, while steaming a few hundred miles off the Brazilian coast, the ship was caught by the British ocean liner *Carmania*. Like so many other merchant and passenger ships, the *Carmania* had been converted for war and was being used to hunt German merchant ships and smaller vessels. Far from home and badly in need of resupply, the *Cap Trafalgar* was heading to the island of Trindade. Portuguese for "Trinity," the small archipelago of volcanic islands off the Brazilian coast was secretly being used by Germany as an emergency supply base. At roughly nine thirty in the morning of September 14, the *Carmania* spotted its foe's smoke and began pursuing the *Cap Trafalgar*, ultimately trapping the German ship against the island's anchorage.

The *Carmania* was much more heavily armed. As such, the commander of the *Cap Trafalgar* attempted to flee to deeper waters rather than fight. Orders were given for "full speed ahead," and the German liner attempted to outrun the British vessel. It nearly worked.

The *Carmania* gave chase and closed the distance. A ninety-minute battle ensued, with both ships exchanging a nonstop barrage of cannon and machine-gun fire. The *Carmania* was the first to fire, but the shots fell short of the target. The *Cap Trafalgar* returned fire, and its cannons proved accurate. The German ship landed devastating hits on the British liner, blowing apart sections of the deck. Even though it was outgunned, the *Cap Trafalgar* initially had the upper hand in the battle.

Both ships continued firing and ultimately closed the distance to within a few dozen yards. The *Carmania* was absorbing blow after blow from roughly seventy direct cannon hits. Even though machine-gun fire pinned down the crew, they managed to fire back and scored a direct hit on the *Cap Trafalgar*. The shot struck the German liner below the water line, and the large ship began taking on water. When it was apparent the ship could not be saved, the captain lowered lifeboats, and the crew abandoned ship. After listing to the port, the *Cap Trafalgar* sank bow first. It was the first armed passenger liner of the war to be sunk by another armed liner.

The crew was lucky. The German ship *Kronprinz Wilhelm* was nearby and had picked up the *Cap Trafalgar*'s distress call. After rescuing those sailors who made it into the lifeboats, the *Wilhelm* quickly steamed from the scene. Its commander chose not to linger, worried his ship would also be vulnerable to attack from the *Carmania* or other British warships that might be prowling the waters. He need not have worried. The *Carmania*, although still afloat, was badly damaged and in no condition for battle.

It is estimated that a few dozen sailors were killed on the *Cap Trafalgar*, while the *Carmania* suffered nine killed in the battle. The loss of the *Cap Trafalgar* was one of the first of many devastating setbacks of the war for both the German navy and Hamburg-Süd. Indeed, the company would lose its entire merchant and luxury fleets to military conscription or sinking. Its continuity as a leading shipping company was less the question than whether Hamburg-Süd would even exist in the postwar years.

With grim prospects for any recovery from the war, Hamburg-Süd's directors met in 1920 to discuss the fate of the company. What emerged from the meeting was no less than audacious, if not completely unrealistic. Rather than discontinue operations or pursue a path of austerity to ensure the company's survival, the directors developed an ambitious plan to completely rebuild their line of ships.

Given the weak German economy and limited market for new ship construction, Hamburg-Süd soldiered on with just three small schooners. To supplement its meager fleet, the company creatively chartered ships from other companies in order to continue serving its customers, making it one of the few shipping lines to continue service in those difficult years.

Hamburg-Süd thus managed to keep afloat as a company and gain the confidence and loyalty of merchants eager to fill the postwar gap in trade. Aggressive and well managed, Hamburg-Süd was also one of the few large companies in all of Germany to prosper in the devastated postwar order.*

Despite competition from the Norddeutscher Lloyd Company, which operated in the North Atlantic, Hamburg-Süd continued to prosper and drive Germany's postwar recovery. It even managed to launch a new steamer as early as 1920, the 5,745-ton *Argentina*, which crossed the ocean at ten knots. By 1926 the company had done the unthinkable, surpassing its prewar numbers and enjoying record profits.

It was around this time that the company's directors promoted a bold plan to build one of the grandest vessels on the seas, one inspired by the most legendary ship in history, the *Titanic*. It would be the flagship of the Hamburg-Süd line and the gem of German shipping.

For the task of producing such a large and technologically sophisticated ship, Hamburg-Süd selected the Hamburg-based shipbuilder Blohm + Voss. Not only were the Germans some of the best shipbuilders in all the world, but Blohm + Voss was one of the oldest and most respected builders in Germany. It was a wise decision.

Founded on April 5, 1877, by Hermann Blohm and Ernst Voss, the company's main shipyard was on the island of Kuhwerder, near Hamburg. Known for its quality ship construction and attention to detail, the company's shipbuilders had even studied the *Titanic*'s sinking in order to engineer safer ships. For instance, when they launched the massive 34,500-ton *Fatherland* on April 3, 1913, one year after the sinking of the *Titanic*, they outfitted the then pride of Germany with eighty-four lifeboats. The *Titanic* had only twenty.

Despite the devastation of World War I, by the 1920s the company's manufacturing site on Kuhwerder boasted three massive waterfront construction berths, two of them capable of working on ships more

---

* Two and a half decades later, the company survived World War II. Afterward, Hamburg-Süd again retooled and expanded its portfolio of services to include tanker shipping and refrigerated cargo shipping to go along with its liner and passenger services. In more recent times, the company acquired several other shipping lines and extended its reach to serve North America, the Mediterranean, and the South Pacific. Today, the company continues to grow as part of the Oetker Group, a major shipping firm, and still operates out of Germany.

than three hundred feet in length. Blohm + Voss was so successful that it employed a whopping sixteen thousand workers during the 1920s and, in later years, managed to build some of Germany's most legendary ships, such as the *Bismarck* and the dreaded U-boats that inflicted such a terrible toll on Allied shipping during World War II. The company also built the ocean liner RMS *Majestic*, which was for a time the largest ship in the world and owned by the White Star Line, the parent company of the *Titanic*, and the MV *Wilhelm Gustloff*, a ship that would end up holding the dubious distinction of being the world's worst maritime disaster, with roughly nine thousand lives lost to a Russian torpedo in the final days of World War II.

The Third Reich's official yacht, the *Grille*, built in 1935 and used as Hitler's personal maritime conveyance, was another one of Blohm + Voss's ships, and the company provided ships for Germany's "Strength Through Joy" program. This Nazi initiative offered cruises for German workers as part of Hitler's propaganda efforts. In the 1930s, it even became the largest tourism operator in the world. Even though Blohm + Voss survived both world wars, the same cannot be said of its image, which was tarnished by its association with the Nazis. In 1944 and 1945, the company had its own labor camp and used inmates from that camp to work at a shipyard in Hamburg-Steinwerder. The camp was a subcamp of the infamous concentration camp at Neuengamme, which later figures prominently in the story of the *Cap Arcona* and this book.

The company managed to recover from complete destruction after both the wars and from its association with the Nazis. After the war it continued building some of the world's largest ships, yachts, and airplanes. But perhaps none of its products has been as celebrated as the *Cap Arcona*.*

---

* Blohm + Voss continues today to build warships for the German navy and for export to navies around the world. It has also diversified beyond ship and warplane construction by entering the merchant and luxury craft markets and is now a leading manufacturer of oil drilling equipment. Blohm + Voss retains its preeminent status as an international shipbuilder, manufacturing some of the largest and most luxurious yachts in the world.

Chapter 2

THE QUEEN OF THE ATLANTIC

THE GRAND SHIP WAS christened on May 14, 1927. In a simpler time, the launch of an ocean liner was a public spectacle. Company executives, shipyard workers, prospective passengers, newspaper reporters, and curious onlookers alike came for a glimpse of a hulking ship and to daydream about the far-off, exotic ports it would soon visit. A crowd had gathered to witness the event at the Blohm + Voss shipyards. Excitement was in the air. Germany had had little to celebrate in the past several years.

Before the *Cap Arcona* slid down a ramp into Hamburg Harbor at the entrance to the river Elbe, a bottle of champagne wielded by Beatrix von Amsinck christened the sturdy hull. From an elevated platform, von Amsinck, daughter of the head of the Hamburg-Süd line, spoke of the ship quite poetically, saying: "Out of the waves of the Baltic in the north of the lovely island of Rügen, there rise steep cliffs, crowned by a lighthouse . . . which beams its light out over the sea every night. . . . The name of these cliffs, the only cape which graces Germany's coast—Cape Arkona—will, from now on, be your name. May you sail the seas, to the honor of our dear German fatherland and to the joy of your company, and be a further bond between the new world and the old."

As the largest and most luxurious ship traveling to South America, the *Cap Arcona* earned the nickname the "Queen of the South Atlantic." Others referred to her as the "Pearl of the Atlantic," the "Flower of the Atlantic," and even the "Floating Palace." That it was! It was the latest and the most advanced of the Cap line of passenger ships built by Blohm + Voss for Hamburg-Süd, which included the *Cap Vilano* built in 1906, *Cap Finisterre* built in 1911, *Cap Trafalgar* built in 1913, and the *Cap Polonio* built in 1914.

On October 29, 1927, construction on the *Cap Arcona*, which had begun on July 21, 1926, was completed. Three consecutive days of sea trials were conducted beginning the day prior to the ship's completion. They proved successful. It was a truly remarkable ship. Ever since the christening of the ship, the final preparations were followed closely by German officials and ship enthusiasts worldwide. Indeed, anticipation mounted as Germany's answer to the *Titanic* prepared for its maiden voyage. On November 19, that day finally arrived.

On that bright, crisp autumn day, wealthy passengers and curious onlookers gathered on the docks of Hamburg to witness the newest ocean liner in the German fleet. With three massive smokestacks towering fifty feet above nine shining decks, the *Cap Arcona* sat majestically in port, awaiting its first sailing. The fresh red paint of the funnels glistened in the morning sun, contrasting with the stark black and white exterior of the ship's slender hull, creating a memorable effect for those in attendance to witness the maiden voyage.

The commotion on the docks included workers carrying casks of fresh caviar to the ship's kitchen and vintage bottles of wine for the extensive wine cellar. On board, teams of engineers in the bowels of the ship and stewards scurrying about the hallways prepared to take 1,325 affluent travelers to South America. The *Cap Arcona*'s passengers were all treated to the finest accommodations afloat. Fully 575 of them traveled in first-class suites, 275 traveled in second-class cabins, while the remaining 475 were housed in dormitories. Those traveling among the latter group dined separately from their privileged peers and were not permitted at the musical performances.

First-class travelers benefited from additional exclusive services, personal butlers, and some of the largest staterooms afloat. These spacious accommodations included sitting rooms, sofas, armchairs upholstered in silk, and restrooms with a full bath. Not surprisingly, the ship's passengers included the crème de la crème from Germany and Europe as well as moneyed families from Buenos Aires and Rio de Janeiro. The dashing American actor Clark Gable sailed in one of the ship's first-class suites and noted Hamburg poet Hans Leip, who wrote "Lili Marlene" during World War I, honeymooned on the liner. Leip even dedicated the poem "Honeymoon in the Sea" to the ship while on board the liner. One wealthy patron from Argentina booked two first-class suites for her fourteen dogs, while a prominent family from Brazil paid to have cows and chickens stowed in the ship's hold so that their children would be assured fresh milk and eggs every morning.

The ship's logs* from South American cruises in the 1930s indicate that most of the affluent passengers came from Germany, England, Brazil, and Argentina, but the *Cap Arcona* attracted guests from numerous other countries as well. The passenger manifests, which listed passengers by the class cabin in which they were traveling, also show that several female guests traveled alone and that passengers both boarded and exited the cruise from several ports of call such as Vigo, Lisbon, Madeira, and Montevideo, not just Buenos Aires and Hamburg. Elegant multipage programs and itineraries were given to guests, featuring photographs of the ports of call, distances to each port, fares, disembarkation information, listings of the ship's agents in each port, the names of all the ship's officers, menus, and lists of the passengers traveling on the voyage by class and section of the ship.

Sailing from its home port of Hamburg, the impressive new liner presented a new standard of luxury and engineering for the shipping world. A marvel of technological progress, the *Cap Arcona*

---

* The logbooks and itineraries for the passengers still exist and are in the archives at Hamburg-Süd in Germany.

was not only the largest ship transporting passengers to South America, but also one of the world's fastest liners. The shipbuilders had managed to fit it with the most advanced propulsion system of the time. Two steam turbines generated an astonishing 24,000 horsepower, allowing the twin propellers to push the massive luxury liner across the Atlantic Ocean at twenty knots, a speed nearly unequaled at the time. It raced from Hamburg to Buenos Aires in a mere fifteen days.

The fourth largest ship in the German merchant fleet, the *Cap Arcona* measured roughly 676 feet in length and 189 feet from its keel to the topside flags. Its specs included a beam of nearly 85 feet with a draught of 50 feet. It displaced 27,561 tons and was crewed by 475 handpicked sailors, chefs, concierges, and other service professionals. As a result, the luxury liner ended up costing a staggering thirty-five billion reichsmarks. In short, it was a ship worthy of the adulation.

Hamburg-Süd selected the best officers for the new flagship. The *Cap Arcona* was commanded by Commodore Ernst Rolin, an experienced captain who had previously served as master of the *Cap Polonio*; his chief officer was Richard Niejahr, who was being groomed for higher command. In addition to the experienced crew, masseurs, physicians, and chaplains were on hand to further serve the guests. The *Cap Arcona* even had its own postmark and a seaplane that brought regular mail service to the ship regardless of its location on the planet. First-class passengers were told that their every request would be fulfilled, no matter how fantastic.

The ship's top three decks boasted an assortment of recreational amenities, including regulation-size tennis and shuffleboard courts, an indoor heated pool, chaise longues, spacious decks book-ended by large potted palms, and a walking track stretching one fifth of a mile along the Promenade Deck. Passengers enjoyed everything from leisurely games and gambling to an expansive collection of art that adorned the ship's elegantly decorated corridors and lobbies. After a day of swimming, sunning, and fun, guests relaxed at the Winter Garden Club, perhaps the ship's most popular drinking establishment, and reveled in the individualized attention that came from a ratio of two crew members to every first-class passenger. The daily pampering also included British high tea with an assortment of cakes and beverages, three elegant fireplaces, jazz music performed at the Palm Court, and performances of Mozart, Strauss, and other great composers by the ship's orchestra. Because of the popularity of Argentina as a destination and the growing number of Argentines traveling on the ship, the *Cap Arcona* also offered tango music and dancing. Famous Argentinean band leader and pianist Enrique Lomuto performed on board the ship and served as its musical director.

One of the highlights of sailing on the *Cap Arcona* was the food. The ship was known for epicurean dinners in the Grand Salon, an elegant parlor capable of seating 436 guests at one time. For many years, executive chef Sibilius and assistant chef Nowak prepared the finest meals afloat. A transatlantic crossing in 1937 featured a multiple-course dinner menu with chateaubriand and Bernhardt potatoes, shish kebabs garnished with herbs and spices, fresh fish, veal, grilled hens, Irish bird soup, salad, and California pears in syrup. The dessert selection included ice cream with a fruity, nutty nougat; pastries; Carmen cakes; and jelly Miss Helyett.*

A Christmas menu from a holiday cruise in 1933 offered an array of options, including three soups (double-broth soup, broth with Caracu, and Irish bird soup) and several courses. Passengers selected from silverside fish fried à la Romana; veal with truffle sauce, hearts of palm, and royal potatoes; pork ribs; lamb chops with goose liver, celery, and spiral potatoes; and grilled hens. They also enjoyed cauliflower, ham croquets, pasta Palmir, a salad with yellow beans, and a cold buffet selection that included boned chicken in jelly Nancy and pickled quail with capers and onions.

Before any dinner seating, guests enjoyed drinks, hors d'oeuvres, and entertainment in the Jockey Club and afterward relaxed with fruits and coffees in either the Grand Hall, Ballroom, Smoking Room, or Winter Garden Club. Champagne and iced Beluga caviar were available for every meal and occasion, and the ship celebrated

---

* The jelly dessert was named for an operetta in 1890.

the passengers' last night aboard with a grand farewell banquet in the main Banquet Hall.

The transatlantic voyages, with their many ports of call, typically lasted five weeks.* In addition to the ship's South American itineraries, the *Cap Arcona* also sailed to such ports of call as Casablanca, Russia, Santos, and Hafen, an island off northern Germany. One voyage, departing on July 4, 1935, from Hamburg to Buenos Aires, traveled to Boulogne-sur-Mer in northern France, Southampton, La Coruña, Vigo, Lisbon, Madeira, and then to South America, with stops in Rio de Janeiro and Montevideo, Uruguay.

These cities excitedly announced each arrival and departure of the famous ship. For instance, in 1934 when the *Cap Arcona* visited Puerto Vigo in Galicia, Spain, one of the largest fishing ports and busiest shipping centers in the world, newspapers and public bulletins eagerly documented the occasion. Boasted one account: "It just left to Lisbon. This is the first trip of the German ship *Cap Arcona!*" Reporters even announced the ocean liner's speed and tonnage.

THE *CAP ARCONA* departed from Hamburg on its maiden voyage at the scheduled time on November 19, 1927. Amid the popping champagne corks and stringed instruments on the upper decks, passengers waved enthusiastically to the crowds below on the docks. This would be but the first of the ship's ninety-one transatlantic crossings, traveling from 1927 to 1939 from Germany to Buenos Aires, La Plata, Montevideo, and Rio de Janeiro.

Hamburg-Süd bet its future on the ship and the continued passion among Germans for the balmy weather of South America. Indeed, the *Cap Arcona* appeared destined for greatness. It seemed a safe bet. And for a time it was, until an urgent message arrived.

---

* For example, the ship's logbooks show trips from September 1 to October 10, 1933; October 20 to November 24, 1933; and April 3 to May 12, 1938.

Chapter 3

AN URGENT MESSAGE

THE MAIDEN VOYAGE WAS a roaring success, garnering for the ship instant notoriety as one of the world's premier ocean liners. The *Cap Arcona* soon appeared on postcards and in magazine stories throughout Europe. It was, after all, a romantic period for cruising, a time when the captains of luxury ships were household names in Germany and such magnificent vessels were celebrated around the world.

However, by the 1930s the *Cap Arcona* and its sister liners also emerged in Germany as prominent symbols of a new and dangerous form of ultranationalism. One of the many admirers of these grand ships was a former corporal from World War I and radical politician named Adolf Hitler. And he had big plans for the celebrated ocean liner.

German emigration and tourism to South America peaked in 1929. Although the alarming rise of National Socialism in the country and increasingly disturbing news coming out of Germany deterred some Europeans from cruising out of German ports or on German ships, a vigorous travel and trade business continued somewhat unabated during the initial years of Hitler's reign, which began in January 1933.

Within Germany the *Cap Arcona*'s popularity grew. While other industries were increasingly brought under state control, the führer allowed the *Cap Arcona* and other luxury liners to operate freely, as they had done before the Nazis swept into power. For example, because of Hitler's passion for these huge ships, their captains and owners were not required to "sign off" with the Nazi high command regarding the details of their voyages, nor were they prohibited from visiting ports around the world or booking non-Germans in first-class cabins. On the contrary, Hitler held these liners up as symbols of German power.

Just about the only change occurring with the operation of the *Cap Arcona* when Hitler assumed power was that the well-respected commodore of the ship, Ernst Rolin, resigned his command. Rolin had been sailing with Hamburg-Süd for forty-three years. On October 20, 1933, Richard Niejahr, the first officer who had been with the company since 1910, assumed command of Hamburg-Süd's flagship. He would be promoted to commodore in 1937. Heinrich Bertram, who would soon figure prominently in the tragic story of the *Cap Arcona*, was promoted to Niejahr's second in command.

By 1936 reports around the world began surfacing of the growing fanaticism inside Hitler's regime. News of the shocking details of the Nuremberg Laws that disenfranchised Jews, combined with negative publicity generated by the ominous display of ultranationalism during the Berlin Olympics, deterred prospective passengers from around the world. Bookings on the *Cap Arcona* declined precipitously by year's end. The Nazi regime compounded their own problems by placing prohibitions on their citizens' ability to travel outside of Germany. Nazi ideology also began discouraging such "frivolities" as vacations, instead maintaining that Germans should be hard at work for the fatherland.

One exception to these new Nazi policies was the "leisure vacation" for German workers. German industrialists were therefore encouraged to both reward productive workers and celebrate nationalism by sending their most loyal laborers on Nazi cruises. Led by Dr. Robert Ley, a Nazi politician and head of the German Labor Front, ships were rented for the purpose of accommodating workers on vacations to Norway and the Baltic, Italy, Madeira, and

Yugoslavia. The Nazi regime, through its Strength Through Joy initiative, subsidized these affordable vacations while subtly indoctrinating workers on the cruises. The problem for companies like Hamburg-Süd was that these leisure vacations competed with the South American cruise business. Ships were diverted from their previous, vastly more profitable, routes to accommodate German laborers.

Nevertheless, at the start of 1939, Hamburg-Süd was, despite the competition from Nazi Party leisure vacation bookings, still operating fifty-two ships with a total capacity in excess of 385,000 tons. Impressively, 57,859 passengers had traveled aboard the *Cap Arcona* across the South Atlantic, helping to position the company as one of the world's leading cruise and shipping lines. However, all that was about to change.

As summer approached in 1939, emotions ran high on the *Cap Arcona*. Commodore Richard Niejahr had taken ill with a serious bout of typhus, business had slowed, and rumors swirled among sailors and shipping executives alike that German liners and commercial ships were being reassigned to the German navy. However, good news arrived to temporarily lift the spirits of the *Cap Arcona*'s crew. Commodore Niejahr returned that summer from a leave of absence to inform his crew that the ship had been assigned a new cruise—its ninety-second—and that Hamburg-Süd planned to build a sister ship to the *Cap Arcona*. The announcement from the ship's parent company came on August 21, a mere ten days before the start of World War II. The ship embarked on its scheduled cruise, but that ninety-second excursion would never occur.

The appearance of business as usual only temporarily cloaked the reality of the coming war. Of the ship's many passengers traveling to Argentina, Uruguay, and Brazil on that round-trip voyage, only two of them had booked their cruise all the way back to Hamburg. The rest were disembarking in France prior to the ship's return to Germany. It was clear to the captain and crew that the public no longer viewed Germany as a safe or desirable place. Sure enough, the voyage would be the *Cap Arcona*'s last as a passenger ship.

After disembarking most of the passengers, the *Cap Arcona* sailed from France en route to Hamburg. On the evening of August 24, Commodore Niejahr turned command of the massive liner over to a junior officer and retired to his cabin to sleep. But in the wee hours of the morning, the worst fears of the captain and crew were realized. As the ship was approaching Hamburg, a radio message marked "urgent" was delivered to the captain.

Commodore Niejahr called a meeting of his senior officers. Those present were the first and second officers, the ship's physician, head engineer and second engineer, steward, chef, and purser/paymaster. The officers likely suspected the worst. In compliance with the order, Commodore Niejahr removed from the ship's safe an envelope. Grimly, he informed the crew that the envelope was marked "Special Orders for the Event of War for Cargo Vessels."

Over the next few days, a series of radio messages arrived. Message QWA 7, on August 25, ordered "No transmission to all stations" and that all ships must "deviate from scheduled routes by 30–100 nautical miles as security precaution." Message QWA 8 ordered all ships to camouflage their hulls and avoid sailing through the English Channel. On August 27, message QWA 9 required them to return to their home harbor within four days. The *Cap Arcona* raced to Hamburg. Ships were to avoid the ports of several countries, one of which was the United States, which was permitted to be entered "only in cases of extreme necessity."

Over the next several days, Commodore Niejahr received three more of the urgent QWA messages. They notified the officers of the outbreak of war with France and England; advised ships to return to Germany by Norway and Shetland, preferably at night and without using lights; and established the protocol for going to war. Niejahr announced to his men that he would pray.

When the ocean liner returned to its home port, noticeably absent were the usual fanfare and cheering crowds gathered at the docks. Very few people were visible anywhere near the harbor to greet the returning ship. Nazi officials ordered the crew and two passengers off the ship. Commodore Niejahr's protestations of "What will happen to my ship now if we have war?" were met with stony silence. Despite his earlier hopes and prayers, his beloved ship was ordered to be placed under the command of the German navy, the Kriegsmarine.

ONE OF THE MANY affectionate nicknames that emerged for the *Cap Arcona* during the 1920s and 1930s was, ironically, the "Lucky Lady." However, the ship's fate, along with the course of world history, changed on September 1, 1939, when Hitler's army marched into Poland.

In a coordinated lightning strike by land and air, tanks, artillery pieces, and warplanes stormed across the border. The Polish army, which attempted to fight German tanks with men on horseback, was crushed in a matter of days. The formal surrender came on September 27, marking the first domino to fall in the führer's mad game of global domination.

Nearly every German vessel afloat was officially reassigned in 1939 to the Kriegsmarine as a naval accommodation ship. The *Cap Arcona* was placed in the service of the Nazis' "Fortress Command" and sent to the occupied Baltic port of Gotenhafen, site of present-day Gdynia on the northern Polish coast, near Danzig. The port city had been taken by the Nazis in 1939 and was now a bustling naval base. Military operations at Gotenhafen flourished during the first few years of the war when the base was largely spared from Allied bombing. As a result, a number of warships and other converted accommodation or "help" ships soon joined the *Cap Arcona* in port. Hamburg-Süd was ordered to close the file on its highly profitable flagship.

In 1941 control of the former luxury liner was again transferred, this time to the Nazi "Coastal Control Office for the Mid-Baltic." Nearly all its officers and crew were ordered off the ship. Commodore Niejahr experienced additional health problems and took another leave of absence. He briefly returned to "command" the rusting hulk moored on the Polish coast on February 11, 1942, but died of his malady on April 4. That September an interim captain was appointed to the ship. However, he was "voted off the ship" exactly one year later by the officers of the naval base. The first officer took command of the *Cap Arcona* for the remainder of the month. In October 1943, a new captain finally assumed command. His name was Johannes Gerdts, and he would preside over one of the most tragic periods in the ship's remaining history.

The once-proud ocean liner would spend most of the war—from November 29, 1939, until January 31, 1945—in port, docked at Gdynia quay. Its new role: a floating barracks for naval personnel and an ad hoc training platform for naval exercises. It was quite a demotion for the pride of Germany. Its dining rooms now functioned as a mess for sailors in uniform. Many of its luxurious furnishings were stripped from the ship, and the "Queen of the South Atlantic" was painted military gray, although the name "CAP ARCONA" remained in large white capital letters on the stern of the ship. Its glory days were gone.

But the monotony of serving as a floating barracks for the Kriegsmarine during the war was soon to be interrupted. The *Cap Arcona* had caught the attention of Hitler's propaganda minister and one of Germany's greatest movie directors. They wanted to cast the ship in the starring role of an epic Nazi propaganda film.

Starring Role

NAZI PROPAGANDA FILM

Chapter 4

REWRITING HISTORY

MOORED ON THE NORTHERN coastline of Poland from 1940 onward, the *Cap Arcona* was spared from direct involvement in the naval battles of World War II. That meant that the pride of Germany was not an active participant in the nation's successful military conquests at the outset of the war. But it also meant that it was spared when the war turned bad and the Kriegsmarine lost countless ships. The ship was not permitted to leave the dock, but it was partially crewed, with Commodore Niejahr still nominally in command, supported by his first and second officers, a steward, and a ship's cook. It seemed that its fate was to rust in obscurity. All that changed, however, in late 1941 on account of an unlikely series of events.

WHEN SOLDIERS FROM the Soviet Union took Berlin at the end of World War II, they not only destroyed the city but also indiscriminately ransacked records, museums, and German state archives. Anything deemed to be of material value, including furniture, gold, and tires, was sent back to Russia. However, in the passion of the moment, war-weary soldiers mistakenly threw out official reports, looted buildings, and burned important files.

It was a terrible time for Berliners, who suffered from the brutality of the occupying Red Army and were reduced to scavenging in order to stay alive. One of those scavengers made an important discovery. Amid the mess created by days of constant shelling and marauding soldiers were loose-leaf papers that littered the courtyard of the Nazi Ministry of Propaganda. They were part of a diary, and many of the pages were singed; others were likely burned and lost to history. In the days after Berlin fell, Soviet soldiers had removed the diary's pages from roughly eighteen handwritten notebooks that were stored in filing cabinets. Ironically, they discarded the papers on the floor but confiscated the filing cabinets.

A scavenger collected the papers and binders for safekeeping. The priceless find included nearly six thousand pages of handwritten personal and official writings, speeches, letters exchanged with top Nazi officials, tax documents revealing the financial troubles of its owner, receipts for purchases (including a payment to a jeweler to replace a damaged Nazi Party emblem), and thousands of additional sheets of dictated typed notes that formed a diary. The contents of the diary were even more shocking and disturbing than the discovery of its existence. It contained cold, calculating comments on the murder of millions of Jews and revealed a man with a bloodlust not easily quenched. It belonged to Joseph Goebbels, Hitler's propaganda minister and one of the driving forces behind the hatred that fueled the Holocaust.*

Goebbels's notorious megalomania and callousness extended to the manner by which he kept his diary. Even though Germany was suffering during the war from severe shortages of natural resources and a variety of common consumer products, including paper, Goebbels triple-spaced his diary and used a heavy watermark paper virtually unavailable in the country at the time. The treasure trove of papers eventually made its way to Frank E. Mason, the former military attaché assigned to the U.S. Embassy in Berlin after the war, who identified Goebbels as the author of the diary and made sure the important find was preserved.

---

* The diary contents are held today at several sources, including Stanford University; the National Archives in Washington, DC; the Moscow Archives; and the Institut für Zeitgeschichte in Munich.

It turned out, however, that some of Goebbels's writings were taken back to Moscow after the war, where they remained for decades in a file. A relatively recent discovery of a microfilm containing lost sections of Dr. Goebbels's diary by a researcher in the Russian state archives has rekindled interest in the propagandist. The documents, which are now held in the Institute of Contemporary History in Germany and are difficult to decipher because of the sloppy handwriting, have proved to be a helpful supplement to understanding the writer's maniacal hatred of people and his motives behind the Holocaust. The institute's Dr. Klaus Lankheit sums them up by saying simply that Goebbels's "hatred of Jews screams out of every page."

The "Little Doctor," as Goebbels was known—sometimes affectionately, sometimes disparagingly on account of his diminutive stature—comes across as vulgar and vicious in the diary.* A thin-skinned monster who enacted cruel vengeance on anyone who crossed him, and even those who did not, Goebbels abused fellow Nazi officials. Using gutter language, he spoke of colleagues as "nitwits" and called them names such as "pig," "stupid camel," "scoundrel," and "fat, complacent swine!"

These documents also reveal that Goebbels was a man haunted by his own secrets and past. A victim of polio as a child, his right leg never fully developed, which limited his ability to walk and run like other boys. This disability prevented him from serving in World War I. Therefore, unlike others of his generation, including leaders of the Nazi Party and German military, he was neither a veteran nor a hero. He was physically weak and had no medals to prove his worth in the zealously patriotic and rabidly militaristic hierarchy of Nazi Germany. Described as "fragile" and "sickly," Goebbels was anything but the strong, tall, blond Nordic ideal that he and his fellow Nazis celebrated. But he had other skills that would serve Hitler and the Nazis in even more effective and violent ways.

Joseph Goebbels was born on October 29, 1897, into a quiet but stern middle-class family that resembled so many other families in

---

* Goebbels was five foot five.

Germany. His working-class parents lived in the village of Rheydt in the Rhineland, where his father, Fritz, worked at a factory and as a bookkeeper. His mother, Maria Odenhausen, was the daughter of a blacksmith and was a thoroughly devout Catholic. Though socially insecure and possessing a volatile personality, Goebbels was very creative and intelligent. He developed a passion for poetry and the arts early on in his life and, like Adolf Hitler, had a flair for the theatrical, a gift for oratory, and a passion for film. Even though he ended up attending eight different universities, Goebbels finally graduated from the University of Heidelberg. He also completed his PhD at the age of twenty-four in 1921, studying, ironically, under the renowned scholar Professor Friedrich Gundolf, an expert on Goethe and literary history and a Jew. By all appearances, young Joseph's childhood seemed rather normal, not one that would produce one of the truly evil personalities of the twentieth century.

Goebbels suffered a number of setbacks in his early career. He longed to be a writer, but his dark novel, *Michael*, published in 1926, and two plays—*Blutsaat* (Blood seed) and *Der Wanderer* (The wanderer)—did not enjoy any commercial or artistic success. His other literary efforts were rejected by publishers and newspapers, and he was even turned down when he applied to be a reporter with the *Berliner Trageblatt*. Such literary and intellectual rejection further fueled the darker side of his emotional development and his growing inferiority complex.

Indeed, a healthy social life eluded the maladjusted young man, who found an outlet for his pain and resentment in railing against those who were popular and privileged. Goebbels shared such tendencies with the man who would one day lead Nazi Germany, and, in 1922, he discovered the National Socialist German Workers' Party (NSDAP) and rose quickly to prominence in the movement. One of the main reasons for his success was his alliance with Hitler, but their relationship transcended the business of the party. Both men held radical views against capitalism, had a deep hatred of Jews, and were driven by personal insecurities. Goebbels's intellectual and literary ambitions, like Hitler's artistic pursuits, failed, leading both men to blame their personal failures on Jews. The relationship was also mutually beneficial. Hitler recognized the Little Doctor's skills and elevated him to the senior ranks of the Nazi Party. Goebbels did not disappoint and quickly emerged as a loyal deputy and brutally effective instrument for Hitler's larger goals.

Goebbels's successes continued to benefit Hitler, who increasingly came to rely on his propagandist. Wrote Hitler on June 24, 1942, "Dr. Goebbels was gifted with the two things without which the situation in Berlin could not have been mastered: Verbal facility and intellect." As the head of propaganda in Nazi Germany, Goebbels intoxicated the masses using an alarming but effective elixir of hate, fear, blamemongering, and scapegoating. He fabricated an array of alleged Jewish abuses of and attacks on Germans in order to incite the public. To those political leaders who did not succumb to his propaganda, he simply co-opted them through bribes and thinly veiled threats. In the ensuing years, Goebbels developed a fanatical devotion to his führer, once writing of him, "As long as he lives and is among us in good health, as long as he can give us the strength of his spirit and the power of his manliness, no evil can touch us."

Goebbels drew inspiration from Hitler. When periods of time passed without seeing his leader, the propagandist often became filled with self-doubt; that is, until he once again met or spoke with his beloved führer. Such meetings always infused Goebbels with fanaticism. "I am so happy Hitler is coming. I venerate and love him," Goebbels once confessed in his diary. He became flush with emotion and pride when Hitler praised him, defeated when Hitler ignored him, and jealous whenever Hitler paid attention to another senior official. "I have him all to myself," swooned Goebbels after gaining a private audience with the führer. "Hitler embraces me. His eyes are filled with tears. I am happy."

Hitler even served as the best man at Goebbels's wedding. Moreover, had it not been for Hitler's intervention in the Goebbels' marriage, it is likely Joseph and Magda would have divorced because of his many highly public affairs. Because Hitler wanted Germans to have large families, Goebbels stated that he and his wife would have one child a year—they ended up having six children, Hilde, Holde, Helga, Heide, Hedda, and Helmuth—all of whom were instructed to refer to Hitler as uncle.

It was Goebbels who rewrote German history and forged the myth of the führer, bestowing on the former corporal a "halo of infallibility." Goebbels was a master propagandist who understood the adage that "the greater the lie, the more of a chance it has of being believed." And the Nazis proceeded to construct what would seem to be the most irrational and unbelievable "truths." For such outrageous lies to be effective, Goebbels knew they needed to be repeated at every opportunity and reinforced by any and all means available. Yet such shocking messages had to be framed in a clear, simple manner in order to dupe the masses and were most effective when they appealed to raw emotions like hatred and fear. And he was just the spellbinding orator, masterful showman, and mass manipulator to do it.

Two facets of history Goebbels sought to rewrite were an imagined international Jewish plot against Germany and the "Aryan superman" who were the rightful masters of Europe. Goebbels branded Jews as untrustworthy traitors who supported an alleged "Jewish-Bolshevik" alliance in Moscow and used a number of methods to craft his alarming message, including the 1935 Nuremberg Laws, pogroms such as Kristallnacht, and control of the artistic and cultural life of Germany, including films.

Jewish caricatures began appearing in propaganda messages throughout Germany and in numerous films. Goebbels boasted of his "total war" against Jews and other opponents of the Reich. Emboldened, he sought to launch his most ambitious propaganda effort yet. It involved movies and a famous ocean liner.

Chapter 5

HOLLYWOOD ON THE RHINE

FROM 1939 TO 1942, THE *Cap Arcona* fell into disrepair. Without maintenance or regular use, the powerful turbines eventually stopped working properly, and the ship began to rust. But Germany's propaganda minister would soon have an outlandish idea that would thrust the old liner back into the limelight. It would involve his passion for film, a diabolical plot to win the war, and an epic movie.

ADOLF HITLER RELIED ON Joseph Goebbels to build support at home for Germany's international aggression and the steep sacrifices necessitated by war. Both men "saw propaganda as a political weapon and also during the war as a military weapon." As such, Hitler charged his trusted deputy with the grand mission of opening a propaganda front against the Allies. Goebbels found the answer to this new phase of the war in movies.

Perhaps more than any other propaganda vehicle or cultural expression, it was the silver screen that captured the attention of Hitler and Goebbels. In the words of one expert, "For the Nazis, film was an extremely important way of mobilizing audiences, of conveying ideas, and Hitler was fascinated by the power of film." Filmmaking thus emerged as a central tool for both internal Nazi propaganda efforts and new psychological operations against their enemies.

Two of Goebbels's most ambitious films were released in 1940, the year after the war started. They shared the same simplistic plot: there was a "Jewish threat" to Germany, one that necessitated an aggressive response. The first of these anti-Semitic propaganda films was *Der ewige Jude* (The eternal Jew). It presented Jews as parasites living off the host—the German people—and as a plague on German society. Lest anyone miss the message, the film even showed swarms of rats running across the screen when Jews appeared.

Another film, *Jud Süss* (Suss the Jew), depicted an innocent girl from a village (which could have been any small community in Germany) who was raped by a Jew. To no avail, the girl begged her attacker to stop. The message in this film was equally overt and unmistakable: Jews were villains who would likely attack again and again. As a result, villagers ultimately took matters into their own hands. With screams of "The Jews must go!" the residents expelled the Jewish population from their community. Goebbels used the film to deliberately attempt to incite the German population to commit violent anti-Semitic acts.

Jud Süss was one of the most commercially successful anti-Semitic propaganda films in history, with an estimated twenty million viewers, an astonishing number at the time. Proud of his accomplishment, Goebbels boasted that it was "an anti-Semitic film the kind we could only wish for!" However, *Der ewige Jude* was a flop. Goebbels felt that neither film realized its true potential. He needed a new approach to moviemaking and something on a grander scale if he wanted to brainwash the German public. The inspiration came courtesy of Hollywood.

Goebbels's private diary reveals that he and Hitler saw themselves as connoisseurs of film. They watched as many films as possible, oftentimes together. For instance, on December 22, 1933, Goebbels recorded in his diary, "I gave the Führer 32 super films." Because of Goebbels's own strict censorship laws, however, foreign films were not readily available in Nazi Germany. As a result, Goebbels ordered his agents to confiscate movies from elsewhere in Europe. He then arranged private screenings for Hitler. Interpreters were organized, ready to whisper every line in German to the Nazi leaders. Together, the two film buffs watched as many Hollywood blockbusters as possible, enjoying a diverse array of classics, including their personal favorites *King Kong* (1933), Disney's *Snow White* (1937), and *Gone with the Wind* (1939).

In early December 1928, Joseph Goebbels watched a movie made in Hollywood for the first time in his life. The experience horrified him. Goebbels revealed the cause of his rage, saying, "Virtually all you saw were Hebrews." He described the film as "Sheer Hell." A few months later, perhaps in response to his growing resentment of the success many Jews enjoyed in the arts—which was in marked contrast to both his and Hitler's failures in the same fields—the propagandist recorded a foreboding entry in his diary: "The Jewish question is the question of all questions."

However, neither Hitler nor Goebbels appears to have fully grasped the degree to which Jews had succeeded in the American film industry until several years later. While watching the concluding film credits after one of their many sessions viewing Hollywood movies in 1942, two realizations dawned on them. The first was the discovery that many of Hollywood's most successful directors, producers, scriptwriters, and actors were Jewish. Tempers flared in the private screening room, with Goebbels complaining, "I have received statistics about the number of Jews in the American radio, movies, and press. The percentage is truly terrifying. The Jews are 100 per cent in control of the film, and 90 to 95 per cent of the press and radio."

The second realization was that Hollywood's action films and dramatic story lines were far more successful than the pseudodocumentaries Goebbels had been producing in Germany. In particular, the box-office success of *Casablanca* (1942) during a critical year in the war greatly disturbed Goebbels. Not only was the movie highly successful commercially and a masterpiece of filmmaking, but it was effective in promoting a negative image of Nazi Germany during the war. And *Casablanca* was only one of many blockbuster films coming out of Hollywood with powerful messages about the war.

Goebbels recognized that American propaganda efforts were far more effective than his own because they were not anti-German but anti-Nazi, whereas his films were simplistic and attempted to portray entire groups of people and countries as evil. Likewise, American films were far less ham-fisted and obvious in their propaganda message. Remarked Goebbels after what he claimed was a careful study of American filmmaking, "The fact of the matter is that the Americans have the ability of taking their relatively small stock of culture and by a modernized version to make of it something that is very appropriate for the present time." American filmmakers understood that people wanted to be entertained. Epic action films were far more effective in achieving the goal of mass mobilization through propaganda, especially if the viewers did not consciously realize they were watching propaganda. Something needed to be done, and something would be done.

Goebbels needed to develop a film industry that would rival America's and produce blockbuster action and dramatic films. In short, he needed to create "Hollywood on the Rhine." Under his leadership, the German film industry would compete with Hollywood and prove itself superior to the Jewish artists and businessmen that composed much of Hollywood's elite. And thus an obsessive rivalry began.

It was not so much that Goebbels had to invent the German film industry as much as he hoped to re-create it and focus it on propaganda. The German film industry had prospered before the war. Studios such as UFA churned out successful films, and the school of cinema known as German expressionism was invented there. In fact, as early as World War I, German leaders understood the propaganda value of film and encouraged the nation's film industry to make pro-German movies. But the German film industry was hit very hard during the economic downturn between the wars. Undeterred, Goebbels hoped to rebuild it and make it, in the words of one writer, the "once-triumphant German rival of Hollywood."

The location for Hollywood on the Rhine was Babelsberg, on the outskirts of Berlin. Once the largest studio in Europe, this is where

Marlene Dietrich made *Der Blaue Engel* (*The Blue Angel*) in 1930, considered to be perhaps the famous actress's best work. Babelsberg is also where Fritz Lang filmed *Metropolis* in 1926, a film widely considered to be one of the greatest science-fiction movies ever made. Many other great films were made in Babelsberg, and Germany featured a number of talented filmmakers, including Friedrich Murnau, who reinvented cinematography and special effects "with cameras strapped to the torsos of bicyclists and fire-engine ladders" and other innovative techniques.*

Recognizing the power of movies, the Nazi Party created a film department in 1930, and Goebbels pronounced himself a "patron of the German film." He began consuming every Hollywood film his agents could procure. One of them, which he watched on the evening of May 3, 1942, was *Swanee River*. The film, which was in Technicolor, used a number of innovative filmmaking techniques that Goebbels studied in order to incorporate them into German films.

Goebbels created a cultural office and film office, both of which worked with his Ministry of Propaganda. To encourage studios and filmmakers to make products that furthered Nazi Party ideals, he taxed films that did not reflect his preferred "cultural value" and gave subsidies through a national film bank to those that did. A professional organization akin to a Screen Actors Guild was formed and confirmed the status of "Reich filmmaker" on select individuals. The propagandist organized meetings with Germany's filmmakers and even ordered them to study Hollywood films.

To encourage people to go out and see movies, cinemas were not nationalized. Private theaters were allowed to operate, but strict rules were placed on them. For instance, cinemas had to show Goebbels's documentaries and newsreels, and all films were screened by the Ministry of Propaganda. Goebbels understood that film offered people escape from their work and the war. Male actors were pardoned from military service if they were popular among the people. Actor Heinz Rühmann, however, served in uniform but

---

* Hitler also planned to build an enormous film studio near his hometown of Linz in Austria.

was accompanied during the war by film crews eager to get news-reel footage for public consumption. Films were also shown in military barracks and factories and to groups such as the Hitler Youth and at Nazi Party functions.

Large movie audiences were assembled when Hitler, Goebbels, and other leaders were in attendance, oftentimes with beautiful young actresses at their sides. Hitler often attended dinner parties in the company of leading actresses such as Lil Dagover and Olga Tschechowa. Hermann Göring even married a famous actress, and one of Goebbels's mistresses was the Czech actress Lida Baarova.

In short, Goebbels proposed a complete restructuring and re-thinking of the German film industry, even expressing alarm at the anti-German content of Swiss and Swedish films. He wanted Nazi agents to look into possible action against the International Moving Picture Association for these reasons. When he watched Italian films, he was aghast to discover that Germany's supposed ally also produced films with content contrary to the Nazi mantra. He therefore hatched a plan to "lay our hands on the entire Italian movie export in Europe," gleefully adding in his diary, "I hope the Italians fall for it."

The propagandist also complained about the quality of acting in his country. Believing that the French had all the talented actors, Goebbels suggested to his directors that they "be hired by us for German film production." He also reminded his directors that, unlike Germany, French films celebrated French culture in great films. It was time to celebrate German cultural superiority through film. After Marlene Dietrich, Greta Garbo, and other stars fled Germany for Hollywood, Goebbels oversaw an effort to promote new German stars. He also ordered his Ministry of Propaganda to make a star out of the beautiful Swedish actress Zarah Leander by devising a massive public relations campaign for her. She became the highest-paid actress in Germany.

Goebbels was motivated by more than just Hollywood blockbusters. He also attempted to reproduce the work of Leni Riefenstahl, whose documentary *Triumph of the Will* was both a commercial and a critical success and has been widely credited with playing a key role in promoting Adolf Hitler as a visionary leader among the German people. It is also one of the most disturbing motion pictures ever made, as it helped usher in one of the world's darkest and most terrifying political movements.

Triumph of the Will, which premiered on March 28, 1935, at Berlin's Ufa Palace Theater, made Riefenstahl one of the most well-known yet reviled filmmakers in history. She had been a popular German actress who had directed her first film in 1932, a project titled *Das Blaue Licht* (The blue light). She was not particularly political but had heard Hitler speak around the time he attained power and was deeply moved by his words and charisma. Inspired and perhaps seeking to advance her own career, she began writing to Germany's new führer.

When Hitler discovered that the alluring actress and gifted filmmaker was an admirer, he asked Riefenstahl to direct a grand project to document the 1934 Nazi Party Congress rally in Nuremberg. Riefenstahl had no experience with political or biographic documentaries, but Hitler's powers of persuasion mixed with her own ambition led the young filmmaker to agree to turn her talents to supporting the Nazi cause. It seemed an odd selection, but in Riefenstahl Hitler found the person he needed to help him launch his movement to international fame.*

Hitler was not interested in an established filmmaker or "the usual" approach to making a documentary. Rather, he wanted the celebration in Nuremberg to be filmed by "a non-expert eye" in order to capture the experiences of ordinary people. As Riefenstahl remembered, "He wanted a film which would move, appeal

---

* In an interview in 1964, the director claimed that she was not helping to promote Hitler and Nazism but rather was simply documenting the reality of events in Germany. She offered the following revisionist account of her work: "If you see this film again today you ascertain that it doesn't contain a single reconstructed scene. Everything in it is true. And it contains no tendentious commentary at all. It is history. . . . It reflects the truth that was then in 1934, history. It is therefore a documentary. Not a propaganda film." Her efforts to repair her reputation, however, do not have merit. Even after her death, Riefenstahl remains controversial.

to, [and] impress an audience which was not necessarily interested in politics."

Hitler would get his wish. *Triumph of the Will* brilliantly and powerfully chronicled Hitler's massive rally, portraying it as the crucible marking the rise of the Nazi Party and Germany as a resurgent world power. The highly scripted and choreographed event presented Riefenstahl with both a challenge and an opportunity, as the rally was attended by an estimated seven hundred thousand people, an audience of unprecedented size at the time. Riefenstahl proved worthy of the task. Every aspect of the film was touched by Riefenstahl's hand. She wrote, directed, and edited the project. Her crew of 172 ended up shooting more than sixty-one hours of film for the two-hour documentary.

The film allowed Riefenstahl to display her creativity and talent for cinematography. For instance, in order to capture the power of the rally and exuberance of the Nazi faithful, she ushered in new filming techniques such as blending choreographed scenes from the rally with unrehearsed moments of raw emotion. She even instructed her crew to dress in military uniforms in order to blend in with the crowd and experimented with new camera angles. These included aerial shots that highlighted the enormity of the event and moving cameras placed on tracks that followed the sea of sharply dressed soldiers in formation. In order to enhance Hitler's natural charisma, the director ordered that pits be dug in the ground near the main dais, allowing the viewing audience to look up at the speakers in a way that reinforced their status and reflected the admiration of the audience.

Riefenstahl opened the film with commentary on the rise of Germany, presented in the form of bold, blocked written text on the screen, an approach recognizable to contemporary fans of the George Lucas *Star Wars* series. It read:

On 5 September 1934
20 years after the outbreak of the World War
16 years after the beginning of German suffering

19 months after the beginning of the German rebirth
Adolf Hitler flew again to Nuremberg to review
the columns of his faithful followers

Hitler was the star of the film. After the prologue, audiences were treated to the image of an airplane descending like a god or angel from the skies. Emerging from the plane was the führer, who, like a "Nazi Messiah," greeted the great multitude awaiting his arrival. The intended message worked.

Others were motivated by the film's alarming content in an altogether different way. During World War II, legendary filmmaker Frank Capra produced *Why We Fight*, shown as a series of newsreels commissioned by the U.S. government and designed to counter the propaganda of *Triumph of the Will*. Extraordinary comedian and actor Charlie Chaplin used Riefenstahl's film as inspiration for the brilliantly irreverent and effective spoof *The Great Dictator*. Released in 1940, the comedy was a success for lampooning Hitler. Likewise, two years later, British filmmaker Charles A. Ridley made a short film for the British Ministry of Information called *Lambeth Walk— Nazi Style*. Using the popular dance song named in the title, Ridley edited Riefenstahl's film in a way that made Nazi soldiers appear to be dancing in a silly fashion to the song. It has been said that when Goebbels watched Ridley's parody, he stormed out of the room, kicking over chairs and screaming in anger.

Nonetheless, with its striking visuals and the power of the film's message, *Triumph of the Will* established an enduring image of the Nazis and solidified Hitler's power. The documentary and both the American and the British war films made a lasting impression on the Nazi Party's master propagandist, Joseph Goebbels, who vowed to answer Capra, Chaplin, Ridley, and others with his own masterpiece of misinformation. In his diary Goebbels revealed, "It is my ultimate goal to establish the German film as the dominant cultural world power." From 1933 to 1945, a whopping 1,094 movies were produced through the Ministry of Propaganda, although not all of them were propaganda films.

Inspired by Leni Riefenstahl, a woman the Little Doctor saw as "the only star who understands us," Goebbels intended to replace her as the new master. Hitler and Goebbels mobilized every resource available to Nazi Germany in order to produce the most powerful propaganda film of the war. One of those resources would be Germany's most famous ocean liner.

Chapter 6

RAISING THE *TITANIC*

FOR MORE THAN SEVENTY-THREE years, the discovery of the resting place of the RMS *Titanic* eluded researchers, in part because of the technical challenges of searching the ocean floor at a depth of more than twelve thousand feet and in part because the coordinates given by the crew that fateful night in April 1912 were inaccurate. Finally, on September 2, 1985, thanks to sophisticated robots with remote-controlled cameras and sonar-mapping systems capable of operating in pitch blackness and the extreme pressure of such depths, a team of American and French researchers led by Dr. Robert Ballard of the Woods Hole Oceanographic Institution located the remains of the infamous ocean liner. What they found was remarkable. Though deteriorating, much of the ship was intact.

Multiple missions to the ocean floor were launched in subsequent years to photograph the wreckage and collect artifacts. Thousands of items ranging from china dishes and cooking utensils to a large section of the hull have been recovered. Yet it is likely that untold riches still remain below on the ocean floor. The *Titanic* sank with millions of dollars' worth of diamonds as well as jewelry and family heirlooms owned by the wealthy passengers aboard the ship.*

Movies have been made about the *Titanic*, numerous exhibits of the recovered artifacts have been organized, and there is a 3-D effort to "virtually raise" the ship. Recovery efforts continue at the site, but experts believe that every salvaging mission degrades the resting place, as does the passing of time. Ironically, the discovery of the ship may be the very thing that quickens its final destruction.

Hamburg-Süd never intended to raise the *Titanic*, but the company did intend for it to be the inspiration for the queen of its fleet. In the 1920s the designers of the *Cap Arcona* even studied the plans of the British ocean liner not only in hopes of replicating the elegance and allure of the world's most famous ship, but also in order to improve upon any flaws in safety. They could never have imagined that their ship would one day help raise the memory of the *Titanic* by starring in the most expensive propaganda film in history.

THE DOMINOES FELL FAST. After their successful blitzkrieg strike in Poland in 1939, Nazi Germany commenced with the invasion of Denmark and Norway on the morning of April 9, 1940. These quick victories were followed in May 1940 by the invasion of France and then of Belgium, Luxembourg, and the Netherlands. Within days the "Low Countries" surrendered. Paris fell on June 14, 1940. In the wake of their ruinous effort to defend France and after sustaining massive casualties, British forces were evacuated across the English Channel in late May and early June 1940.† While some in England pondered a conditional surrender to Germany, Hitler and his commanders turned their attention to the last major power still opposing

---

* The passengers included John Jacob Astor, one of the world's wealthiest men, and Isidor Straus, owner of Macy's. Both men went down with the ship, as did Mrs. Straus, who refused to leave her husband for the safety of a lifeboat. Remarkably, the bodies of Astor and Straus were among the few that were later recovered by ships sailing to the scene of the wreck.

† Pushed to the edge of the Continent, British forces were evacuated at Dunkirk, France. Well over three hundred thousand British and French troops were forced back across the English Channel after suffering roughly forty thousand casualties and the loss of hundreds of tanks, trucks, and artillery pieces.

them. Great Britain, standing virtually alone against the Nazi war machine, was the next target.

On July 16, 1940, Hitler ordered preparations for Operation Sea Lion—the invasion of the British Isles. The initial motive was to scare the British into negotiating an armistice. It nearly worked. Nazi leaders had even begun planning for the celebrations that would mark Britain's capitulation. Hitler's planned invasion of Britain included massive aerial bombings by the Luftwaffe, designed to soften British defenses, whereupon the grand amphibious invasion would commence. Hitler hoped to have troops in London by Christmas 1940.*

The pivotal battle waged by the Luftwaffe against Britain occurred in August 1940. More than twenty-five hundred German aircraft crossed the Channel in wave after wave, targeting British shipping, ports, industry, infrastructure, and airfields in order to undermine Britain's ability to wage war. The massive air attack also struck cities and political targets in a campaign of terror designed to bring the British to their knees and to the negotiating table. The campaign was known in Germany as the "air battle for England." The name history remembers—the Battle of Britain—comes courtesy of a famous speech delivered by Prime Minister Winston Churchill in the House of Commons, where the great orator said, "The Battle of France is over. I expect that the Battle of Britain is about to begin."

The Battle of Britain was, at the time, the largest air campaign and aerial bombing effort in history. But Nazi planners did not count on the courage and tenacity of Royal Air Force Hurricane and Spitfire fighters, who were waiting for them in the skies above the British Isles. It proved to be a horrifically bloody campaign for both sides. The RAF suffered 544 airmen killed and more than 400 wounded, with more than fifteen hundred aircraft destroyed. There were also tens of thousands of civilian casualties, and the bombings

---

* On May 10, as the German invasion of France began, a new leader came to power in London. Replacing Neville Chamberlain was Winston Churchill. The new prime minister would hear nothing of negotiations or surrender, instead digging in for battle and inspiring the British people and military to mount an unwavering defense of their island home.

took a terrible toll on Britain's cities and industry. However, German casualties were worse. Nearly 2,700 Luftwaffe pilots and crew members were killed in the attacks, almost 1,000 were captured, and hundreds more were missing or assumed dead. Nearly two thousand aircraft were destroyed. The Battle for Britain did end up being a turning point in the war, just not in the way Hitler or Goebbels intended. Britain was saved; the Nazis suffered their first major setback of the war. On September 14 Hitler postponed (for the time) plans to invade Britain.

Just over one year later, a facet of that plan was reactivated. Joseph Goebbels was tasked by the führer to open a propaganda front in the fight against Britain. Around that same time, a German screenwriter named Harald Bratt had an idea for a film. It would be an action and drama film based on the sinking of the *Titanic*. Bratt had been inspired by the book *Titanic: Tragedy of an Ocean Liner*, written in 1936 by Josef Pelz von Felinau. The book was an instant hit in Germany.*

Bratt was a most unlikely ally for Goebbels. Born August Christian Riekel in 1897, the veteran of World War I had been dismissed from his job as an educator, fell on hard times, and decided to assume an alias. Bratt also started writing propaganda scripts for the Nazis under his new pen name. But his timing and vision were perfect. Goebbels immediately recognized the film's potential to be *the* blockbuster he and Hitler desired. It would accomplish two other vital objectives as well: such an epic film would spearhead the new propaganda front in the Battle of Britain and also help launch their dream of a Hollywood on the Rhine.

The script was based on the 1912 sinking of the RMS *Titanic*, Britain's worst maritime disaster. Billed as unsinkable, the *Titanic* was a technological marvel. Yet a mix of human error and engineering flaws doomed the most luxurious passenger ship of the time. In a cruel twist of fate and a blow to human ingenuity, a ship that took more than three years to build was lost in less than three hours.

---

* A few weeks after the *Titanic* sank, a thirty-minute silent film, *At Night in Ice*, was made in Germany and was a hit.

While on its maiden voyage from Southampton, England, to New York City on April 14, 1912, the ship struck an iceberg. The time was near midnight. A few hours later, the ship sank with more than fifteen hundred people still aboard.

Other devastating losses of ships and man-made machines such as the explosion of the German zeppelin *Hindenburg* in 1937 or the loss of the U.S. space shuttle *Challenger* in 1986 pale in terms of the number of lives lost on the *Titanic*. Yet even other large tragedies with large numbers of casualties, though heart-wrenching, fail to capture the world's imagination as does the sinking of the *Titanic*. Perhaps only the terrorist attacks at the World Trade Center and Pentagon on September 11, 2001, are equivalent in terms of the special memory afforded them by history. Not surprisingly, the story of the ship's sinking has been made into several films, a few of them blockbusters, including Jean Negulesco's 1953 film *Titanic*; the critically acclaimed British film *A Night to Remember*, released in 1958 and adapted from the Walter Lord book; and, most recently, James Cameron's award-winning movie in 1997. Although there have been other more deadly disasters, the *Titanic* remains one of the most well-known and irresistible stories of all time.* It would now serve the Nazi cause.

Bratt's idea resonated with Goebbels for yet another reason—Hitler was fascinated by big ships and took great pride in them. Both Hitler and Goebbels understood that shipbuilding was one of Germany's top industries and also saw the propaganda value of the industry, which was apparent in the fourfold increase in the number of ships built in Germany during the Nazi reign and the eightfold increase in gross tonnage under Hitler.

In 1938 the führer made a point of being on hand for the launch of the massive *Robert Ley*. There were only four ships in Germany larger than the *Robert Ley*, one of them being the *Cap Arcona*. With thirty thousand workers gathered in a grand staged event, Hitler named the 25,000-ton ship for Dr. Robert Ley, the leader of the

---

* The *Titanic* has also appeared on the small screen in the 1979 miniseries *S.O.S. Titanic* and another TV miniseries in 1996.

German Labor Front. Armed with a bottle of champagne and appearing with a young working girl at his side, Hitler dedicated the ship as part of the Strength Through Joy fleet. These ships, built for German workers, included the *Wilhelm Gustloff*, a sister ship of the *Robert Ley* and *Cap Arcona*, named for the Nazi leader killed in Switzerland by a Jew.

As would be expected, Goebbels approved Bratt's script for *The Sinking of the* Titanic and ordered that the film be made right away. The thirtieth anniversary of the famous maritime disaster was approaching, and Goebbels saw his propaganda film as softening English resolve to fight and so tarnishing their image that Britain would be isolated by the international community. As such, the central theme for the Nazi *Titanic*, as described by one film historian, was to present it as "a national disaster hugely embarrassing for Britain." This would be accomplished by portraying the *Titanic* as "a story about stupidity, a story about cowardice and a story about greed." According to Friedmann Beyer, author of *Der Fall Selpin*, a book about Herbert Selpin, the man chosen to direct the film, Goebbels "expected the *Titanic* movie to become a very spectacular film with a lot of special effects but he also of course expected that the film would have a clear message against the main enemy of Germany—Great Britain."

The epic film would not only open a propaganda front against the British, demonstrate Germany's superiority to Hollywood, and help Nazi Germany win the war, but, to Goebbels's mind, also establish him as the world's greatest film producer and further ingratiate him to Hitler. At least that was the plan.

But Goebbels was not the only one devising propaganda during the war. Churchill's soaring rhetoric was complemented by a concerted and effective propaganda campaign by the British. This included several lavish feature-length films and numerous shorts developed through the British Ministry of Information. In effect, even though the British had but a fraction of the extensive budget and resources as Goebbels, Britain's cinematic countermeasures trumped Germany's.* The propagandist recognized the superior quality, commercial success, and propaganda value of the British films and was immediately consumed by the need to best not just Hollywood but now the British propaganda films as well.

One of the most successful British films of the war was *Went the Day Well?* Adapted from a story by Graham Greene and directed by Alberto Cavalcanti, the film was released in 1942 and inspired both British and American audiences to resist Nazi militarism and ideology. The plot of the ninety-two-minute film was that German paratroopers managed to parachute into England undetected. In disguise they found their way to a quiet village called Bramley End. However, the villagers and home guard fought back and defeated the invaders. *Went the Day Well?* was filled with stirringly patriotic and memorable scenes. For instance, at the end of the film one of the victorious English villagers paused and looked at the graves of the defeated German soldiers. The character then remarked, "This is the only bit of England they got."

Another popular British war film and, indeed, one of the most successful films of the entire war was *In Which We Serve.* The Noel Coward classic was also released in 1942 and told the gripping and realistic story of the crew of a British destroyer that was torpedoed by a German U-boat. The film emphasized an important message: the crew survived by working together and depending on one another. In the words of Professor James Chapman, a film historian at England's University of Leicester, the film "comes to represent a national community pulling together as powerfully expressed for all the men, regardless of rank or class, they cling together desperately to a life raft."

Hollywood had also entered the war film business. The U.S. government established the Bureau of Motion Pictures and charged it with supporting the film industry's efforts to produce not just films for entertainment but pictures that served the war effort. Sure enough,

---

* It is estimated that the Nazi budget for propaganda was twelve times that of the British Ministry of Information.

Hollywood found the perfect villain for their movies—the Nazis. The end result was some of the most effective films and propaganda of the war. Several major studios released war films, and leading stars were employed to promote the war. This included Jimmy Stewart, who was photographed in uniform; Ronald Reagan, who made training films; and James Cagney, who starred in several war films.

One of the most successful of the war-propaganda films was *Casablanca*. Released in the same year as *Went the Day Well?* and *In Which We Serve*, the epic action and drama film starred two of Hollywood's biggest names, Humphrey Bogart and Ingrid Bergman, and was directed by Michael Curtiz. The film told the story of two lovers caught in Nazi-occupied North Africa, a story line enhanced by the fact that the film's release coincided with the Allied liberation of North Africa. *Casablanca* was an immediate blockbuster, setting the standard for war-propaganda films. It remains a classic film even today.

The commercial success of the American and British efforts put additional pressure on the Germans. Even though both the invasion of Britain and the development of his grand propaganda film were delayed, Goebbels remained optimistic. He believed he had the right vehicle to best his enemies. An event as momentous as the sinking of the *Titanic* offered Goebbels the sweeping historical theme necessary for an epic movie.

Goebbels had ample funding and the führer's blessing for his ambitious project. He found his subject and his scriptwriter. Plans for the epic propaganda film began in 1940, although Goebbels had considered the sinking of the *Titanic* as a possible film project back in the 1930s. However, the propagandist still needed two key ingredients, a star for the film and a director capable of bringing to life his grand vision. Both ingredients were at hand: the first in the form of an old ocean liner rusting in a German-held port on the Polish coast, the second courtesy of a bombastic former boxer and ballroom dancer.

Chapter 7

THE CELEBRATED SELPIN

IF HE WAS IN A POSITION to do so, noted German movie director Herbert Selpin could have cast himself in the role of director. He looked, dressed, and acted as if he had come straight from central casting, fitting the stereotype of a famous film director. Selpin was enigmatic and eccentric in his lifestyle, difficult and demanding on the set of his movies, and fastidious and flamboyant in his mannerisms and tastes. But he had a gift for moviemaking. These traits would lead him to make what he thought would be the greatest decision of his flourishing career, one that would catapult him to fame as one of the world's greatest directors. And it involved the *Cap Arcona*.

Nicknamed "the Hedgehog" because of his diminutive size and prickly demeanor, Selpin was described by one observer as a man who was "short, spunky, and loved his liquor." The director was oftentimes aloof and condescending, but he was also capable of being extremely charming. Indeed, there are as many varied accounts of Selpin as there were dimensions to his personality, yet most descriptions of him focus on his temperamental disposition. The director had a legendarily quick temper when he did not get his way.

In 1936, for instance, while filming *Spiel an Bord* (Play on Board), Selpin banned the producer from the set and insulted the

51

management team of the studio making the film.* The incident happened because the difficult director wanted to review the scenes he had shot by himself. However, when the producer and officials from the studio arrived as originally planned, Selpin ordered them out of the studio, screaming, "All scum here!" Selpin's friend and scriptwriter Walter Zerlett-Olfenius tried unsuccessfully to calm the director while the others ran out the door to avoid being hit by the chair thrown at them.

Even though the testy director succeeded in angering and alienating most everyone involved with the film, this particular movie would plant the seed for the production that would soon be the Nazis' most ambitious propaganda film. *Spiel an Bord* was a whodunit that took place, ironically enough, on board the German ship *Bremen* while traveling to New York. Selpin fell in love with the ocean liner and expressed an interest in again using a luxurious ship in one of his films. In a few years he would get his wish. But his temper would, this time, prove to be his undoing.

Selpin was born on May 29, 1904, in Berlin. After studying medicine in the city of his birth, he came to the realization that he was ill-suited for the occupation and spent the next few years drifting through an odd collection of jobs. These positions included boxer and ballroom dancer, as well as librarian and art dealer. In the mid-1920s, he found a job in the film industry, serving as an intern at Berlin's UFA Studios, where he was assigned the task of cutting film.

Not long afterward, while working on the set of Friedrich Wilhelm Murnau's production of *Faust* in 1926, Selpin discovered his calling. Selpin's artistic inclinations, eye for detail, charisma, and intelligence caught the attention of producers and directors in the industry, and he was offered a job with Fox's European film division in 1927. At Fox he gained experience working on various aspects of moviemaking, eventually serving as an editor. Later that year he was given the opportunity to serve as an assistant to Walther Ruttmann, an acclaimed German director, on the set of his movie *Berlin*.

---

* The studio was Neucophon-Tonfilm GmbH.

A highly ambitious young man, Selpin jumped at the opportunity to direct his first film, *Chauffeur Antoinette*, which was released by Excelsior Films in 1931. As his career was taking off, however, Selpin found himself the target of Hitler's Nazi Party, which was gaining power in Germany. His sympathetic portrayal of Britain and his sometimes realistic and critical depictions of Germany aroused suspicion among the übernationalists in the Nazi movement.

Selpin recognized the threat. At the same time, Germany's film industry, like every other part of society, was being put in the service of the Nazi Party. There was less money available for filmmaking. A notable exception was Goebbels's Ministry of Propaganda and Public Enlightenment, which was investing in film. So Selpin started making propaganda films for UFA Studios and the Ministry of Propaganda. In that capacity Selpin came to the attention of Joseph Goebbels.

Although Selpin was directing films with regularity and some of his efforts were making money for the studios, his propaganda films were unsuccessful.* What finally brought Selpin acclaim was his 1941 film *Carl Peters*, an adventure film whose protagonist was an explorer in Africa. The film's anti-British story line and subtle criticism of British policy on the Continent were not lost on Hitler and Goebbels.

The ambitious movie was filmed in 1940 in the Bavarian countryside, which Selpin ordered to be transformed to look something like an African landscape. The Hollywoodish action-drama format was what Goebbels wanted for his new propaganda films, so he arranged to have the German army build Selpin's elaborate sets, assist with the extensive relandscaping, transport the large crew, and even stand in as extras. *Carl Peters* was a huge hit and made Selpin a favorite among Nazi leaders.

Selpin followed the success of *Carl Peters* with another well-received propaganda film, *Geheimakte W.B.I.* In the words of one film historian, "Selpin was a young dynamic director, very skillful and he specialized . . . in movies with action content. Goebbels liked

---

* His films *Schwarzhemden* in 1933, *Die Reiter von Deutsch-Ostafrika* in 1934, and *Alarm in Peking* in 1937 were widely panned by critics.

his work, he liked his films." Therefore, in September 1941, he dispatched Friedrich Kienzl, the man who would serve as the production manager for the planned propaganda film, to the set of *Geheimakte W.B.I.* to offer Selpin the opportunity to direct what was described as a masterpiece about history's most famous ship. Selpin did not refuse. After three days of negotiations, a deal was struck.

In some ways, Selpin was an unlikely selection to direct Goebbels's epic film. The director was anything but a loyal Nazi in good standing with the party. But he was very ambitious and was eager to solidify his status as one of Germany's greatest directors, even if it meant a high-profile alliance with Goebbels . . . or precisely because of such a relationship. The paranoid Goebbels usually demanded that everyone associated with him and with the party be completely devoted to Nazi ideology, yet he was willing to gamble with Selpin.

On the other hand, Selpin's selection as director was a logical choice. Selpin was talented and had made action films with heroic, adventurous characters. This was exactly what Goebbels wanted and needed. Yet there was another reason he was chosen to direct the grand film. In the years after 1933 when the Nazis established the Ministry of Propaganda and Public Enlightenment and gave Goebbels absolute control over all cultural pursuits in Germany, most of the nation's talented directors, actors, and artists—many of them Jewish—chose to flee the country. There was a vacuum of directorial talent, which allowed Selpin to rise quickly up the ranks to become one of Germany's most successful and prolific directors. He made more than thirty films in just one decade and was enormously popular with the public.

In September 1941, Herbert Selpin began assembling his team to make Goebbels's propaganda masterpiece. It would be produced by Tobis Studios in Berlin.* Given the budget and resources allocated for the film by the Ministry of Propaganda and the project's high profile, Selpin was able to recruit the best actors and crew in

---

* Tobis, like many German companies, had suffered through the economic downturn between wars, but by the end of the 1930s was a powerful studio. In 1942 it was merged with the UFA Group.

Germany. For instance, he cast Sybila Schmidt, one of the country's leading actresses, as Sigrid Olinsky, a rich heiress traveling on the *Titanic,* and signed matinee idol Hans Neilsen as the leading man, a German officer named Petersen.*

Although the story for the film would be the sinking of the *Titanic* and would be based on Harald Bratt's script, Goebbels wanted it laced with propaganda messages, and Selpin wanted a romantic subplot along with a more powerful dramatic interpretation of the characters on the ship. Both he and Goebbels also wanted more action. Accordingly, in December 1941, Selpin requested a rewriting of Bratt's script. For this important job, Selpin demanded the services of his good friend Walter Zerlett-Olfenius. As was the case for all documents and public cultural pursuits, from radio broadcasts to operatic scores, every change and detail of the film had to be approved by the Nazi Party and the Ministry of Propaganda.

Initially, the Ministry of Propaganda and studio were hesitant to delay the production in order to rewrite the script. Everyone knew that Hitler and Goebbels wanted the film to be ready as soon as possible. Selpin, however, was unflinching. To ensure the project would be a blockbuster, the script needed more drama and action, and Selpin maintained that Zerlett was the best scriptwriter in Germany. The request was eventually approved by Goebbels, who was eager to complement his anti-British message with as much drama and action as possible. Moreover, Zerlett was a fanatically loyal Nazi who had been awarded the Iron Cross for bravery in World War I. Zerlett was given the job.

Zerlett was born on April 7, 1897, in the German countryside at Wiesbaden. He was educated at schools in Hanover. Smart and hardworking, the young man was given the opportunity to continue his studies at Friedrich-Wilhelm University in Berlin, although he never graduated. War intervened, and Zerlett enthusiastically joined the fight, enlisting with Fusilier Regiment 80 in 1914. He rose to the rank of lieutenant and because of his fluency in English and

---

* The cast also included Ernst Fritz Fürbringer as Bruce Ismay, Karl Schönböck as John Jacob Astor, Charlotte Thiele as Madeleine Astor, Otto Wernicke as Captain E. J. Smith, and Kirsten Heiberg as Gloria, Ismay's girlfriend.

French was assigned to the German Intelligence Service. He also held staunch anti-British views.

Zerlett had been working as secretary-general for the German Radio Technical Association, but after the Nazis seized power in 1933 he was offered a position in the Reich Broadcasting Company. Zerlett's older brother, Hans, was an established screenwriter and director. Thanks to the family connection, from 1936 until the end of the war the younger Zerlett worked on a variety of UFA films as a screenwriter. In this capacity, Zerlett had developed a working relationship with director Herbert Selpin. The two had collaborated on seven other film projects. Indeed, letters between the two men and Selpin's home movies (which survived the war) reveal that the two men were more than colleagues—they were good friends.

Yet it was an unlikely friendship. Selpin was an extrovert, whereas Zerlett was an introvert. Selpin was attractive and charismatic. Popular with women, vain, and ambitious, he was a snappy dresser and was highly conscious of his image and the status of those around him. Zerlett, on the other hand, was a chain smoker, frail and skinny, and suffered from poor health. In public he was nervous and shy. He also had a rather quirky side, such as when, in 1935, he suddenly hyphenated his parents' last names and adopted it as his last name for the remainder of his life. Despite their differences, the odd couple worked well together, and it was Selpin who was responsible for Zerlett's success. The dashing director invited the awkward writer to join him at social events and introduced him to the most influential members of the German film industry.

As Selpin had predicted, Zerlett turned Bratt's script into the film Goebbels wanted.* After combing through every word in the script, in February 1942 the Ministry of Propaganda approved Zerlett's changes to the story. It was properly Nazified. Interestingly, however, unlike Goebbels's earlier propaganda films, this one was not overly or overtly anti-Semitic, although one Mediterranean character

---

* The script is housed today at the University for Film and Television in Berlin.

was involved in a murder on the ship. It was implied that he was Jewish. It was also an unusual topic for a propaganda film.

Zerlett rewrote the script in a matter of days, adding several exciting plot twists and dramatic dialogue to enhance the impact of the film's anti-British message. The new script contained a cadre of coldhearted British capitalists, self-serving officers and crew members, cowardly passengers traveling in first class, and numerous ethnic stereotypes, including hotheaded Latins; rowdy, drunk Irish; sultry Gypsy women tempting married men; and calm, chivalrous Scandinavians, even when the ship was sinking. There was even an invented character: a brave German. The fictitious hero's name was Petersen, the lone German among the all-English crew. The script never explains how the German came to work on the ship. Throughout the film, it was Petersen who attempted, to no avail, to warn others of the dangers of steaming too rapidly through the iceberg-infested waters of the North Atlantic.

In Zerlett's reinvention of history, the script featured Bruce Ismay, the president of the White Star Line, which owned the *Titanic*, demanding that the ship's captain sail faster through iceberg-littered waters in order to break the record for the quickest transatlantic crossing. Doing so would increase the value of the company's stock, even if it endangered the passengers.

Alas, it was Petersen—the German—who seemed to be the only person on the ship who recognized the dangers. Of course, he was unsuccessful in getting the English officers and captain to slow the *Titanic*. With his odd encyclopedic understanding of icebergs, Petersen explained the dangers to the ship's crew: "Some icebergs can stretch on for kilometers. Furthermore, seven-eighths of them are hidden underwater." Yet his warnings went unheeded. At one point in the film, an unconcerned English officer responded, "A threat to the *Titanic*? Laughable! The *Titanic* is unsinkable!" To which Petersen added, "Proof of that has yet to be established."

The propaganda message was inescapable throughout the film. Zerlett and Goebbels were particularly interested in portraying the British capitalists, the shipping company, and even the British people as corrupt and motivated only by greed and money. Foremost among them was Bruce Ismay, the head of the White Star Line. As such, scenes were added to the film showing Ismay gloating about his ship's invincibility, boasting to his associates before the tragedy, "At this very moment what you are experiencing is the *Titanic* cruising at 26½ knots—a world record speed." The ship's investors celebrated the news by proclaiming, "Ismay is a genius." Ismay informed his investors that the ship would make them all unimaginably rich because the *Titanic*'s success would "cause our shares to skyrocket." They all agreed, saying, "Let's go to the telegraph and buy all the shares we can." One greedy investor even urged them to do it right away, "before it hits the papers."

As such, Bruce Ismay put his personal wealth and company's profits above safety. Despite the lurking danger, the ship was urged onward in order to break the record for the fastest crossing of the Atlantic. While doing so, Ismay enticed Captain Smith: "For arrival on schedule in New York, I will pay you five thousand dollars. And for every hour ahead of schedule another one thousand dollars. So the faster your ship, the greater the reward." American millionaire John Jacob Astor was also depicted in the film, boasting greedily to his young wife, Madeleine, that he could easily buy the *Titanic* for her as a birthday present. Ismay's girlfriend, Gloria, cared little for her beau but was careful to collect as much jewelry as possible before departing the sinking ship in a lifeboat with many empty seats.

Later in the film as the ship was sinking, it was Petersen who risked his life to rescue passengers trapped belowdecks. Braving the rising water, the German was shown helping others escape, including a very cute little girl screaming for someone to save her. The noble Petersen was so committed to justice that he even arranged for Ismay to get into one of the last lifeboats. He wanted the head of the White Star Line to be saved so that he could stand trial for his crimes. At the end of the film, Ismay and the other defendants are acquitted. Lest the audience miss the steady dose of propaganda, Zerlett concludes his script with a frustrated Petersen giving a speech against the British and their capitalist greed.

In the capable hands of Zerlett and Selpin, all the ingredients of a blockbuster were brought together. Filming would begin immediately in the Johannisthal Studios in Berlin.

Chapter 8

A NEW STAR

GOEBBELS HAD LOFTY EXPECTATIONS for his grand propaganda film. Therefore, it is surprising that the paranoid propagandist, who was prone to micromanaging everything, gave Selpin complete control of the film. Goebbels also authorized an enormous budget for the undertaking: 4 million reichsmarks, which is the equivalent of roughly $180 million in today's currency. At the time, the Nazi *Titanic* would be the most expensive film ever made. The risks were high, but so were the stakes in the war, and Goebbels's fixation with producing the greatest propaganda film in history factored into decisions that otherwise would likely not have been made. Both men—Goebbels and Selpin, like their führer—were consumed by megalomania, and the film was the perfect vehicle for their ambitions. Each man had a stake in the film and wanted to claim credit for its success. They would soon butt heads.

Selpin's grand vision for the film drove him to make outrageous demands of his crew and the Ministry of Propaganda, including a request for eighty-seven days of shooting, which would run from February 23 to August 14, a large number even by the standards of today's blockbusters. The testy director demanded that nine enormous sets be built to replicate the interior of the *Titanic* as well as some invented rooms for the movie. Crews immediately began construction on an enormous ballroom, which was not a part of the *Titanic*, and the ship's famous grand staircase, which featured polished oak, wrought iron, and boutique glass below a glass dome that provided natural lighting. The center of the staircase included a large panel with a clock, which was considered to be the ship's crowning glory and whose fame was later featured in the James Cameron film.

These elaborate sets were constructed in Berlin, where the filming began in early 1942. Several delays, however, postponed the filming, largely on account of the extensiveness of the sets and numerous demands from the director.* This included Selpin's interest in a large cast to portray the passengers aboard the ship. Goebbels agreed to the request and, even though war was waging, reassigned men in uniform to serve as extras for the film. The booklet released by Tobis Studios to promote the film explained the challenges: "It was no easy task to film the disaster, which is the focal point of the film, [and make it] as realistic as possible." It also indicated that "the technical preparations were of the most difficult sort and demanded a staff of experts, a lot of time, and even more patience."

The art director for the film was Fritz Maurischat. Fortunately for history, Maurischat kept meticulous notes during the filming of the movie. His production diary reveals the extent of Selpin's demands, but also the director's commitment to quality filmmaking, both of which contributed to the numerous delays. Maurischat's diary also notes the ever-present need to imbue the film with Nazi propaganda.

By April 1942 Selpin was halfway through his production schedule. The first two months had gone remarkably well, given the scope of the project and the truncated time frame for filming. However, a number of problems were about to occur that would threaten the entire project. One of the main obstacles involved filming the actual sinking of the *Titanic*. From his initial shots, Selpin realized that the small models would not allow him to capture the realism of the world's largest ship sinking. So Selpin requested that a model of the *Titanic* be built

* The first day of filming was March 12, 1942.

for him, one that would be at least twenty to thirty feet in length and be an exact replica of the celebrated liner. And the director wanted it built immediately. Goebbels again approved the request, and another massive construction project was ordered, involving a naval training workshop and numerous engineers and artists.

The Germans were the most skilled builders of scale models in the world, and the studio in Berlin managed to make a huge and exact replica of the *Titanic*, accurate to the smallest detail, in less than one month. Filming the grand finale with the large model, however, would have to wait. This time the problem was that there were no pools or tanks large enough to accommodate the model. Initially, a water-filled basin covered by a tent roof was used for the sailing and sinking scenes, but Selpin wanted something more realistic. The director therefore decided to film the sinking scene on a lake at Scharmützel in Brandenburg on the outskirts of Berlin. However, to do so required twenty-five trucks be procured in order to transport the massive model and all the equipment from the studios in Berlin. Goebbels again approved the request.

When the film crew arrived at the lake, they realized that they needed to construct a slipway on the lakeshore in order to launch the model ship. But then everything went wrong, starting with the model, which was a work of art but not a marvel of technology. The sinking of the *Titanic* was the highlight of the film, so it had to be realistic. Day after day, the crew tried sinking the ship, but Selpin was not happy with the outcome. It was not realistic enough. A rail system running from just below water level to a depth of roughly thirty feet was constructed in the lake. The idea was that the ship would be pulled along the rails by a steel cable and then submersed in a way that approximated the real sinking. A crane was brought in to put the ship in position and a fake floating iceberg the size of a speedboat was manufactured. Selpin even had smoke from wood burning inside the first chimney pumped into the air to resemble the *Titanic* at steam. When water poured into the chimneys during the sinking scenes, Selpin had them covered with a transparent tarp.

But Goebbels and Selpin could not control every facet of the film; they could not control Mother Nature. The weather failed to cooperate, as rain, storms, and a thick fog rolled over the lake throughout the month of April when Selpin planned to film his ocean scenes and the dramatic sinking. Filming was repeatedly disrupted, further delaying a film that was already well behind schedule.

Another problem concerned historical accuracy. In order to present the details of the sinking of the *Titanic* as they really happened, Selpin needed to film at night. The problem, of course, was that the Royal Air Force had begun nighttime bombing raids, which required Germany to be under a strict blackout order each evening. One of the many demands made by Selpin in his contract was that he wanted to film the sinking at night. So, unfazed, Selpin began preparations to film at night and with large, bright studio lights arrayed around the lake. Of course, the presence of the crew with their lights provided an inviting target for the Allies. The military command wisely denied the request, but Goebbels intervened to overrule them. Selpin would be allowed to film the sinking at night, despite the imminent threat of Allied bombing.

As the war dragged on, Goebbels had become even more paranoid and desperate. He was under mounting pressure from the military and his führer to produce results from his propaganda program. The movie had to be made, regardless of the costs and risks. When the weather improved and air raids slowed, Selpin quickly resumed filming the scenes with the model ship on the lake. However, after repeated setbacks caused by air-raid sirens, power outages, and Allied bombings, this time it would be the electronics on the model ship that halted production. The rushed production schedule for the huge model proved problematic; the electronics on the ship repeatedly malfunctioned. Selpin was forced to send the model ship by truck back to Berlin for repairs. Days turned into weeks of delays. The budget ballooned, and complaints grew both on the set and back in Berlin.

Seemingly oblivious to the mounting tensions, Herbert Selpin demanded more lights, new props, additional time, and a larger budget. Among his outrageous requests was to have the Kriegsmarine transfer complete control to him of the sailors being used as extras on the set. Against his better judgment, Goebbels continued to support every request made by his director. The Little Doctor was now desperate for results and had invested much into a film he saw as his triumphal contribution to victory.

When the model ship was finally repaired and working, Selpin resumed filming. However, when viewing the footage of the model on the lake, Selpin realized the ship looked like what it was: a model. The scale proved to be a problem, even when shooting at twenty-four frames per second (a cinematographer's trick to make the image look life-size). Selpin's answer to the dilemma was to change the speed of filming and use a more expensive film in order to make the ship appear larger. The request was sent to Goebbels, but the director soon discovered that years of war had ended the production of such film and the stock was depleted. The country was running out of everything, including film. Selpin would have to make do with what he had or come up with another solution. He opted for the latter.

The model would not do. The director would make his most outlandish demand yet; this time he wanted a full-size luxury ocean liner as a stand-in for the *Titanic*. Goebbels again complied and sent officials from the Ministry of Propaganda to the Kriegsmarine offices to locate a suitable ship.

WITH THE FILMING IN the studios in Berlin finished, Selpin wanted to move the crew to the coast to film exterior scenes on an ocean liner. Goebbels had become so desperate for his masterpiece to be made that he ordered the naval high command to hand over one of their largest ships. One of the first ships recommended for the job was the *Cap Arcona*, which had been removed from service three years earlier because of the outbreak of war and had been rusting at the naval base at Gotenhafen on the Gulf of Danzig on the Polish coast.

Stripped of its elegant furnishings and painted a drab military gray, the ship was being used by the Kriegsmarine as a floating barracks for sailors and as a U-boat training school. It still had a skeleton crew under the command of Commodore Niejahr and First Officer G. Müller. Moreover, Selpin recognized that the *Cap Arcona* would be the perfect double for the *Titanic*. Its construction and design had been inspired by the legendary ship, and the *Cap Arcona* had been one of the largest, most elegant liners afloat during its heyday. It was only slightly smaller than the *Titanic*.* Selpin, along with Maurischat, Zerlett, and other members of the crew, traveled to see the new star of their film on December 13, 1941. Despite the noisy military base and crowded harbor at Gotenhafen, Selpin knew immediately that the *Cap Arcona* was the right ship.

Filming in the Berlin studios was completed in mid-March 1942, so Selpin now turned his attention to the external and deck scenes. In preparation for its new role as the star of the film, the large German liner was refitted to its former grandeur and repainted to resemble the *Titanic*. The German navy was uncooperative at first, not wanting the smokestacks to be painted white† and opposing night filming for obvious security reasons. They were also reluctant to tilt the ship on its side to simulate the sinking. Without regard to cost or the threat of war, Selpin relocated the entire cast to the southern Baltic, where filming would begin again on April 29, 1942. At least that was the plan.

---

* The *Titanic* was roughly two hundred feet longer and six feet wider than the *Cap Arcona* and had four funnels to the *Cap*'s three.

† The *Titanic*'s smokestacks were black at the top and ochre colored at the bottom, but for a black-and-white film, Selpin needed them to be gray and white.

Chapter 9

THE SINKING OF
THE *TITANIC*

WHILE THE U-BOAT OFFENSIVE in the Atlantic Ocean was proving effective, nearly every other facet of the war was meeting with stiff resistance or failure for Adolf Hitler. Back in Germany, Allied airstrikes intensified in May 1942. Waves of American and British bombers were flying over German territory nearly nonstop, inflicting massive damage to key cities, military bases, and munitions factories. The German people, suffering from severe shortages of food and other essentials, were losing their appetite for war, and the German economy was now teetering on total collapse.

The complexion of the war had changed. It was no longer an expansion of Nazi influence across Europe and into northern Africa; it was now a fight for Germany's very survival. One of the few operations in the Nazi war effort not in crisis mode was the naval training facility on the occupied Polish coast. The southern Baltic had been spared from Allied bombing, and Soviet forces had not yet started their drive westward. The training schedule of the cadets stationed at Gotenhafen was shortened in an effort to help replenish the losses suffered by the Kriegsmarine and warships came and went, but otherwise it was quiet: no sound of gunshots, roar of bomber engines, or the scream of air-raid sirens.

One of the ships that remained in port was the *Cap Arcona*. Sailors and cadets drilled on the massive ocean liner, but such was the relative calm along the southern Baltic that the ship was now rusting badly. It had been moored there for roughly three years of quiet, dull service. But orders arrived from Berlin for naval personnel to be ready to assist with the film and for them to restore the decks of the ship to its sailing heyday.

DESPERATION CAUSED HITLER and Goebbels to impose an even tighter grip on all sectors of German society. Decision making became increasingly centralized, and paranoia ran amok through the Nazi chain of command. Pressure also built for Goebbels to rally public opinion in Germany in support of the war. Hitler awaited the launch of his overdue propaganda front against the British and the release of Goebbels's epic propaganda film, which was now way over budget and behind schedule. Desperate, Goebbels ordered his film about the *Titanic* to continue shooting and demanded it be completed immediately, even though, ironically, people had virtually stopped going to the cinema in Germany.

At the same time, German state media were told to hype the upcoming film. A Berlin newspaper ran a featured story saying, "Thirty years ago the ship of the White Star Line sunk . . . due to the sheer foolishness of irresponsible [owners] and stock market speculations. Tobis is now producing a film about the night of the catastrophe under the direction of Herbert Selpin." Other news reports baited the public with promises of an accurate depiction of the sinking based on "conscientious facts." As a mouthpiece for Goebbels, Tobis Studios promoted the film as also one about "boundless British greed" and "decadent British lords" who were "without scruples." Anticipation for the grand film mounted.

A train loaded with movie equipment, cameras, and crew, including many beautiful actresses from Berlin, headed north. Selpin moved the crew to the German naval base at Gotenhafen, in northern Poland, and assigned his friend and scriptwriter Walter Zerlett-Olfenius the task of preparing the scenes using the *Cap Arcona*.

Zerlett was happy to help and went in advance to oversee preparations for filming. Workers were told to rush the restorations for the
old ocean liner, refurbishing it so that it could serve as a stand-in for
the star and namesake of the grand film. Zerlett was also charged
with auditioning extras from the German navy, rehearsing the cast,
and making sure all preproduction concerns were completed.
Selpin would join his cast and crew later, after finishing business
with Goebbels in Berlin.

Without Selpin's firm hand overseeing the rehearsals, however,
the film set fell into disarray. Already disheartened by the curse that
seemed to plague the film, cast and crew partied rather than rehearsed. The German sailors, delighted to be freed from the drudgery of their training and, most especially, from combat, drank to
excess. They harassed the actresses and wrecked the expensive sets.
The film was now hopelessly behind schedule.

By this time, Selpin was drinking too much and was beginning
to loathe his own film. The director, who had been uninterested in
Nazi Party politics, had grown tired of the invasive presence of
Nazi uniforms and symbolism on his set and in every facet of life in
Germany. Further delays occurred because the film for each scene
shot had to be sent from the coast back to Berlin for approval and
for production. But the director continued to make outrageous requests, such as wanting eighty large spotlights for filming the night
scenes, despite the fact that such lights would make the port an inviting target for Allied attack.

Over the preceding weeks, Selpin had met with Goebbels to
discuss the progress of the film. Goebbels was not happy with the repeated delays, and it showed in his treatment of the director. Trau-
matized by the interrogations he received in May and June, Selpin's
emotional well-being and mental health appear to have deteriorated.

So too had his scriptwriter become a problem. The relationship
between the two collaborators was fraying. When Selpin arrived at
the Polish coast from Berlin a few weeks later, he expected to find
his cast and crew prepared, rehearsed, and ready for filming. The
demanding director was greeted by a far less acceptable site. His

movie set, crew, and film were in complete chaos. It was July, work on the film had essentially come to a standstill, and the director would have to struggle to complete the climactic final scene of the movie—the sinking of the *Titanic.*

Selpin's volatile temper exploded when he arrived on set on April 30. The weather deteriorated as Selpin tried to resume filming, and the background noise in the harbor continually disrupted the shoots. During one shoot, naval personnel curious to see the filming walked through the live scenes. In other scenes, hungover actors and extras missed their lines and marks. The demanding director became more and more irritated. A letter from the production manager, Willy Reiber, to Tobis Studios describes the situation. "Bad weather, rain, web cables, no night filming possible, mood average."

The problems continued through May. Beautiful twenty-seven-year-old actress Monika Burg continually flubbed her lines but attracted enthusiastic crowds of young sailors. Many came on set to get her photograph or request a kiss. Selpin's mood deteriorated, and he openly criticized everyone associated with the film. However, back in his hotel the night of May 15 and likely drinking with senior members of the film and navy, the director had words with his screenwriter. In front of his crew and cast, the feisty director lashed into Zerlett for being unprepared to resume filming and chastised the extras from the Kriegsmarine for their unruly behavior. At one point, the director exploded at his screenwriter and a soldier, "You and your shit soldiers. You shit Lieutenant with your shit Wehrmacht!"

Zerlett came to the defense of the sailors. After the war he testified, saying that Selpin "described me as a 'former shit officer' with your 'shit Iron Cross.' . . . When I told him he could not offend me, he attacked, in meanest forms, the German infantry soldiers, calling them cowardly, pathetic guys who would not destroy Russians, because they shot out of fear into the air and not at the Russians, and then ran away." The decorated veteran of World War I and former intelligence officer with the German General Staff maintained that they were heroes and were thus entitled to a little romance and fun. But Selpin shot back, suggesting that the sailors' military commendations were earned not for bravery in battle but for the number of women they seduced. He then proceeded to loudly condemn the military, the war itself, and even the leadership of Nazi Germany.

Selpin's harsh words for his old friend and screenwriter were, perhaps, deserved. However, his tirade against the sailors and disparaging tone for the military crossed the line. Even if Selpin had not criticized the sailors and ship's captain, his comments on the war and Nazi leadership were tantamount to verbal treason. Snitching had become rampant across Germany and was both encouraged and rewarded by the Nazis. The entire country had succumbed to extreme paranoia. Even an inopportune joke or comment could earn for the individual a death sentence. Nazi spies and members of the Gestapo, the Nazi state police, were everywhere. Most especially, they kept tabs on the film industry.

One of the Germans assigned to spy on Selpin for the regime in Berlin was Zerlett. Even though he and Selpin had always been on good terms, the screenwriter's relationship with his director was secondary to his deep loyalty to the Nazi Party, his ultranationalist views, and his allegiance to men in uniform. Zerlett handed Selpin his resignation on May 15 and walked off the set of the film. The morning after the director's outburst, Zerlett boarded a train for Berlin and informed the Gestapo of his old friend's remarks and accusations.

It is uncertain whether Selpin knew he was being watched by the Gestapo or whether he was aware that Zerlett would inform the Gestapo about him. Selpin trusted Zerlett and was likely emboldened by orders that had been passed down from Goebbels that everyone involved in the film was to offer full cooperation to the director. Such artistic license was rare in Nazi Germany and, when mixed with Selpin's natural disdain for authority and monstrous ego, may have contributed to his carelessness and lack of appreciation for his precarious situation. However, Selpin did comment to his friend and artistic director Fritz Maurischat that he expected Zerlett would report him.*

---

* Maurischat remembered that Selpin had even said that before the Gestapo could arrest him, "I'll jump out of the window."

Prior to the film, Selpin had not been particularly interested in politics, one way or another. As has been noted by Sabine Hake, a film historian at the University of Texas, "[Like Selpin], the vast majority of film professionals who were working in the Nazi film industry were not particularly political. They were careerists, opportunists. They just wanted to do their job and do it well."

Yet Selpin knew only too well that Goebbels and Hitler were deeply and personally invested in his film. Moreover, for months he had made unreasonable requests and been given an unprecedentedly large budget and broad artistic license for his film. Selpin's surviving home movies, filmed during the time he was making the *Titanic,* show him partying excessively. While the German people were struggling with rationing, Selpin seemed oblivious to the war. He ordered lavish meals and hosted grand parties overflowing with alcohol and attractive young women. While filming the *Titanic,* he even commandeered the Grand Casino Hotel, a five-star resort with a swimming pool in the seaside resort town of Aoppot, for his headquarters, even though the cast and crew were housed aboard the *Cap Arcona.* So too did Selpin befriend Oskar Wipper, the ship's chef, who provided the director with as much food and alcohol as he desired. Selpin even took supplies home with him during his weekly trips back to Berlin, while the rest of the cast and sailors struggled on sparse rations. The director's extravagant lifestyle was also at odds with Nazi Party doctrine and had finally caught up with him.

By the time the report of Selpin's "verbal treason" was sent to Goebbels, the propagandist's patience with his director had worn thin. In late July the Gestapo again ordered Selpin to come back to Berlin. His wife and friends were distraught, but Selpin told them not to worry, that he would be back. Yet he knew what was about to happen, commenting to a friend, "I know what will happen—but I have accomplished everything in life, had success, women; it has been good for me. What else is left?" He arrived by train on July 30 and was driven to the propaganda minister's office by the film's production manager, Willy Reiber.

At one o'clock on that very day, Selpin was brought to Goebbels's office by two uniformed guards for a face-to-face interrogation. Leaving the car, Selpin remarked to the driver, "Reiber, the 'heini' has not been nice to me."* A guard told Reiber not to bother waiting. The director was brought before Goebbels, who said, "Mr. Selpin, on May 5 you have made the following statements in front of many witnesses." The interrogation was witnessed by a secretary, who noted that the propagandist proceeded to tick off a colorful but damning list of charges Selpin made during his temper tantrum. It included calling a lieutenant colonel a donkey, a group of pilots "a bunch of assholes and braggarts," and naval personnel "shitters on their submarines."

After finishing the accusations, Goebbels asked, "Is that correct, what is written in this document?" Selpin responded that, if it was the statement he signed, "it is correct." The propagandist repeated, "Do you still stand by these statements?" Without hesitation and in a clear voice, Selpin responded, "Yes, I do." It is not certain exactly what else Goebbels said to his director, but it is likely the meeting was meant to frighten him. It is also likely the director was drinking when he arrived for his final meeting in Berlin. Even though Goebbels was losing patience in Selpin, he gave the director a chance to save his life, asking him to recant and to "correct" the charges made against him. But the director, having become increasingly despondent, remained unapologetic and even admitted every charge read to him from the report. Goebbels was outraged at the display of arrogance and disloyalty. He had placed his trust in Selpin, along with his reputation and the fate of his grand film.

In a desperate and brave attempt to save Selpin, the director's friend Fritz Maurischat, a well-known art director, attempted to appeal to Zerlett. Maurischat's diary survived the war and indicates that he knew he was risking his own life by intervening. Maurischat begged Zerlett to disavow his charges against Selpin in order to save the man's career and life. Zerlett refused, leading Maurischat to accuse him of digging the grave for their old friend.

---

* *Heini* is a German slang term with a derogatory meaning.

Likewise, General Hans Hinkel, a senior official in the Ministry of Propaganda and, since 1944, superintendent of the National Film Office, suggested that the affair simply be swept under the rug. But Goebbels refused his colleague's request, writing on July 31, "I find myself obliged to arrest the film director Selpin and to hand him over to the Volksgerichtshot [People's Court]. He has been found guilty of inept remarks about the Wehrmacht and the conduct of the war in general. He will probably have to be given a long custodial sentence."*

It is likely Goebbels and Selpin knew they were both in hot water. Selpin was risking everything he had worked for and his life. Goebbels was finished with his difficult and demanding director. Not wanting the case to attract attention and unwilling to engage in a political tug-of-war with the Gestapo over the sensitive matter of the treasonous director, Goebbels did not defend Selpin and decided to hand him over to the state police. The Gestapo ordered that Germany's famous director be arrested on July 31 and placed in a prison cell in the basement of the Berlin police prison. He was charged with treason and disloyalty. An account of what happened next exists: "Near midnight on Friday, July 31, 1942, two guards went to Selpin's cell and proceeded to tie his suspenders to the bars of the window high in the ceiling. They brought in a bench. They told Selpin to stand on it and grasp the bars, then tied the suspenders around his neck and took the bench away. When the unfortunate man could no longer hold on, he was strangled to death."

Goebbels had his agents photograph and record the death. The photo shows Selpin in shorts and loose socks, his back against the wall while hanging from a high bar. Goebbels later sent a letter to the director's wife, claiming that her husband had "committed suicide." The propagandist wrote in his diary simply that "Selpin has committed suicide." Of course, it is highly unlikely the diminutive director could have managed to hang himself from the high bars near the ceiling of his cell. The only account that exists about

---

* The People's Court was established in 1934 by Adolf Hitler because he was dissatisfied with the normal judicial process. It tried political offenses and handed down an unusual number of death sentences.

Selpin's death does little to persuade anyone that it was indeed a suicide. The issue remains unresolved.

On August 2, Dr. Otto M. Eppenaur, Selpin's family doctor, examined the corpse and stated that "no traces of external influences could be seen." In 2005 a pathologist with the Forensic Institute at the University of Vienna examined the photographs of Selpin's body and concluded, "We have no evidence of strangulation." However, the physician also stated that further evidence was needed to make a reliable conclusion.

The consensus by Selpin's friends was that it was murder. Members of the cast and crew on the set of *Titanic*, who had no doubt been on the receiving end of Selpin's demanding style, were nonetheless angered by his death. The propagandist notified the crew of Selpin's film that their director had "violated the ethics of war by despicable slander and insults to German soldiers and officers at the front." Nevertheless, Selpin's death angered the German film industry to the extent that Goebbels felt it necessary to issue a defiant warning. It said that anyone who had an issue with Zerlett or anyone attempting to hold Selpin's death against the screenwriter would be summoned to see Goebbels in person. Goebbels also ordered that Selpin's name be banned from the film credits.

So much money, time, and effort had been invested in the making of the *Titanic* that Goebbels needed the film finished without the famed director. He selected a replacement. Werner Klinger, a somewhat unknown director, was tasked with quickly finishing the film. Klinger, who was born in Stuttgart on October 23, 1903, was an actor with few directorial credits to his name. One of them, *The Home Guardsman Bruggler*, was released in 1936 and was a patriotic story about the home guard during World War I. The heroic themes adopted by Klinger for his movies along with his low profile likely factored into Goebbels's decision to hire him.

When Klinger arrived on set of *Titanic*, he found the cast and crew in turmoil. Paranoia and suspicion ran wild, and everyone felt the pressure to finish the project. Most of the filming had already been completed and the script firmly established, so Klinger's role was to shoot the final scenes and oversee the editing of the grand film. He did so, finally finishing it in October 1942.* The finished product ran just shy of one and a half hours in length.†

Goebbels had yet to see his long-awaited masterpiece. The moment came on December 17, 1942, the same day as the worst bombing raid on Berlin at the time. After watching the film in his own private screening room, Goebbels realized the entire project—which had run over budget and long past the due date, and had been plagued by problems of all manner—was a catastrophic mistake!

In his diary, Goebbels noted that he showed a few invited guests the film, but he was alarmed by the possible interpretation of the film by the German public. A film about helpless people on a sinking ship commanded by a foolish leader mirrored the situation in Germany. Also, the country had lost too many sailors during the war, and the sinking scenes were too graphic and realistic. The film would be received by those who had lost loved ones at sea to be, at best, callous and, at worst, a cold slap in the face. In the ultimate twist of irony, the propaganda film designed to be the perfect screen metaphor for all that was wrong with Britain ended up reflecting Nazi Germany.

Emotionally distraught and embarrassed, Goebbels ordered the film banned.‡

Titanic WAS EVENTUALLY shown on a limited basis, after Goebbels authorized its distribution outside of Germany. Released by Tobis Productions for UFA Films in 1943, it was first shown in Prague and then in other German-occupied territories, followed by its release in Switzerland, Sweden, Finland, Greece, Spain, and Belgium. The

---

* The last day of filming was October 31, 1942.

† The film's credits—Director: Herbert Selpin/Werner Klingler; Script: Harald Bratt; Walter Zerlett-Olfenius; Producer: Willy Reiber; Music: Werner Eisbrenner; Camera: Friedl Behn-Grund; Editor: Friedel Buckow.

‡ Werner Klinger survived both World War II and Goebbels's anger over the film. Klinger went on to direct a total of twenty-nine films, most of them action and espionage thrillers of mixed success. He died on June 23, 1972, in Berlin.

film broke box-office records and finally premiered in Paris on September 24, 1943, and shown there throughout the fall. Large crowds turned out for the film in France and generally agreed that it was extremely well made. The film, however, was never screened inside Germany while the Nazis were in power. Goebbels, claiming it lacked any artistic or commercial value, refused to allow it to be seen in the fatherland. *Titanic* was locked away by the propagandist for the remainder of the war until it was rediscovered in 1949 in the Nazi archives. The film was finally shown in a limited engagement in West Germany in 1955.

The Nazis' *Titanic* fell back into obscurity until the year 2005, when it was once again made available to the world. Despite its political message, the finished product is impressive from a technological perspective. Complete with a star-studded cast, elaborate props and sets, and innovative cinematography techniques, the Nazi *Titanic* had many of the ingredients for critical acclaim. Over the ensuing years, many films were made about the world's most infamous ship. One of the most acclaimed films on the topic is *A Night to Remember*. The black-and-white film was released in 1958 by the British company Rank Film Productions and was directed by Roy Ward Baker. Interestingly, for the climactic scene of the ship sinking, Baker chose to use the footage shot by Selpin because of its quality and realism.

Third Role

EVACUATION SHIP

Chapter 10

THE TIDE OF WAR CHANGES

ONE OF THE MAIN TURNING points of the war was Operation Barbarossa, Nazi Germany's invasion of the Soviet Union, which was
named for the medieval Roman emperor and launched on June 21,
1941.* Hitler sent his forces east in what would become an all-or-
nothing campaign. Indeed, the fate of Germany, the Soviet Union,
and Europe hung in the balance. More than three million German
soldiers, a half-million Axis troops, and hundreds of thousands of
trucks, tanks, and horses crossed into Soviet territory in the largest
invasion in world history.

The initial months of the operation went well for the Germans.
They captured vast amounts of land and numerous cities along
Russia's western border while inflicting serious casualties on the
outmatched Soviet forces. The numbers are without precedent in
the annals of military history. More than three million Soviet soldiers were taken prisoner in 1941 alone, most of whom later perished from starvation, and millions more were killed in combat.
Hitler confidently predicted the Soviet Union would fall within a

---

* The operation was announced on national radio the following morning by Goebbels, who said, "At this moment a march is taking place that, for its extent, com-
pares with the greatest the world has ever seen. I have decided today to place the
fate and future of the Reich and our people in the hands of our soldiers."

few weeks. However, the German advance was about to be halted. It would then come completely unhinged when a mixture of impassably muddy roads courtesy of Russia's inadequate infrastructure and a rainy autumn, a bitterly cold winter, shortages of food and supplies, and Hitler's megalomania doomed the invasion.

The powerful Nazi war machine was stopped just miles from Moscow by all these factors and the Red Army's seemingly inexhaustible supply of men, which helped turn the tide of the invasion. In the single most deadly military operation in history, millions of Soviet soldiers and civilians were dead, but the Soviets held and Germany never recovered. It would only get worse for the Nazi regime and the German people.

Almost one year after the ill-fated invasion of the Soviet Union commenced, the director of the epic Nazi propaganda film Herbert Selpin was summoned to Berlin, where he was later found dead. The finished product was soon banned inside Germany. Meanwhile, the movie sets were removed, the actors and film crew headed back to Berlin to begin another propaganda project, and the grand film was largely forgotten—at least inside Germany. The *Cap Arcona* was relegated once again to the dull drudgery of housing German sailors on the Polish coast, just as it had done before being cast as the *Titanic* in the film.

Captains and crews came and went, and the *Cap Arcona* rusted on the Polish coast from September 23, 1942, until March 1945.* During the two and a half years in dock, the ocean liner again fell into disrepair. But the star of the propaganda film was about to get another leading role. The reason: the war was getting even worse for Germany.

BY 1944 YEARS OF WARFARE had drained Germany's finances and the will of the populace, who had suffered through years of severe food and fuel rationing. Throughout the country electricity and water systems no longer functioned, while in Hitler's Berlin residents

---

* Captain F. Seeger was forced to abandon his command by his crew on January 21, 1943, whereupon First Officer G. Müller temporarily assumed control. Roughly one year later, Captain J. Gerdts took command of the ship, followed by Captain H. Bertram, who took control on March 1, 1945.

queued for hours at food shops. The Nazi economy had collapsed, and the German people were reduced to scavenging for food. The reichsmark was not worth the paper on which it was printed, and a crude system of barter had emerged, whereby alcohol, cigarettes, and supplies were exchanged like currency.

It had become difficult to travel anywhere inside Germany, whether by car, boat, train, or airplane. Fuel was scarce, and roads, bridges, and railways were destroyed. Perhaps the main deterrent to travel, however, was the constant bombing campaign by the Allies, which made it unsafe to leave one's home. Few cities in the country were safe from bombing; the Americans attacked by day, and British bombers came at night. Germany's air defenses ceased to exist, yet the air-raid sirens continued their eerie call, reminding Germans of the hopelessness of their situation.

Both the western and the eastern fronts had collapsed. Indeed, the bloody but successful D-Day landing of the Allies at Normandy in June 1944 marked the beginning of the end for Nazi Germany. By August Allied forces had fought their way through France and had liberated Paris. The march to Berlin continued but was fraught with peril. One of the obstacles was the "Siegfried line."

Germany's vaunted defensive line included hundreds of miles of tank traps, machine-gun nests, mines, and other defensive measures organized to deny the Allies entrance to German soil. Like the "Atlantic wall" on the European coast, it proved to be a formidable defensive network. Even though the "wall" and the "line" proved to be only temporary hurdles to the liberation of Europe, they did slow Allied gains and inflict many casualties.* The result of the delay in the march to Berlin allowed the Russians to enter the important city first. Also, each day the Allied invasion was delayed

---

* One effort to subvert the Siegfried line was Operation Market-Garden, the largest airborne campaign at the time, overseen by British general Bernard Montgomery and launched on September 17, 1944. But, tragically, it too stalled and caused further delays. General Dwight Eisenhower was hesitant to undertake an "all-out offensive" that would incur high casualties. Rather, he reluctantly opted for a more cautious strategy for getting to Berlin. Sure enough, on the other side of Berlin, the Soviets ended up suffering perhaps three hundred thousand casualties in the battle for the German capital.

meant more suffering in the concentration camps. The death toll of the Holocaust climbed as the Allies clawed their way across the Continent. Every day mattered.

Another factor impacting the Allies' plans for invading Germany was the rumor that Hitler might retreat to Bavaria, the Austrian mountains at Tyrol near Innsbruck, or elsewhere to make a last stand. Reports suggested that his forces were stockpiling food and weapons in bunkers deep in the mountainous Austrian landscape. Other reports suggested that the Nazis planned to flee to Norway by way of the Baltic Sea in order to use the peninsula with its deep fjords and snowy peaks as a final redoubt. Either scenario would have resulted in the continuation of the war in terrain advantageous to the Nazis. Some Allied commanders advocated a lightning strike to prevent German forces and the Nazi command from escaping to Austria or Norway, but others favored a more methodical approach in order to limit Allied casualties. As the debate raged over a strategy on how to get to Berlin, few military planners factored in the loss of prisoners inside Germany's concentration camps.

But the Allied bombing command did make a decision that would soon have grave consequences for many prisoners inside the camps. For months, American and British aircraft had been conducting a savagely effective air campaign, bombing targets deeper and deeper into Germany. The British air chief, Sir Arthur "Bomber" Harris, hoped the bombing campaign would destroy the will of the German people and military to fight. Accordingly, the targets were not restricted to just military units and bases or trucks, trains, oil refineries, weapons factories, and industrial targets. They also targeted cities.

On the evening of February 13, 1945, nearly 800 Lancaster bombers of the Royal Air Force dropped thousands of tons of bombs in two massive attacks. The target was the historic city of Dresden in the far East of Germany, near the Czech and Polish borders. The following night, 311 American B-17 bombers from the VIII Air Corps hit the city again. The city was leveled, and countless civilians, Allied prisoners of war, and inmates who had the misfortune of being detained nearby in the concentration camp at Muehlberg were killed. The day the bombings ended, a reporter at the Allied Expeditionary Force headquarters filed a dispatch claiming that he had been told that the Allies had adopted a deliberate terror campaign targeting German civilians with the goal of bringing about the end of the war.

A month later, Prime Minister Winston Churchill signaled a shift in British policy when, on March 28, he drafted a message for his senior staff that said, "It seems to me that the moment has come when the question of bombing of German cities simply for the sake of increasing the terror, though under other pretexts, should be reviewed." In part because of the controversy, the British command decided on April 16, 1945, to formally end the widespread bombing of nonmilitary targets. Churchill also shifted primary responsibility for targeting along Germany's northern and coastal airspace from bomber command to fighter command. The problem was that the latter did not have the intelligence or aerial reconnaissance capabilities that the bomber command enjoyed. Fighter command also lacked detailed data on the location of the concentration camps, an oversight that would, in a bizarre twist, soon jeopardize the *Cap Arcona* and thousands of prisoners.

THE WEHRMACHT WAS IN full retreat, as the Allies advanced from all directions into Germany and ultimately to Berlin. Some units fled back toward Berlin. The strict discipline that had defined the Nazi war machine was also in collapse, replaced by disarray and desertion among the troops and miscommunication at the top of the command structure. In Berlin many soldiers lacked weapons or adequate ammunition for the defense of the capital city, while troops on the front lines found that their resupply lines had become nonexistent.

Exactly three years after Germany invaded Russia, Operation Bagration began, when two million Soviet troops counterattacked. By late August 1944, the Soviets had seized Bucharest. In September they were in Estonia. That October the Red Army marched through Belgrade. Later that same month, they entered German East Prussia and began a ruthless campaign, plundering villages and murdering civilians. One of the first German communities taken by the Red Army in 1944 was Nemmersdorf, in the Gumbinnen district of East Prussia. Soviet troops set about brutalizing the population to the extent that any German villager shot outright was lucky.

Women were raped by Soviet soldiers, and their naked bodies were left strewn about the ground both as a warning to others and out of an utter disregard for humanity. Other victims were crucified or thrown into icy ponds and lakes to drown as a form of sport, while Russian soldiers callously wagered bets on the time it would take villagers to die. Other civilians suffered the fate of being tied down while Soviet tanks were driven over the bodies. One account of the Red Army's assault on the people of East Prussia recorded that "children were shot indiscriminately . . . old men and boys castrated and their eyes gouged out before being killed or burned alive. . . . Women were found nailed to barn doors after being stripped naked and gang-raped, their bodies then used for target practice."

Another eyewitness described countless gruesome murders and Soviet soldiers dragging families out of their homes. Those not killed were never heard of again. Another account told of an elderly couple who were "chased into the village pond and forced to stay there until they drowned in the icy waters. A man was hitched to a plow and driven until he keeled over, when a burst from a submachine gun finished him off. The proprietor of the Grumbkow estate, Herr von Livonius, had his arms and legs hacked off and was thrown, still alive, to the pigs."

It was payback time for Nazi aggression. As these stories spread, panic ensued in eastern Germany and Prussia. Many Germans rushed westward and to the south to surrender to American and British forces rather than be caught on the eastern front. Others fighting in East Prussia committed self-inflicted wounds in hopes of being transferred back to Berlin. By 1945 entire communities were fleeing to the Baltic Sea to board ships headed out of Prussia and away from the Russians.

The Allied advance on all fronts meant that concentration camps were liberated. On July 24, 1944, the Soviets arrived at Majdanek, in Poland, the first concentration camp to fall into Allied hands. Like so many camps in Poland, Majdanek was unimaginably gruesome. As early as April 1942, the Schutzstaffel (SS) had killed 2,800 Jews there in one mass orgy of death. On November 3, 1943, a staggering 17,000 inmates were murdered, many with machine guns. Of the roughly 500,000 prisoners to arrive at or near Majdanek, about 200,000 of them died. Of those lost, roughly 125,000 were Jewish.

The Soviets also liberated the notorious camp at Auschwitz on January 27, 1945. They found much of the camp destroyed and deserted, but there were still roughly 1,200 prisoners clinging to life. In haste, they had been abandoned as the Nazis fled the advancing Red Army. Just two weeks earlier, many of the prisoners were marched out of the camp in a last-minute effort to avoid their falling into Soviet hands. More than 1.5 million Jews had died at Auschwitz.

To make matters worse, some German units continued fighting and mounted spirited counteroffensives that stalled the Allied invasion. Throughout Nazi-occupied territories, partisans were murdered in alarming numbers in late 1944 and through the waning months of the war in 1945. Hitler also gave orders to "shoot any officers who retreated," and the SS responded. At the same time, many of the young boys who were drafted to fight were quick to flee when the front lines collapsed. Any such soldier caught deserting was hanged with a sign around his neck reading, "I am a deserter. I was a coward in the face of the enemy."

Every day and every delay by the Allies mattered.* For the Allies, the final days of the war brought with them a series of questions and additional challenges beyond the obvious goal of destroying the

---

* In February 1945, Franklin Roosevelt, Winston Churchill, and Joseph Stalin met at Yalta on the shores of the Black Sea. After much wrangling, the Crimean Conference produced an agreement to conduct coordinated attacks on the remaining forces in Germany.

last vestiges of Nazi resistance. Both sides were faced with the question of what to do about the concentration camps. For the Allies, the march to Berlin contained evidence of the shocking reality that the Nazis had established an extensive system of ruthless concentration camps and had murdered countless innocent people across the Continent. The sheer number of camps and the inhuman conditions of them shocked even the most battle-tested soldiers. Most military units were unprepared to handle the conditions of the camps. It also became apparent to the Allied forces that there might still be hundreds of thousands of prisoners in concentration camps throughout Germany, Poland, and other Nazi-occupied areas not yet liberated. The march to Berlin meant that each victory and each liberated camp spared lives from the crematoriums.

The fate of countless Allied and German soldiers as well as civilians inside Germany also hung in the balance. Soon, the timing of the Allied march to Berlin would even matter for an old ocean liner.

Chapter 11

EVACUATION

RECOGNIZING THE THREAT TO soldiers and civilians in German-occupied territories, in late 1944 Admiral Karl Dönitz of the Kriegsmarine began planning for their evacuation. The situation further deteriorated when the Soviets entered Germany's eastern borders in January 1945. Germans were looking to get out of the region by any means necessary. But any escape by land for those trapped behind the rapidly advancing Red Army would now be impossible. The evacuation would have to be by sea. With limited warships available for the operation, Dönitz would end up relying on any available craft, including a few famous ocean liners. It would be perhaps the largest evacuation in history.

Only a few years earlier, the Germans had driven the British army off the Continent, necessitating another massive naval rescue operation at Dunkirk. The date was May 26, 1940, and the war had come within a few miles of ending in a Nazi victory during the Battle of France. German forces were able to overrun France's border defenses to the east known as the "Maginot line" and also invade the Netherlands to the north. The lightning speed with which the Nazi war machine was able to accomplish these objectives caught the French, British, and Belgian armies by surprise. Allied counterattacks failed, and the tip of the German spear drove ever deeper through France and ultimately to the western edge of the Continent.

The result was that the Allied armies were separated and trapped in narrow corridors with their backs to the sea. With the Germans turning north and seizing port after port, there was little chance of reinforcement or rescue. The remaining Allied troops were surrounded and cut off from escape by land. However, with the war hanging in the balance, the Nazi command issued what history calls the "Halt Order." The German advance stopped, allegedly in order to consolidate their forces before driving the British and French into the sea. This gave the British a brief window of opportunity to organize an escape. Churchill acted.

Beginning on May 26 and lasting for eleven remarkable days, the Royal Navy sent every craft that would float to the French coast to evacuate the British and French forces. Roughly 338,000 men were saved, including 123,000 French soldiers. Even though the Allies suffered an embarrassing defeat, the armies lived to fight another day. The massive naval evacuation denied Hitler a quick and complete victory in the war.*

This time it would be the Nazis who undertook a mass rescue operation for soldiers and civilians from conquered territories. It began in January and included civilians, members of the army, and SS officers and soldiers, many of whom had been living with their wives and children in confiscated homes in the occupied East. The effort was organized by Dönitz and Vice Admiral Konrad Engelhardt and has been called "the greatest evacuation operation in history."

In contrast to the British evacuation in the English Channel in 1940, the German evacuation of 1945 was launched from ports in the Baltic. Nearly one million Germans were able to board transport ships from the port of Danzig, headed to locations in the West such as Nazi-held Copenhagen. The operation also involved the

---

* Allied casualties included approximately 11,000 dead and 40,000 captured, along with the loss of numerous tanks, artillery pieces, and trucks, abandoned during the rushed evacuation.

port at nearby Gotenhafen, the site of present-day Gdynia on the Polish coast. It was the home port for two of Germany's celebrated ocean liners: the *Cap Arcona* and the *Wilhelm Gustloff.*

MOST OF THE FIGHTING BETWEEN the Germans and Russians during World War II occurred on land. However, there were critical naval campaigns, including the battle for the control of the Baltic. Germany had controlled the Baltic for much of the war, taking key ports such as Gotenhafen, where the final scenes of the Nazi propaganda film about the *Titanic* were shot. Kriegsmarine torpedo boats, warships, and U-boats were based there and patrolled the frigid waters for most of the war. The Allies prioritized other fronts during the war and made little progress on the Baltic because Hitler deployed thousands of mines in the sea, which also served to deny the Soviets the ability to move troops or conduct trade, and to bottle up the Soviet fleet in the Gulf of Finland. With control of the Baltic, Germany was able to supply and reinforce troops on the eastern front with relative ease.

All that changed at the end of the war. By early 1945, the Kriegsmarine was broken, and Soviet submarines prowled the Baltic. Alerted to the massive evacuation from Gotenhafen and other locations, Soviet subs began hunting every German ship. One of them was the infamous *Wilhelm Gustloff.*

With thousands of refugees crowded onto ports along the Baltic, Captain Friedrich Peterson of the *Gustloff* was ordered to pick up soldiers and civilians fleeing the Red Army and transport them to Kiel in the West, near the border with Denmark. The *Gustloff* was an unlikely transport craft. Much like the *Cap Arcona*, in its heyday it had been a grand liner. One of its famous cruises, which happened to be up the River Thames in April 1938, was even covered by media outlets across England and Germany. It was a favorite of many top Nazi officials and had personally been inspected by Adolf Hitler, who proclaimed it one of the world's foremost ships. The liner was also part of the Strength Through Joy program that provided German workers with inexpensive cruises and vacations.

Measuring 684 feet in length and displacing nearly 26,000 tons, the *Gustloff* was equipped to carry 1,463 passengers. Built by Blohm + Voss, the company responsible for the *Cap Arcona*, it was one of the largest ships assigned to evacuate the eastern front.

The large white ship with one thick funnel was named for the forty-one-year-old former head of the Nazi Party in Switzerland, who happened to be a close friend and ardent supporter of Hitler. Gustloff was a controversial figure whose brutality led to his assassination in 1936. The man who pulled the trigger that ended Gustloff's life was David Frankfurter, a young Croatian Jew who had been studying dentistry in Germany but fled to Switzerland. The death of Gustloff at the hands of a Jew sent Hitler into a rage. Moreover, the details of the murder—Frankfurter had approached the Nazi leader at his home and shot him five times in the head, neck, and chest in Gustloff's private study—provided fodder for propaganda.

Hitler and Goebbels used the commemoration of Gustloff's death to ratchet up their vicious war against Europe's Jews. Goebbels orchestrated a highly public funeral for the fallen Nazi politician, held on February 12, 1936, and attended by a large cadre of Nazis, including Hitler and Goebbels. "Heil Hitler" salutes memorialized Gustloff, and the führer announced to those in attendance that the murder was part of a larger Jewish plot against Germans, describing "the hate-filled power of our Jewish foe, a foe to whom we had done no harm, but who nonetheless sought to subjugate our German people and make of it its slave—the foe who is responsible for all the misfortune that fell upon us in 1918, for all the misfortune which plagued Germany in the years that followed."*

In 1938 Hitler named a ship after his late friend. It was christened by Gustloff's widow in a highly propagandized ceremony. Since 1940 the *Gustloff* had been reassigned to Gotenhafen, where it functioned briefly as a hospital ship and then served alongside its famous sister ship *Cap Arcona* as a U-boat training platform. Its

---

* After the funeral, Frankfurter was convicted of murder and sent to a prison in Switzerland. He served through the war but was later pardoned, whereupon he moved to Israel where he resided until his passing in 1982.

demotion was viewed by some as proof the ship was cursed. After all, reasoned the crew, the *Gustloff* was named for a controversial slain leader and its captain, Carl Lübbe, died of malaria on the bridge of the ship on the maiden voyage in 1938.

Like the *Cap Arcona*, the *Gustloff* had fallen into disrepair while docked in Gotenhafen. The luxurious interior was stripped, the paint had chipped away, and the ship now carried antiaircraft guns. In January 1945, in preparation for the massive evacuation mission, the ship's engines were repaired, and it was once again seaworthy. But nothing could have prepared the ship's crew for what lay in store for them.

Panicked crowds of passengers were waiting for the *Gustloff* at Gotenhafen's port. People had come from miles around with little more than the clothing on their backs while fleeing certain and barbaric death at the hands of the Russians. Refugees were dying of hunger or disease while waiting to board the ship. News of the Soviet advance on the outskirts of the city only contributed to the anxiety most refugees felt. When it was finally time to board, thousands of refugees, suffering from freezing temperatures and little or no shelter, shoved and clawed their way onto the large liner.

The ship was dangerously overcrowded. Passengers outnumbered lifejackets and lifeboat capacity. Food and water were scarce, and toilets no longer worked; the smell caused even seasoned members of the crew to be sick to their stomachs. A few of the refugees, already weak and ill, died while the ship was still docked and preparing to sail. Yet despite the conditions and a bitterly cold day in January, the ship held out hope of survival for the throngs of refugees pouring into the port. However, after accepting thousands of refugees, the crowded ship was forced to sit in port for three days on account of Soviet submarine activity throughout the southern Baltic. The British Royal Air Force was also now patrolling much of the Baltic, having sunk eighteen German ships in these waters during the month of January alone. It was too dangerous to go to sea. Yet as reports arrived of the progress made by the Soviet army marching toward Gotenhafen, it was clear that it was too dangerous to stay in port.

Just as the ship was about to cast off its lines and set sail, air-raid sirens came screaming to life. Allied aircraft had been spotted in the skies above Gotenhafen. The order came down from the bridge: "Everybody off!" Passengers were hurried down the gangplanks; others were too weak to stand, much less walk, and remained behind. It proved to be a false alarm. Ultimately, the passengers were reboarded, and the ship set a course for Mecklenburg and Kiel. It was its first voyage in roughly four years. It sailed at night along the Pomeranian coast in an attempt to elude submarines and warplanes that might be waiting deeper in the Baltic.

As the ship traveled out of the bay and into the blackness of the Baltic on the freezing cold evening of January 30, Captain Peterson ordered that a speech by Hitler be broadcast over the ship's intercom. The führer was commemorating the occasion of his twelve years in power. But it is likely his words rang hollow to the refugees crammed onto the ship. The captain made another, more fateful, order that evening. Due to the murky weather, he ordered the ship be illuminated to avoid a collision with another transport. Unknown to the crew and passengers, lurking just below the water was a Soviet sub. It homed in on the brightly lit liner.

Only minutes after Hitler's speech ended, the *Gustloff* was fired upon. Four torpedoes were launched from the nearby Soviet submarine. One torpedo jammed in the launch tube, but the other three found their target on the starboard side of the ship. Freezing water rushed through the gaping holes in the hull of the liner. Already overcrowded, the ship immediately began listing. Most of the refugees were trapped belowdecks and at the waterline. They therefore had no chance. Many of those traveling in the deep holds of the ship died instantly. Those lucky enough to get to the top deck discovered several of the systems for deploying lifeboats had failed. Maintenance on the ship was long overdue. Others jumped or were knocked overboard into the freezing water, where they drowned or died within minutes from hypothermia.

The *Gustloff* sank in under an hour. Because they were not far from the Polish coast, transport ships from a passing convoy would have been in a position to respond to the distressed ship. However, due to the risk of being torpedoed by the same sub, the large transport ships in the convoy abandoned the *Gustloff*. A few smaller craft did come to lend assistance to those who managed to make it into lifeboats. Roughly 900 people were saved, including the captain and three most senior officers, who chose not to assist their passengers, but an estimated 9,000 perished.*

Less than two weeks later, on February 10, the 550-foot ship *Baron von Steuben*, named for the Prussian military officer who helped train the fledgling colonial army during the American Revolution, was torpedoed and sank while sailing from Gotenhafen to Copenhagen. It was hit with two torpedoes by the same submarine that attacked the *Gustloff* and sank in the same waters.

Like the *Gustloff*, the *Steuben* was fleeing the advancing Red Army and transporting refugees. Also like its sister ship, the hospital ship had sailed only a few miles into the Baltic before being intercepted by a Soviet submarine. Nearly 3,000 wounded German soldiers and more than 1,100 civilian refugees from East Prussia filled the overcrowded decks, rooms, and hallways. Built in 1922, it was a sturdy ship. But the torpedoes struck at an angle that caused the hull to split. The *Steuben* took fewer than twenty minutes to sink. Roughly 3,500 people were lost; only 659 were rescued by passing transport ships, making the incident another one of the worst maritime disasters in history.†

The submarine that sank the *Wilhelm Gustloff*, *Baron von Steuben*, and many other vessels was the *S-13*, one of history's most feared and infamous submarines. It would later hunt the *Cap Arcona*. The sub was captained since 1942 by Alexander Marinesko, who was

---

* Estimates of the tragedy vary because of the chaos surrounding the final months of the war and overcrowded conditions on board the ship. Death toll estimates vary from a low of 5,400 to a high of 9,400. One thing most scholars agree on is that many of those lost were women and children.

† An interesting note to this tragedy is that the *Baron von Steuben* was not discovered until 2005, the hull split but resting on its side in 170 feet of water.

both a legend in the Soviet navy and one of the more controversial figures of the war on account of his ruthless attacks on civilian ships. Raised in Odessa by a Ukrainian mother and Russian father, Marinesko rose rapidly through the military ranks.

Marinesko had been motivated to become a submariner by a fateful incident that had occurred back in 1939. It also involved a passenger ship and a submarine. The British liner SS *Athenia* was sailing in the Irish Sea, roughly two hundred miles off the Welsh coast. Little did its captain or crew know, but it was being hunted by the Nazi submarine *U-30*, commanded by Fritz-Julius Lemp. The British liner was carrying more than 1,400 passengers and crew, many of whom were Jewish refugees. Approximately 300 Americans were also on board. Although unprovoked, Lemp attacked and fired what were perhaps the first shots in what would become the Battle of the Atlantic. Roughly 120 people, including many women and children and 22 Americans, were killed in the surprise attack. It was the first British ship sunk by Germany in the war.

Newspaper accounts in the United States and Europe expressed shock and condemnation at the attack. But the tragedy of the *Athenia* was soon forgotten, overshadowed by the Nazi invasion of Poland and start of the war, and thus largely forgotten by history. But it was not forgotten by Marinesko, who was both angered over the attack and intrigued by submarines. He decided to become a submarine commander and would end up being one of the most successful of the war. The sinking of the *Athenia* also caught the attention of Joseph Goebbels, who rewrote history with claims that the British sank their own ship in order to bring the United States into the war.

With Marinseko's submarine being but one of many operating in the Baltic at the end of the war, it was a very dangerous place. Even though there were international agreements against targeting hospital ships and those on humanitarian missions, the Soviets—like the Nazis before them—actively hunted and destroyed them, ignoring international standards such as The Hague Convention and often completing the attacks by shooting any survivors in the water or on lifeboats. In total, about 25,000 lives were lost during the evacuation from Prussia and eastern Germany, many of them on the *Gustloff* and *Steuben*. Several other German hospital and transport ships were lost, along with many warships and submarines.

Despite the loss of ships and constant threat from Soviet submarines and British bombers, the evacuation continued through the winter. The name given to the massive evacuation was Operation Hannibal. It began in January with the knowledge that the approaching Red Army was unstoppable. In total, from January 23 until May 8 when the war ended, more than eight hundred ships evacuated a total of 2 million civilians and refugees as well as 1 million soldiers from the advancing Red Army. With the war all but over and Germany in ruin, the Kriegsmarine still managed in April 1945 alone to evacuate 254,887 people. This feat was accomplished even though the German army was nearly defeated, the command structure was largely hunkered down in Berlin, and the Allies had complete control of the skies above the Baltic. Indeed, Admiral Dönitz and Vice Admiral Engelhardt had to contend with limited resources (Germany was running out of fuel, ammunition, and ships) and the constant threat of naval and air attacks on their convoys.

The admirals faced another problem. There were not enough ships. Because of severe shortages of coal, the Kriegsmarine was forced to conscript oil-burning ships, including several ocean liners, for the mission. As a result, in January 1945, after three years of serving as a floating barracks and naval training platform in Gotenhafen, the *Cap Arcona* was restored and reactivated for the operation. The interiors were stripped of any remaining furnishings in order to make room for additional refugees. The old ship was barely seaworthy, but the times were desperate for Germany. The ship was about to begin another intriguing role in its fascinating life.

The mission: Load refugees from the swelling population at Gotenhafen and do so while the port was struggling with shortages of food and fuel as well as riots sparked by the threat of the approaching Red Army. That done, the liner would transport the refugees to Denmark or other German-occupied areas, where they would be housed at temporary camps hurriedly set up by the Nazi command. The empty ship would be refueled (if fuel was available); loaded with food, medicine, and supplies; and sent back for more refugees. Each crossing of the Baltic required the ship to navigate a gauntlet of Soviet submarines and British bombers.

The *Cap Arcona* was now commanded by Johannes Gerdts. On January 31, it departed its berth in Gotenhafen, where the ship had been docked since November 29, 1939. For the first run, the former luxury liner was overloaded with ten thousand refugees. During that initial evacuation across the Baltic, the *Cap Arcona* struck a Soviet mine. Luck was with the old liner, as damage was minimal and, although it was without any guns or defenses, it managed to elude any warplanes and submarines.

The *Cap Arcona* arrived in Copenhagen and unloaded its passengers. Captain Gerdts and his crew were under tremendous stress during the crossing. All aboard knew the end was at hand for Germany. Passengers were starving and homeless; most were sick, and several died during the voyage from a lack of food and water. Seeing so many desperate refugees and hearing their stories of Russian atrocities on the eastern front further unnerved even the hardiest of veteran sailors. While in port awaiting refueling and repairs, the captain was visited by Nazi officials and other ship commanders, all of whom shared similar stories of despair and rampant destruction in German cities.

On February 20, Gerdts was visited in his cabin by a Captain Mende, whose team was inspecting the ship. Mende passed along the order that the *Cap Arcona* would again have to navigate death alley to pick up more refugees. The two officers also discussed the repairs needed for the ship. After the brief meeting, Mende put on his overcoat, holstered his duty weapon, and departed the cabin. Without warning at around ten that evening, Captain Gerdts shot himself in the head. The ship's physician, Dr. Appelbaum, was unable to revive him and pronounced his senior officer dead.

Captain Gerdts's body was removed from the ship at approximately four thirty the following morning. The local Nazi police force boarded the ship and conducted an investigation of the shooting. Gerdts had some minor health problems and was not a young man, but there were no plans to replace him and no reason to question his fitness for command. After interviewing the crew and Captain Mende, it was determined that there was no sign of foul play, and Gerdts's death was declared to be a suicide brought on by "intense depression" over the stressful evacuation and the prospects of another dangerous trip across the Baltic.

Gerdts was replaced as captain on March 1 by Heinrich Bertram, commander of the *Monte Rosa*, another liner converted to function as a transport ship. Bertram, a stocky, squared-jawed, experienced sailor, had previously served on the *Cap Arcona* from October 1933 to the spring of 1938 as second officer and later as first officer under Richard T. Niejahr. Before the *Cap Arcona* could sail out of Copenhagen for another evacuation mission, however, its turbines and engines had to be overhauled. The ship was not in its prime and was showing signs of age and neglect.

After the repairs, the liner undertook another round-trip crossing. Bertram sailed his ship at full speed in order for the *Cap Arcona* to outrun Soviet submarines that pursued it, which likely included Captain Marinseko's *S-13*. The ship completed the mission, but its engines, which had received only patchwork repairs, were again failing. It appeared that the once-proud ocean liner would end its service in Copenhagen. However, Nazi officials wanted one of their largest ships back in service.

Captain Bertram received an urgent radio message that another 300,000 refugees were waiting along the German and Polish coasts and time was of the essence. A third mission was undertaken on March 27. The *Cap Arcona* crossed the Baltic and was met in port by crowds of panicked civilians and wounded soldiers, who then clambered aboard, packing the ship far beyond its capacity. Hundreds of refugees were lined up on the decks, thousands were jammed into the holds, and hundreds more filled the grand salon.

In total, the *Cap Arcona* picked up an additional 8,000 to 9,000 refugees and transported them back to Denmark, arriving on April 5.

However, it was no longer possible to sail into Gotenhafen or Danzig, as Soviet troops had seized the region and submarines lay in wait for any German ships on that route. The *Cap Arcona* made a total of three harrowing round-trips across the Baltic. An estimated 25,795 wounded soldiers, civilian refugees, and Nazi officials from East Prussia were safely evacuated by the liner from the advancing Red Army.

Even though very few ports remained open for German shipping, Captain Bertram received a vague and cryptic order to report to Lübeck Bay at Neustadt, in north-central Germany. On April 13, the *Cap Arcona* made its last voyage. The former luxury liner arrived safely the next day, the turbines completely worn out. It was joined off the coast of Neustadt by two other ships, both of which had also helped to evacuate refugees across the Baltic: the *Thielbek*, a 2,800-gross-ton freighter, and the *Deutschland*, an ocean liner a bit smaller than the *Cap Arcona*. They anchored next to their sister ship, but the crews were unaware of the reason they were ordered to the bay.

Chapter 12

NEUENGAMME

AMONG THE PRISON POPULATION suffering during the Allies' slow and difficult march to Berlin were those housed at Neuengamme. Located by the Elbe River just southeast of the city of Hamburg in northern Germany, Neuengamme was part of the *konzentra-tionslager*—the system of camps built by the Nazis in the 1930s and 1940s. It was originally opened as an annex of Sachsenhausen concentration camp in December 1938. The first large group of prisoners—roughly one hundred in total—arrived on December 12 and 13 of that year. Ironically, the new prisoners at Neuengamme were forced to build the camp and facilities where they and thousands more would be detained. As if the years spent in detainment and hard labor had not been harsh enough, the prisoners from Neuengamme were about to be thrust into one of the most shocking incidents of the war. It involved a once-luxurious ocean liner that, in the final days of the war, was ordered into port near the camp.

Neuengamme was a work camp where bricks and other construction materials were produced to meet the need for the Nazis' ambitious economic development plan. The concentration camp also served the German firm Earth and Stone Works, which had purchased the defunct brickyard in Neuengamme in September

1938. The company functioned largely as an extension of the SS and entered into a contract in April 1940 with the City of Hamburg to provide bricks for public works and building projects. One of the first large infrastructure efforts Earth and Stone Works undertook was to dig a canal linking the old factory with a tributary of the Elbe and a nearby railway system in order to transport the bricks produced in the camp out to cities in the region.

The brick factory was reopened, and on June 4, 1940, Neuengamme became an independent camp. With numerous construction projects planned for Hamburg and the vicinity, the concentration camp grew rapidly. In time, it expanded into a massive community of fences, barbed wire, and guards surrounding large barracks. Just one month after Neuengamme was established, the prisoner population had grown to more than 1,000. By late 1940, there were roughly 3,000 prisoners in Neuengamme.

The population continued to grow in the fall of 1941 when thousands of Soviet prisoners were transported there. In fact, for much of the camp's existence, Soviet prisoners of war and refugees constituted the largest segment of the inmate population. A total of 34,500 Soviet soldiers and citizens passed through the camp and its subcamps during the war, nearly 6,000 of whom were women. The population reached 10,000 by the end of 1943; they were now coming from everywhere in Europe.

An extensive system of subcamps was needed because the prisoner population at Neuengamme had grown too large. The bustling camp would end up having about ninety subcamps, such as Fuhlsbutte and Wittmoor. By the end of the war, there were more prisoners living and working in the subcamps than in Neuengamme proper. Approximately 12,000 prisoners were in the camp in 1944, with twice that many in the subcamps; by the end of that year, the overall population had swelled to 49,000. This included female prisoners, who first arrived in November 1943.*

---

* Neuengamme was unique in that, eventually, one-quarter of its subcamps were designated for female prisoners.

Initially, few Jews were imprisoned at Neuengamme. Even as late as 1942, there were only about 300–500 Jewish inmates, many of them political prisoners. However, a group of Jewish prisoners was transferred that summer from Auschwitz. In the chaotic final year of the Holocaust, the SS brought roughly 13,000 Jews to Neuengamme, most of them from Hungary and Poland via Auschwitz. About 3,000 of the Jewish prisoners were women. In total, about 106,000 prisoners were brought to Neuengamme from its opening until the end of the war. The camp housed sizable populations of inmates from all walks of life and faiths and from many countries across Europe, reflecting the bewildering magnitude of the Holocaust.* When the camp was liberated on April 10, 1945, there were only 13,500 prisoners remaining.

When entering Neuengamme for processing, a prisoner's initial experience was with the SS guards and *kapos*. Established by camp commandants, *kapos* were prisoners who cooperated with the commandants and SS guards in supervising the other inmates. In return, they were afforded slightly better living conditions, including extra food rations, and were typically not put to death. Tragically, history is filled with examples of the *kapos* acting as brutally as the guards themselves; the complicity of some Jewish *kapos* in the Holocaust proved to be a difficult subject during the war-crimes tribunals and remains a deeply troubling moral dilemma in the Jewish community even today.

Indeed, Neuengamme was among the camps that suffered from a few especially brutal *kapos*. These overseers doled out savage beatings and punishments, including whippings, solitary confinement, forcing prisoners to stand at attention for hours on end in freezing temperatures, and hanging inmates from posts for the most minor

---

* Neuengamme's population included Soviets (28,450 men, 5,900 women), Poles (13,000 men, 3,900 women), French (11,000 men, 500 women), Germans (8,800 men, 400 women), Dutch (6,650 men, 300 women), Belgians (4,500 men, 300 women), Danes (4,800 men), Hungarians (1,400 men, 1,200 women), Norwegians (2,200 men), Yugoslavs (1,400 men, 100 women), Czechs (800 men, 580 women), Greeks (1,250 men), Italians (850 men), Spaniards (750 men), Australians (300 men, 20 women), Luxembourgers (50 men), and others. There was even an Icelander.

of alleged offenses. The *kapos* were not the only threats to the prisoners of Neuengamme. The camp's staff and guards were vicious practitioners of torture, detainment, and death. This includes one of the camp administrators, Major Christoph-Heinz Gehrig, who was notorious because of his record of having many children put to death. He would later terrorize prisoners on board the *Cap Arcona*.

The prisoners at the camp also suffered under the leadership of savage commandants. The first of them was Major Walter Eisele of the SS, who was appointed by Heinrich Himmler to organize and construct the camp. In April 1940, Eisele was replaced by Lieutenant Colonel Martin Weiss. However, Commandant Weiss was sent to Dachau at the end of the summer of 1942, whereupon Lieutenant Colonel Maximillian Johann Pauly became the commandant of Neuengamme. He would prove to be the worst of the lot.

The son of a hardware store owner, Pauly was born on June 1, 1907, in Wesselburen, Germany, and, at age eighteen, the young man became a clerk in the store. A few years later, in 1928, Pauly's father died, and he assumed control of the family business. That same year Pauly joined the Nazi Party. Two years later he married and began working for the SS, where he was assigned to organize local SS branches. Pauly demonstrated proficiency in promoting the Nazi cause and was rewarded with a post as the police commandant in Danzig. Climbing the Nazi hierarchy and becoming increasingly fanatical in his beliefs, in 1936 Pauly decided he no longer had the time to run the family hardware store. Management of the store was passed to his brother, and Pauly dedicated his life to the Nazi Party. He would soon get another promotion of sorts.

When the Nazis began building concentration camps, the father of five children was made one of the first commandants. His appointment came in September 1939 when he was made commandant of Stutthof, a labor camp composed mostly of Polish prisoners. Described as "a cruel man," Pauly was a ruthless disciplinarian. He even handed out severe reprimands to his own staff. For instance, in November 1944, a human jaw bone was discovered in the soup cooker at Neuengamme. It turned out that the *kapos* in charge of the kitchen and crematorium had made a deal to sell the camp's sparse meat rations to nearby businessmen. The kitchen *kapos* then replaced the meat in the soup with the flesh from dead inmates at the camp. Pauly put his officer in charge of the *kapos* on trial. However, the lieutenant colonel was less concerned with the nightmarish scenario in the kitchen than he was with the fact that he had not authorized the act. He charged his guard with "committing an atrocity without permission." Tragically for the inmates, Pauly stayed in his post until the end of the war. Thousands would die because of his actions.

The main work being done by the prisoners at Neuengamme was producing bricks, mining clay, and building and maintaining canals to transport the bricks to the nearby river. But the camp also served a number of other industrial and war efforts. In 1942 several private companies with ties to the SS such as Carl Jastram Motorenfabrik, Messap, and Walther-Werke established operations at Neuengamme and its many subcamps for the purpose of manufacturing an array of war products, including armaments and ammunition as well as U-boat parts and antiaircraft shells. Later, Bremen and Hamburg, a machine, tool, and shipbuilding company, began production at the camp. Germany's capitalists were eager to exploit the "free" prisoner workforce, including women, who constituted roughly one-third of all laborers involved in armament and industrial production.

Inmates worked exceedingly long days through any weather conditions—from the heat of the summer to the snow and cold of Germany's winters—in their tattered striped uniforms. They worked without sophisticated equipment, digging the rich, heavy peat with old shovels and making bricks with crude tools. The labor was hard; the beatings they suffered were worse. Prisoners were also given jobs that put their lives in danger. During Allied bombings, cities in northern Germany were destroyed. Inmates from Neuengamme were sent to collect the unexploded ordinance and clean up collapsed buildings and piles of rubble in the city streets. Yet when air-raid sirens sounded, the prisoners were not able to join civilians in the shelters. Consequently, on April 17, 1943, when Allied bombers struck the city of Bremen, six prisoners from Neuengamme were caught out in the open and died in the attack.

Prisoners endured physical abuse and emotional intimidation from the SS guards, a lack of hygiene, unsanitary water, starvation, virtually no health care, and even less access to any material comforts and the outside world. Diseases such as tuberculosis and typhus ran rampant through Neuengamme and its subcamps. Most inmates struggled with pneumonia at some point during their incarceration, and a bout with typhus at the camp killed a thousand prisoners in December 1941 alone. Mortality rates stayed so high that a cremation station was constructed at the site in April 1942. Prior to having their own mortuary, inmates were taken to Hamburg to be cremated.

Neuengamme is remembered as a labor camp rather than a death camp, such as the notorious camps at Auschwitz, Birkenau, Treblinka, and Sobibor. Yet conditions were brutal and violent at the camp, and evidence exists that the camp commandant authorized both deplorable medical experiments and the use of poison gas on the prisoners. The commandant also enforced Operation 14f13, which began in April 1941 and was authorized by Heinrich Himmler, head of the dreaded Gestapo. Also known as "Special Treatment," the order required those prisoners deemed unsuitable to be sent to killing centers and gassed. This included what Himmler deemed "excess ballast"—the elderly, the weak, the mentally ill, and those too sick to work. Consequently, a prisoner euthanasia center for Neuengamme was established at Bernberg an der Saale. From 1942 until the camp's demise in 1945, roughly two thousand prisoners were brought there expressly for the purpose of being killed by lethal injection or medical experiments.

Evidence for these horrors was uncovered during the war-crimes trials conducted by the British Military Tribunal in Hamburg in 1946. In one instance, a former medical orderly at Neuengamme named Wilhelm Bahr stated that two hundred Russian prisoners were gassed with prussic acid (a.k.a. Zyklon B) in 1942. While testifying against war criminal Bruno Tesch, Bahr claimed he was instructed to "open a couple of harmless looking tin boxes, the directions read 'Cyclon, vermin destroyer. Warning, poisonous.'" He described the boxes being filled with small pellets that he said resembled blue peas. Bahr dispensed the prussic acid through "apertures" in the roof throughout the gas chamber. He noted that "in each case the cover is carefully replaced on the aperture. . . . Cyclon works quickly, it consists of a cyanic acid compound in a modified form."

Quickly indeed. At the postwar trials, Bahr remembered what happened next. "After about two minutes the shrieks die down and change to low moaning. Most of the men have already lost consciousness. After a further two minutes . . . it is all over." When cross-examined about why he had gassed the prisoners, Bahr stated the usual refrain, "I only obeyed orders." He claimed he was told to do so by a camp doctor. When the British military prosecutor asked what happened next, Bahr claimed he did not know because he departed the gas chamber. His reason: it was lunchtime and he was hungry.

Another horrific part of life at Neuengamme was the medical experiments. In addition to producing bricks and armaments, the camp was used for so-called scientific and medical research. A number of notorious Nazi physicians and researchers worked out of the camp or visited it, reflecting the priority given by the Reich to Neuengamme's experiments. Nazi Germany's Institute for Maritime and Tropical Diseases also used Neuengamme's prisoners to test a variety of diseases, including typhus and those transmitted by lice.

Several cruel experiments were conducted in the winter of 1944 and 1945 by Dr. Ludwig-Werner Haase, who was working on a water filter. To test the effectiveness of the device, he gave 150 prisoners at the camp water containing arsenic at one hundred times the safe dosage and then tried to filter it with his invention. Most of the inmates suffered horribly; a few died.

One of the most tragic experiments conducted at Neuengamme was the tuberculosis tests. In 1930 the nearby city of Lübeck, on Germany's Baltic coast, was stricken by an outbreak of tuberculosis. In hopes of preventing future outbreaks, the city's hospital began experimenting with a vaccination that was administered orally. However, little was known about the disease, and the trials were dangerous. Three researchers ran the trials and administered a schedule of three doses to 251 newborns and children. Fully 73 of the children died, and it was discovered that the vaccine was contaminated with the virulent Koch bacillus. Amid the ensuing panic, the vaccination program was suspended, even though it was the most effective agent in the fight against tuberculosis.

In 1944 doctors and researchers in Berlin and at Neuengamme decided to replicate the hospital trials. For the test, the SS chose Jewish infants and children from the prison population in Germany, most of them from Auschwitz. A total of 25 children ranging in age from six to twelve years of age were sent to Neuengamme for the study. Three weeks after arriving at the camp, they were infected with the disease by making small incisions under the arms in which cultures of the bacilli were placed.

The children were held in an isolated barrack and placed under the care of researchers. Every child came down with the disease and showed numerous signs of the illness, including increased temperatures and swelling and redness in the infected area and glands. The experiment was conceived and carried out by the SS physician Dr. Kurt Heissmeyer, who traveled to the camp from Berlin every week or two to supervise the project. Heissmeyer based part of his research on the pseudoscience of racialism that was promoted by Hitler and espoused the idea that certain races caused diseases. As Jews they were labeled *untermenschen*, or "subhumans"; their alleged weaker state was the source of the disease spreading.

Some of the tests Heissmeyer concocted have also been disproven, namely, the idea that the injection of live tuberculosis bacilli into patients would serve as a vaccine. Various treatments were attempted, and Dr. Heissmeyer's researchers monitored the children for signs of progress, which never materialized. At times the children were even reexposed to the disease. Using only local anesthetics such as Novocain, Heissmeyer would cut out their lymphatic glands. After quickly suturing and dressing the surgical wounds, the SS physician would take the glands and tissue samples back to his laboratory in Berlin for testing. Nazi scientists in Berlin bred new cultures of the tubercular bacilli based on the infections, which Heissmeyer then took to Neuengamme to test on the children.

Most of the children continued to run high temperatures and show signs of the disease. Many developed advanced symptoms such as enlarged lymph nodes; lung incapacitation, including open cavities in their lungs; and damage to other vital organs. The "tuberculosis children" were eventually transferred to the Bullenhuser Damm School in Hamburg, not as a remedy for their suffering but because Neuengamme was a work camp lacking adequate facilities for sick and incapacitated children.

Heissmeyer and his researchers maintained that the suffering and deaths were acceptable sacrifices for "the benefits of progress in medicine." In April 1945, as the nearby camp and city were about to be liberated by the Allies, the children from the medical experiments were hidden in a basement. Then, as British forces liberated the city, the SS guards attempted to destroy any evidence of the medical tests. They injected the children with morphine. They were later found hanging from ropes in the basement of the school, "like pictures hung up on a wall on hooks," in the words of one eyewitness. The four Jewish inmates assigned to care for them had also been killed. The date was April 20, just days before the war ended.

As for Heissmeyer, after the war he disappeared and later resurfaced in East Germany in Magdeburg, where he practiced medicine, specializing in lung maladies and tuberculosis. He was finally convicted at a trial in 1966. During the hearings, the Nazi doctor stated, "I did not think that inmates of a camp had full value as human beings. . . . For me there was no basic difference between human beings and guinea pigs. [That is], Jews and guinea pigs."

With the end of the war apparent and the Allies closing in, prisoners at Neuengamme were forced to relocate to the Baltic. It is hard to imagine anything being worse than life in Neuengamme, but it was about to become an even more deadly ordeal for the prisoners.

Chapter 13

A CRUEL RACE

By THE LAST WINTER OF the war, most of the territory the Nazis had conquered in the preceding years was lost. The Soviets under Marshal Georgy Zhukov had counterattacked, pushing the Wehrmacht out of all of Eastern Europe. At the same time, the Americans had fought their way through Italy and were on Germany's southern border. Americans, British, Canadians, and others in the Allied Expeditionary Force, including Free French units, were now closing in from the Lowlands to Germany's west.

Allied soldiers were not the only ones preparing for the end of the war. SS chief Heinrich Himmler understood that the war was lost. With the end at hand, Himmler, Goebbels, and Hitler were forced to address the fate of the concentration camps. What would happen if the free world learned the extent to which the Nazis operated concentration camps and the full horrors of their crematoriums? The prospects of millions of survivors telling graphically shocking stories was something fanatical Nazis could not allow to happen. Therefore, in March 1945 Hitler informed Himmler and Goebbels that they had to "destroy the concentration camps and their inmates rather than allow them to fall into enemy hands." Himmler shared his fanatical vision with his Finnish massage therapist, Feliz Kersten, who recalled the words of the Nazi propagandist: "If the National Socialist Germany should fall, then our enemies, the traitors of the great Germanic idea, who were imprisoned in the concentration camps until now, should not witness the triumph of being a victor." Himmler promised that the prisoners "won't witness this day; they will die with us all. This is the clear and logical order of our Führer, and I will make sure that it will be executed in all its accuracy and thoroughness." But Himmler had other plans for the prisoners.

On March 19, 1945, Hitler dispatched one of his final official orders to his commanders to liquidate all evidence of the Holocaust. Camp commandants were told to destroy any "indications which might have pointed to the existence of such installations," meaning everything from the camps and barracks to the poison gases and the prisoners themselves

As the man responsible for the administration of the Third Reich's concentration camps, Himmler released his own decree but waited to do so until April 14. It read: "To all Commanders of concentration camps. There will be no surrender. The camp has to be evacuated immediately. No prisoner may fall into the hands of the enemy alive." Even though the orders from Hitler were straightforward, Himmler complicated them by calling for prisoners to be "evacuated" rather than "destroyed."

As a result, some camp commandants believed they were ordered to kill all of their prisoners; others interpreted the latter decree to mean that inmates were to be evacuated. If they were to be evacuated, commandants were not sure where to take the prisoners, at least initially. Nor did they know how prisoners were to be transferred. Questions remained as to whether prisoner relocation was the only option or if commandants were able to decide whether to evacuate or conduct mass executions. Himmler's order did not directly affirm Hitler's dictate that all prisoners be eliminated, nor did it directly countermand it. Rather, the purpose for Himmler's vague decree was to provide him with cover in the event he needed prisoners alive as bargaining chips when negotiating with the Allies.

His ambiguity also served to cloak his disloyalty and effort to save his own hide.

The result of the issuance of two orders was that camp commandants responded with varying interpretations of the decrees. That spring a group of concentration camp commanders met in haste in the Reich security office in Berlin to figure out what to do about the camps, prisoners, and their own survival. Evidence of the confusion and chaos in the Nazi command in the final months of the war is found in the trials at Nuremberg in 1945 and 1946. A Nazi official testifying at the trial of Ernst Kaltenbrunner, the highest-ranking SS officer to stand trial at Nuremberg, reported: "In the middle of April, 1945, Gauleiter Giesler disclosed the fact to me that Obergruppenführer Kaltenbrunner had given him instructions, in accordance with an order from the Führer, that there should be made an immediate plan regarding the liquidation of the concentration camp at Dachau and the two Jewish work camps at Mühldorf and Landsberg."

Other camps were later included on the list, including Neuengamme. As to how the camps were to be destroyed, the witness remembered that "the instructions stated that the two Jewish work camps at Landsberg and Mühldorf were to be destroyed by the German Air Force, since the sites of these two camps had lately and repeatedly been affected by hostile bombing attacks." The Nazis would kill two birds with one stone: liquidate evidence of the Holocaust and, if the deaths were discovered in these camps, blame Allied bombing.

Apparently, the Luftwaffe either never received the order or was hesitant to comply with it. Ultimately, Hitler suggested that all inmates at Dachau except Aryans from Britain and France were to be killed by poison gas. Although the plan to destroy these particular camps never occurred, the general idea would resurface in the final days of the conflict at the Baltic.

Amid the confusion, a cruel race for survival ensued. As the Allies marched into Germany, some Nazi commandants marched their prisoners out of the camps. However, even with the war lost, Allied forces closing in on them, and the Nazi dream destroyed, other fanatical commandants and guards executed their prisoners. Prisoners were gunned down by the thousands in the name of fulfilling Hitler's Final Solution. To save time, many of those shot were killed next to the mass graves that would soon hold their bodies. Other inmates were rushed wholesale into the "ovens" to be gassed. These executions were carried out day and night in hopes of eliminating all evidence of the atrocities. But despite the brutal frenzy of mass murder in the final months of the war, the Nazis were unable to fully erase the record of their cruelty.

When the British liberated Bergen-Belsen on April 15, 1945, they found ten thousand dead bodies in piles waiting to be buried. The prisoners had been murdered in a hurry and not long before the camp fell. The Nazis also failed to eradicate other evidence—this was the camp where Anne Frank had been clinging to life after having been brought there from Auschwitz. Records survived the war indicating that the young girl perished just a few weeks before the end of the war and what would have been her sixteenth birthday.

The grisly scene at Bergen-Belsen was not the only alarming reality the liberators discovered. Another forty thousand prisoners were still alive but close to death. Disturbingly, more than half of those liberated by the British would succumb to the trials of their internment only days or weeks after liberation. Other camp commandants had anticipated the end of the war and had been executing their prisoners since January and February. One such incident occurred at Ravensbrück, where thousands of female inmates were gassed in the early months of 1945. They too were only weeks away from liberation. Such barbarous acts continued literally to the bitter end; thousands of prisoners were gassed at Sachsenhausen the day prior to the camp's liberation.

At other concentration camps, Nazi officers and guards had dropped their weapons, shed their uniforms, and simply vacated the camps, presumably with the hope of blending in with local villagers. Many hoped to be captured by the Americans or British, who would feed and detain them according to international war-time agreements. The Germans did not want to be captured by Russian forces, who returned the Nazi brutality in kind. As a result, these concentration camps were abandoned, and the Allied soldiers liberating them encountered no opposition. Instead, what they witnessed upon arrival at the camps were ghastly mass graves, piles of bodies tossed about with no regard for human dignity, and a stench that moved many to spill the contents of their stomachs. Emaciated prisoners, more dead than alive after having been deprived every human necessity, simply sat waiting for them. They had nowhere else to go.

Knowing the Allies were approaching, some guards, commandants, and others inside Nazi Germany tried to distance themselves from responsibility. One way to accomplish this was to release their prisoners, hoping to curry favor with the Allies or save their own lives by using the prisoners as bargaining chips when their camp was overrun by Allied forces.

THE UNUSUAL ORDERS REGARDING the fate of the concentration camps were given by the same man charged with organizing the camps and implementing Hitler's Final Solution—Heinrich Himmler. Like Joseph Goebbels, Himmler appears time and again in the story of the *Cap Arcona* and shaped the history that unfolded in May 1945.

Himmler was born on October 7, 1900, in Munich to a conservative, middle-class Catholic family. From an early age, he demonstrated some aptitude for learning and developed a knack for organization and a temperament that craved strict routine and order, traits that later made him an effective Nazi administrator. As a teenager, Himmler was captivated by the Great War and longed to serve in uniform on the front lines. Consequently, on January 1, 1918, he withdrew from school and enlisted in the military. However, the young man was still completing his training when the war ended, and he would be denied the chance to serve his country. This missed opportunity would forever haunt him, causing him to overcompensate later in life when surrounded by fellow Nazi commanders who had been heroes of that war.

Himmler's inability to serve left him deeply frustrated, but he remained exceedingly patriotic. He returned to school, completing a degree in agriculture from the Technical University in Munich in 1923. It was while he was back in school and brooding over Germany's "misfortune" that Himmler was exposed to the radical and hateful doctrines that would lead him to the Nazi cause. He joined a far-right student group and began consuming racialist and ultra-nationalist literature. Although Himmler was often described as resembling a mild-mannered schoolmaster, he would turn out to be anything but.

That same year, while working in a demeaning job at a manure-processing factory in Schleissheim, Himmler met Ernst Röhm, the head of a fledgling übernationalist political party. The impressionable young man was easily enticed to join Röhm in their infamous Beer Hall Putsch rally against the German government that would help thrust Adolf Hitler into the limelight.

In 1928 Himmler married Margarete Boden. The couple had a daughter the next year. That same year marked his rise to power within the Nazi Party. On January 6, 1929, Hitler appointed Himmler to manage the party's newly created Security Service with the rank of Reichsführer. The little schoolmaster finally had an opportunity to serve his nation and avenge its defeat during World War I. When Hitler gained control of Germany in January 1933, he rewarded the loyal Himmler by making him the police chief of Munich. By the next year, Himmler controlled police and security services nationwide and began centralizing authority in the secret state police known as the Gestapo. During that same period of time, Hitler appointed Himmler to organize Nazi Party efforts to deal with "the Jewish question." One of Himmler's main tasks in answering the Jewish question was to organize an extensive system of camps throughout Germany and Nazi-occupied territories.

As chief of the SS, Himmler set about ruthlessly marginalizing groups such as Gypsies, convicts, homosexuals, Jehovah's Witnesses, Jews, and others, all of whom he perceived to be both enemies of the Nazi state and threats to his theories on racial purity and superiority. He established offices and policies to purify the German "stock" and promote marriage among Aryans. Ironically, like Goebbels and other Nazi Party leaders, however, he would engage in extramarital affairs and, noticeably, looked nothing like the tall, strong, blond, blue-eyed images of the Aryan "superman" he advocated.

His orders led to the mass evacuation of concentration camps in the waning weeks of the war. For the commandants of concentration camps, time was of the essence. The Allies were closing in. They had to decide whether to flee in an attempt to save their own hides, kill all prisoners in their camps in order to liquidate all evidence of their heinous crimes, or evacuate their prisoners before the camps were overrun by Allied forces.

Relocation plans had been drafted in many camps, but were often derailed because of the rapid advance of Allied forces, the near-complete collapse of the Nazis' command and communication systems, and the limited availability of boats, trucks, and trains for the relocation. But not everywhere. At Mittelbau-Dora, the prisoners were moved on April 10. American soldiers arrived on April 11 to liberate the camp, only to discover that they were one day too late. The situation on the ground was dynamic and thoroughly unpredictable. As a result, some Nazi concentration camp commanders decided to force-march their malnourished detainees out of the camps. If one of the prisoners struggled to keep up with the pace, he or she was killed while in transit. Indeed, there were many mass shootings along the roads leading out of the camps. Others perished from the long forced marches in cold weather, the unhealthy conditions that existed in cattle cars crammed full of dying prisoners, and a critical shortage of food and water. As one scholar noted, the threats of "exhaustion, malnutrition, pestilence, the influence of the weather and deliberate exposure to enemy attacks proved to be far more effective and inconspicuous" than the initial orders to liquidate the prisoners in the camps.

Himmler's order to move the camp prisoners was received at Neuengamme in April by SS general Karl Totzauer, who passed it upward to the camp commandant. Commandant Max Pauly decided to comply with the order and immediately began preparations to abandon the camp. Neuengamme's prisoners would be marched or transported in the only direction not blocked by Allied forces—north. The destination: the Baltic coast, just over sixty miles away.

Graced with the strategic advantage of its bustling northern port, Neustadt had been one of the few German cities to recover from World War I and boast a strong economy. It was also one of the few cities not bombed during World War II. The Baltic coast thus provided the Germans with a possible means for escaping north to Norway by ship and, most immediately, the only viable location for relocating prisoners from the concentration camps.

Neuengamme was a massive camp with many subcamps, which slowed the evacuation. The population at the camp had swelled. By the end of December 1944, roughly ten to fifteen thousand prisoners remained at the main camp, with another thirty-eight thousand at Neuengamme's subcamps. Moving so many prisoners was a logistical nightmare, especially when it had to be done in a hurry, with few trucks, trains, or ships available and without support from the German command. Commandant Pauly's job was, ironically, made a little easier by the death rate at the camp. It is estimated that seventeen hundred prisoners were dying each month during the final winter of the war. Fully twenty-five hundred died in February. But those still living were evacuated.

Prisoners at Neuengamme near Hamburg, along with those from Mittelbau-Dora at Nordhausen and Stutthof by Danzig, were among those being marched to the Baltic. A long, straggling line of death composed mostly of Jews and captured Russian soldiers marched wearily northward. Unbeknownst to them, the British military was also closing in on the Baltic coast. Also, unknown to the prisoners trekking or being transported north from

Neuengamme, four large ships were awaiting them in the southern Baltic port at Lübeck Bay. In fact, not even Pauly and the other camp commandants knew their prisoners would soon be loaded on the ocean liners.

The fateful decisions about what to do with the prisoners once they arrived at the Baltic were still being debated in part because of Himmler's ongoing plans to negotiate a separate surrender and, in part, because of questions about what to do with Germany's ocean liners and freighters now that the war was all but over. Some Nazi commanders did not want to see their ships confiscated by the Allies as war reparations, as had happened after World War I. They advocated sinking all German ships. At the same time, German shipping companies hoped the Allies would allow them to keep their investments and continue business operations after the war ended.

Such issues were complicated by the fact that the Kriegsmarine had a shipping control authority called the Kriegsmarinedienstellen. The KMD was responsible for coordinating wartime merchant marine shipping and transport. The merchant marine had been a somewhat independent authority, but in 1944 Admiral Karl Dönitz placed it under the control of a new agency called the Seetra. This change caused obvious strain on account of their conflicting goals and interwoven chains of command. Officers were uncertain as to whether the *Cap Arcona* should be classified as a merchant ship or military craft. There was confusion as to which command the former liner should report.

It was the Seetra that had ordered the *Cap Arcona* and other ocean liners to rescue tens of thousands of refugees from besieged German ports during Operation Hannibal. After completing its last daring run across the Baltic on March 30, the *Cap Arcona* was in bad shape. Its turbines were worn out, and it was overdue for maintenance. The Seetra thus released the ship from its control. Now decommissioned, the *Cap Arcona* was returned to the Hamburg-Süd company, which operated the liner before the war. The company was eager to save the big ocean liner for their postwar business plans.

However, General Karl Kaufmann, the provincial governor* of Hamburg, ordered the ship to dock at Neustadt Bay, which was near his office at Lübeck Bay and, he claimed, was therefore within his jurisdiction. Born on October 10, 1900, in Krefeld, the governor had been a founding member of the Nazi Party in 1921 and quickly became one of Hitler's favorite officers. Hitler appointed Kaufmann governor of the Gaus Rheinland and Ruhr in the 1920s and then head of the Nazi Party in and governor of Hamburg. Kaufmann served in that position from 1929 to the end of the war, governing with an iron fist.

Kaufmann expanded his base of power in Hamburg and the surrounding region by assuming a number of other commands, including as the Reich commissioner for shipping. In this capacity, he claimed to be in charge of home defense and all shipping in northern Germany—not the Seetra or KMD. It remains uncertain as to whether Nazi commanders intended to destroy all German ships before the Allies could seize them or wanted to return them to the German shipping companies, just as it was unclear who inside Germany had the authority to decide other than Hitler. Kaufmann seized control and ordered four large ships—the *Athen, Deutschland, Thielbek* (whose steering system was barely working after having been bombed the previous summer), and *Cap Arcona*—to steam to Lübeck Bay in April 1945.

Heinrich Bertram, the captain of the *Cap Arcona*, reluctantly ordered his ship back into service and sailed it from Denmark to the bay just off the coast of Neustadt and Lübeck, where it arrived on April 14. The two big liners (the *Cap Arcona* and *Deutschland*) anchored two miles off the coast, while the two smaller freighters (the *Athen* and *Thielbek*) were tethered to the docks. Even though all four of the ships were damaged and badly in need of repairs, Kaufmann ordered the ships' captains to prepare to receive prisoners marching north from Neuengamme.

---

* In Nazi Germany, the title was *gauleiter.*

Chapter 14

SWEDISH SAVIOR

THE *CAP ARCONA* AND other German ocean liners and freighters were not the only ships steaming for the southern Baltic. The port was also the destination of two Swedish hospital ships hoping to rescue prisoners from the concentration camps. At the critical moment during the final months of the war when camps were being either liquidated or evacuated, an unlikely savior along with his hospital ships and white buses arrived, hoping to rescue thousands from the Nazis. His name was Folke Bernadotte.

Bernadotte was the count of Wisborg, a Swedish diplomat, and vice chairman of the Swedish Red Cross, a position he assumed in 1943. Born on January 2, 1895, in Stockholm, he was the son of Count Oscar Bernadotte (formerly Prince Oscar of Sweden), grandson of the late King Oscar II, and nephew of King Gustav V of Sweden. Young Bernadotte looked as if he had come straight from central casting to play the part of a nobleman. Tall, handsome, square-jawed, and impeccably dressed with meticulous bearing and manners, Bernadotte had traveled the world and enjoyed the friendships of many important leaders.

After his schooling, Bernadotte joined the military as a cavalry officer during World War I, rising to the rank of major. In the years between the wars, he represented Sweden diplomatically in a variety of capacities, including at international expositions and at the World's Fair in New York City. At the outset of World War II, Bernadotte helped organize home defenses and negotiated prisoner exchanges with the Nazis that resulted in the release of roughly eleven thousand camp inmates who were placed in the custody of Sweden. He also aided American airmen interned by the Nazis after being either shot down or forced to make emergency landings in and around Sweden. During such missions, he had the opportunity to meet General Dwight Eisenhower, the Supreme Allied Commander, and other influential American generals, who were indebted to him for his work on behalf of the American airmen. Ironically, Sweden's official neutrality during the war would enable Count Bernadotte to render assistance to the Allies in a number of ways, something Eisenhower noted on occasion.

But it was a meeting in France between Count Bernadotte and Raoul Nordling, Sweden's consul general in Paris, that would change history. Nordling had played a role in the negotiations surrounding the liberation of Paris in the summer of 1944, working both covertly and officially with Allied forces, the French Resistance, and Nazi occupiers. In his own words, the count heard that "Nordling had been able to prevent large numbers of women and men from being deported to Germany, and now he had succeeded in persuading the Germans to release a number of Frenchmen who had been imprisoned in France at the time of the capitulation of Paris."

The count found Nordling to be brave, cerebral, and fascinating. In short, he was inspired by the diplomat's tales of intrigue and heroism and hoped to replicate these courageous deeds. Like Nordling, Bernadotte also believed Nazi Germany was finished and correctly guessed that when the regime collapsed, the Nazis would attempt to liquidate all evidence of the Holocaust. Countless Scandinavians and others imprisoned in the concentration camps or trapped in Germany would be at risk. Accordingly, he immediately began working to "persuade the Nazi authorities to let Norwegian civilians be released from the camps in Germany and evacuated to Sweden."

If his negotiations resulted in success, the count then planned to work on the release of additional prisoners. Thankfully, the Swedish Foreign Office agreed and encouraged the count to proceed, but to act on his own or through the Red Cross rather than in an official capacity through the usual diplomatic channels. To do so would likely undermine the effort. Bernadotte decided to personally lead the mission. The first step would be approaching top Nazi officials.

A delegation from the Swedish Red Cross led by Bernadotte traveled to Berlin in February 1945. They were assisted by Christian Günther, the Swedish foreign affairs minister, and Gilel Storch of the World Jewish Congress, who had earlier worked with Bernadotte to collect tens of thousands of packets of food for transport to Jewish prisoners in the Nazi camps. The goal of the present mission was to meet with Heinrich Himmler and request the release of Swedish-born women who had married German soldiers who were either dead or missing.

Meanwhile, while Bernadotte was implementing his plan, another similar effort was under way. Jean-Marie Musy, former president of Switzerland, had also sought a meeting with Himmler to discuss the release of prisoners at Theresienstadt. Musy wanted to bring them to Switzerland. Unfortunately, news of the meeting was reported to Hitler, who ordered an end to any such discussion and summoned Himmler to Berlin. The once-loyal Gestapo chief was in trouble. Hitler was furious and became suspicious of his senior commander.

Bernadotte learned about the failed effort at Theresienstadt, but realized that Himmler was open to such negotiations. However, he reasoned, they had to occur in strict secrecy. The count departed for Berlin by plane in February, claiming he was traveling only to inspect Red Cross operations in Germany. He had his mind on much more than Red Cross relief efforts, though.

One year before Bernadotte traveled to arrange the secret meetings with Himmler and other top Nazi officials, he had heard rumors that alarmed him. He stated in his memoir, "For some time there had been rumors, impossible to ignore, that the German authorities meant to liquidate the prisoners in concentration camps if there should be a collapse of Germany's defenses, and thus to rid themselves of dangerous witnesses."

When the count arrived in Germany, he found the Nazi high command in complete chaos. Hitler was issuing conflicting orders and was facing a complete collapse of German defenses on both his western and his eastern fronts. Even Goebbels had begun to doubt his führer's plans, writing in his diary, "As long as we cannot achieve even semi-stabilization of the Fronts, there can be no question of bringing about a political turning-point to the war." However, the dysfunction and hopelessness in Germany served to facilitate Count Bernadotte's request to meet with Himmler and exploit the Nazis' vulnerabilities and desperation during the negotiations. Even so, at the outset he was justifiably cautious, stating, "I had no illusions as to the difficulties of my task, and little hope of obtaining more than a partial success."

The first contact in Germany was with General Ernst Kaltenbrunner, the Gestapo's second in command behind Himmler. The meeting occurred at Kaltenbrunner's mansion at Wannsee. Kaltenbrunner, whom Bernadotte described as "cool and inquisitive," offered him Chesterfield cigarettes and Dubonnet, all confiscated from Paris. But despite his gracious demeanor, like others in the Nazi high command Kaltenbrunner was deeply suspicious about the request to meet with Himmler.

The count pressed his case with Himmler's top deputy, stating firmly, "You are doubtless aware, relations between Sweden and Germany are extremely bad. Swedish public opinion is intensely anti-German." He reminded the SS officer that the sentiment was "principally because of German cruelty in Norway and Denmark, the scorched-earth policy in North Norway, and above all the taking of hostages." Such actions were, in Bernadotte's words, "in flagrant violation of international conventions." However, he baited Kaltenbrunner, "Himmler occupies a position that would make it possible for him to adopt measures calculated to improve Swedish-German relations." The trap was set.

This argument caught Kaltenbrunner's attention. When Bernadotte asked to see Himmler, he added, "It seems to me that it should be of great importance for Germany not to make an enemy of Sweden, whether Germany wins the war or not." Of course, Bernadotte could not reveal even to Kaltenbrunner the real reason for the meeting. It worked.

The first meeting with Himmler occurred at five in the afternoon on February 12, 1945. Bernadotte was driven to one of Himmler's offices at Hohen-Lüchen, just over fifty miles from Berlin. There Bernadotte met first with Himmler's aide General Walter Schellenberg and then with Himmler. The Gestapo chief had been steadily expanding his portfolio of power and now controlled all police inside Germany and the occupied territories as well as several military divisions. He was functioning as Germany's minister of the interior, which gave him control over the concentration camps. Along with Joseph Goebbels, he was one of the most influential and powerful people in the Third Reich. But he neither looked nor acted the part. Bernadotte remembered Himmler dressed in a uniform "without any decorations and wearing horn-rim spectacles." He said of the man responsible for some of history's worst crimes, "He looked a typical unimportant official, and one would certainly have passed him in the street without noticing him. He had small, well-shaped, and delicate hands, and they were carefully manicured."

At that meeting, Himmler attempted to gain leverage by maintaining that every last German would "fight like a lion" and would never surrender. How much of that blustery rhetoric he truly believed is debatable. The Gestapo chief, needing to keep up appearances and obviously concerned about the possibility of charges being directed at him of being a traitor should word ever escape that he was meeting with Bernadotte, felt the need to constantly state his loyalty to Hitler during the meeting, saying he would never contradict the führer's orders. Of course, the entire purpose of the meeting was to do just that, and both men knew it.

Bernadotte made his request to allow Swedish women who were married to Germans to be released to him along with their children. Himmler hesitated, stating, "I don't feel inclined to send German children to Sweden. There they will be brought up to hate their country, and they will be spat at by their playmates because their fathers were German." He also reminded Bernadotte of the difficult position he was in: "If I were to agree to your proposals, the Swedish papers would announce with big headlines that the war-criminal Himmler, in terror of punishment for his crimes, is trying to buy his freedom." Of course, this is what he was trying to do through the exchanges and his earlier efforts to evacuate the camps.

Bernadotte pressed the matter, requesting that the Swedish Red Cross be permitted access to concentration camps. He added to his initial demands, asking that Norwegians and Danes also be released to his custody. The count stated that the Swedish Red Cross estimated that thirteen thousand such individuals were still in the camps. Himmler countered that only about two to three thousand Scandinavians were imprisoned. The Red Cross estimates were closer to the truth. Ultimately, the Gestapo chief agreed to the release of the aged and ill, mothers who were married to German soldiers, their children, and additional Scandinavians. They would be released, but only to Count Bernadotte.

Himmler wanted reciprocity, demanding assurances that both Norway and Denmark would agree to stop fighting their Nazi occupiers. The reasoning, claimed Himmler rather weakly, was that he needed a quid pro quo to take back to Hitler, which Bernadotte knew would never happen. Himmler could tell no one but his aide General Schellenberg of the real reason for his back-channel deals. The count noted in his diary, "I told Himmler that the concession he had mentioned was quite unthinkable." Himmler withdrew the demand, and the deal was made.

Himmler agreed to release the parties discussed in the negotiations, provided they be interned in Norway and Sweden. Bernadotte was permitted to take a convoy of Red Cross buses to Neuengamme to pick up the prisoners. As a token gesture, the count presented Himmler a piece of Swedish art from the seventeenth century as a gift. In turn, Himmler arranged for his most loyal driver to ensure protection for Bernadotte during his visit to the camps. Half serious, the Gestapo chief quipped, "Otherwise it might happen that the Swedish papers would announce in big headlines: 'War Criminal Himmler Murders Count Bernadotte.'"

ON MARCH 12, 1945, the first of the count's "white buses" crossed the Danish border into Germany; there were twelve buses in a group, three groups per convoy. Bernadotte and his staff of 308 medics, drivers, and volunteers had to travel through areas under heavy attack from Allied bombers. More than once during air raids, they were forced to stop along the side of the road and take cover nearby. Moreover, Bernadotte was not permitted to purchase fuel, food, or medicine within Germany. Any materials in Germany were needed for the waning Nazi military campaign. The white buses had to bring all their own supplies with them. But the lead convoy and the count managed to arrive at Schloss Friedrichsruh, near Lübeck Bay, around sunset and then continued on to Neuengamme. As per the negotiations with Himmler, Scandinavian prisoners from other camps were transported to Neuengamme on March 15. By March 27 a separate and hastily constructed Scandinavian camp had been arranged at Neuengamme for Bernadotte's charges.

Even though Bernadotte had made secret arrangements with Himmler, the Gestapo chief's aides and drivers did not arrive for the prisoner release. Rather, General Kaltenbrunner met Bernadotte at the camp. The general remained suspicious of the count's plans and was angered by the arrangements to release prisoners. Loyal to the Nazi cause to the bitter end, Kaltenbrunner threatened to turn away the convoys; he also delayed the entire mission by several days. But the delay had an unintended benefit. On March 27, while waiting for Kaltenbrunner to acquiesce, Bernadotte received approval from Sweden's foreign minister to open negotiations not simply for the release of Scandinavians, as was originally planned, but also for Jews and others. While the count's intention was to save Swedes and other Scandinavians, it is undeniable that his mission was expanded once he came face-to-face with the horrors of the Holocaust.

After repeated assurances from Bernadotte that he was acting on Himmler's direct orders, Kaltenbrunner finally permitted the convoys to proceed to the camp to pick up the prisoners. It was March 30—Good Friday—when Bernadotte entered Neuengamme, just days before Commandant Max Pauly received the order to evacuate the camp northward to the Baltic. Driving through the large gates with his white buses and staff, Bernadotte became the first representative from a neutral nation or outside organization to visit Neuengamme. But the reception was anything but welcoming. As soon as the delegates from the Swedish Red Cross entered the camp, Pauly ordered the gates be shut behind them.

The horrors that greeted the count made a lasting impression. He noted the great emotion he and his staff experienced at the revolting conditions in the camp, describing Neuengamme as "one of the worst—quite on par with the Dachau camp." Commandant Pauly permitted the count to speak to only Scandinavian prisoners and only in their native tongue. He also severely limited the Swedish party's access to the camp. Bernadotte agreed and said little in order not to arouse suspicion, undermine the release, or disrupt the possibility of future talks.

It worked. Over the next few days, Bernadotte transported prisoners from the camp to freedom, noting the joy and hope in the eyes of some of the inmates, but also the vacant gaze of despair among thousands of others. The count's motor coaches, which were identifiable by their white paint and large Red Cross emblem on the side in order to distinguish them from military targets in the eyes of both the Nazis and the Allies, included roughly twenty-two hundred Danes and Norwegians from Sachsenhausen, six hundred more Scandinavians from Dachau, and sixteen hundred policemen—mostly Danish—held near Dresden. Bernadotte vowed to return for more prisoners. He guessed correctly that time was of the essence.

Bernadotte continued his efforts, flying back to Berlin in April for another round of meetings with Generals Kaltenbrunner and Schellenberg. On April 2 Bernadotte was again taken to Hohen-Lüchen to meet with Himmler. This time Bernadotte found his adversary looking "somber" and "nervous." Himmler asked Bernadotte how well he knew General Eisenhower and other senior Allied commanders. The Gestapo chief revealed the desperation of the situation and his own delusion by demanding the Swedish Red Cross vice chair deliver a top-secret message to Eisenhower that he was interested in negotiating a separate surrender on the western front. Bernadotte knew the supreme Allied commander would never agree to such an action, but he played along and informed Himmler that he would communicate the request, even suggesting that there was a good possibility of negotiating a separate peace. Such false assurances kept the negotiations going.

During the meeting on April 2, Himmler remained guarded and paranoid, again concerned that word of his treasonous actions would get back to Hitler. Trying to have it both ways, he reminded the count of his loyalty to the führer while simultaneously conspiring against him. Bernadotte goaded the Gestapo chief, saying, "Don't you realize that Germany has lost the war? . . . You say that you are willing to do anything for the German nation, and if that is true, and if you consider his determination to continue the war a disaster to your country, involving the death of tens of thousands more on the fighting fronts as well as on the domestic front, you ought to put the welfare of your people above your loyalty to Hitler."

During the four-hour meeting, Bernadotte continued his demands that any remaining Scandinavians and Swedish women who had married Germans be released. He also added requests for additional Danish police officers, Norwegian students being held at Neuengamme, and others, including the sick, weak, and dying. After the discussion Himmler remained quiet and then walked out of the room. He returned a moment later and agreed to the deal, but said that only "some" of the prisoners the count had requested could be released. Too many prisoners would draw attention to the deal. The two haggled further, and Himmler ultimately agreed to all of the count's requests, including that the prisoners could be sent to hospitals rather than detention camps back in Sweden. Himmler requested only that the prisoners remain in Sweden until the war ended. Bernadotte quickly agreed.

After the meeting Schellenberg escorted the count to his car. The general continued to inquire about the possibility of a separate German surrender deal with Eisenhower on the western front. Like so many Germans, Schellenberg was worried about the Red Army advancing into Germany on the eastern front and reports of horrific atrocities being committed by Soviet soldiers against Germans. Bernadotte sounded an optimistic tone in order to continue his act and, upon arriving at Neuengamme, made additional demands; this time he wanted Jews to be released to his custody.

Despite continued opposition from Kaltenbrunner, the count continued visiting camps. On April 17 he wrote to officials back in Stockholm with good news: "Today I can announce that 423 Jews are expected to arrive tomorrow in Sweden, where they are to remain until the end of the war." The prisoners were from Theresienstadt.

Two days later Count Bernadotte removed additional Scandinavian prisoners from Neuengamme. The next day all 4,225 of Neuengamme's Scandinavian inmates were transported to Denmark, Norway, and Sweden. While there to pick up more prisoners, Bernadotte observed that many of the inmates were being transported or force-marched out of the camp, presumably to the Baltic coast. He recalled, "The non-Scandinavians were pushed into freight trains whose destination no one knew. Questioned about it, the German commandant [Max Pauly] shrugged his shoulders: 'Keine Ahnung' [I have no idea]." Bernadotte added, "Of course, he was lying."

As such, the count organized a Red Cross office in Lübeck on the Baltic coast. The location was selected because of the thousands of camp survivors being evacuated by foot, barge, and train to the northern German coast. Major Dr. Hans Arnoldsson was assigned to oversee the office, and the International Red Cross sent staff to assist in the operation to feed the swelling population of starving prisoners.

For the first time, confidence and optimism had crept into the mission.

BERNADOTTE ARRANGED ANOTHER MEETING with Himmler on April 21, again at Hohen-Lüchen. At the six-o'clock breakfast, Himmler appeared completely exhausted, anxious, and defeated. He admitted to his Swedish negotiator that he was not sleeping. However, he ate well. The count raised the topic of prisoners still being murdered in the camps and noted that, when Himmler had met with leaders of the World Jewish Congress, he had promised that no more Jews would be killed at the camps.

Himmler did not answer the question directly, but agreed to release French and Jewish women held at Ravensbrück. Bernadotte moved immediately. The next day 2,873 women were handed over to the custody of the Swedish Red Cross by very reluctant and minimally cooperative camp officials. The one demand Himmler had made, however, was that none of the camp's Poles or Russians be released or even helped. He was insistent. Yet through some sly negotiating aided by the chaos of the final days of the war, Bernadotte was able to include a few Polish women in the exchange.

Bernadotte asked to see Himmler again. The next day, April 23, the two sat down for a final meeting. This time it was at the Swedish Embassy at the coastal city of Lübeck. Himmler had been forced to move his headquarters to Lübeck because of Allied advances, which underscored the necessity of the meetings and further prompted the little schoolmaster's willingness to negotiate. That evening, as if on cue, the meeting was interrupted by air-raid sirens. The negotiators had to take cover in the cellar as the power went off in the building during the Allied bombing.

Himmler continued his requests for the count to transmit his terms for an armistice on the western front. Like other Nazi leaders, he assumed the war was over, that Hitler would simply remain inoperable while ensconced in his Berlin bunker, and that the Allies would be open to separate negotiations on the two fronts. He was correct on the first two.

On April 24 the two men came to terms. The count agreed to take the message "back" to Eisenhower in exchange for more prisoners.* Himmler agreed that more prisoners from Neuengamme could be released, using them as a bargaining chip with the Allies. Apparently, the Gestapo chief was unaware that nearly all of them had already been evacuated. They were crowding into the port and ships at the Baltic coast.

On April 26 news of President Harry Truman's complete rejection of the idea of a separate armistice arrived in Sweden. It read: "A German offer of surrender will be accepted only if it be complete on all Fronts, as regards Great Britain and the Soviet Union as well as the United States." The next day the count informed General Schellenberg that Truman had flatly rejected the deal. Unfortunately, the day after that the Reuters News Agency learned of the back-channel deals between the Swedish Red Cross and Himmler. Their story reported that Himmler wanted to surrender. Word of the report reached Adolf Hitler in his Berlin bunker. The führer ordered Himmler's immediate arrest. The result was that there would be no more meetings or negotiations between Bernadotte and Himmler.

In total, Count Bernadotte's white-buses campaign—a fleet of thirty-six hospital buses, nineteen trucks, fourteen cars and motorcycles, and a tow truck—rescued more than 21,000 prisoners from the concentration camps over a two-month period at the close of the war, including many Jews.† All the while, prisoners from the concentration camps continued to arrive at the Baltic coast in the final chaotic days of the war.

---

* Bernadotte actually transmitted Himmler's request to the Allied command this time.

† Bernadotte rescued 8,000 Swedes, Norwegians, and Danes; 2,629 French; 1,124 Germans; 1,615 Jews; and roughly 7,000 women of American, Argentinean, British, Chinese, Czech, and Polish nationalities.

Final Role

FLOATING
CONCENTRATION CAMPS

Chapter 15

EXODUS

THE *CAP ARCONA* HAD been ordered to anchor in Lübeck Bay in north-central Germany. Preparations were being made to take on thousands of passengers. Yet, the ship's engines were barely functioning, the crew was at inadequate strength for an ocean voyage, and fuel, food, and supplies were scarce. Even so, the captain and crew could not have imagined what was about to happen to their ship.

Meanwhile, preparations for a massive evacuation of Neuengamme began in April 1945 and were ordered by the camp commandant, Max Pauly. Prisoners were readied, and camp records and documents were either destroyed or packed for the journey to the Baltic coast, roughly sixty miles away. As per Heinrich Himmler's order on April 14 to evacuate the camps, the first wave of prisoners from Neuengamme marched out of the camp on April 19, with others following from April 20 to 27. Many lacked shoes and had to tie rags around their bloody feet; all were weak, ill, and malnourished. There was little food or water. Thus began the forced evacuation of the largest camp in northern Germany, part of the largest evacuation of a concentration camp during the war and quite possibly the war's worst death march.

Another sixty-eight hundred of Neuengamme's prisoners were loaded into cattle cars and taken by train north to Lübeck and Neustadt. Emaciated inmates were packed like livestock into the old cars, with guards shouting and violently shoving them. Others were forced onto barges waiting at the Elbe River to be taken to Hamburg. It was far too dangerous to travel during the day due to the Allied bombing campaign. As a result, much of the evacuation occurred at night. This posed a problem for the prisoners on foot, as it was both treacherous and tiring to walk at night. Many inmates tripped over the bodies of their comrades who had fallen along the road from exhaustion. The Nazis were so desperate to hurry their evacuation to the Baltic that SS guards shot anyone who did not keep up, even if the person tripped, stopped to tie a shoelace, or tried to relieve himself. The guards were particularly quick on the trigger if the prisoners were Jewish or Russian.

The Nazis usually kept meticulous records on all facets of the war and Holocaust. However, because of the chaos that defined Germany at the time of the evacuation and the rush to get as many prisoners to the Baltic coast as possible in advance of the approaching Allied forces, there are no reliable reports for the exact number of inmates involved in the death march. It would appear, however, that almost ten thousand prisoners from Neuengamme had been evacuated in the initial wave. In the days to come, many thousands more prisoners from Neuengamme's satellite camps were evacuated north.

Thousands from other concentration camps were also heading to Neustadt and Lübeck Bay, including by transports out of Wöbbelin, near Ludwigslust in Mecklenburg, and from Kaltenkirchen and Reilherstieg. Like their comrades from Neuengamme, they all suffered high death rates during the ordeal. The total number of prisoners who died of starvation and weakness or were shot by guards during the evacuation may have been as high as ten thousand. Prisoners who died while aboard the cramped barges on the Elbe River were simply thrown overboard, and those aboard the cattle cars were tossed off the train.

Witold Rygiel, a Polish prisoner and one of about ten thousand inmates in a group marching to the Baltic, recorded his experience, which began on April 24. "We had absolutely no idea what was happening. It was a death march. People who died were left by the roadside. . . . We walked 170 kilometers to the port of Lübeck and it took a week. When we arrived, there were about 7,000 people left."*

Not all the prisoners were evacuated. Some were too weak to be moved, and there were not enough train cars and barges for the massive operation out of Neuengamme. After the final march departed for the Baltic, around three thousand prisoners still remained at the main camp. Commandant Pauly ordered a few of his guards and some German prisoners to remain behind with them. Their assignment was to destroy the remaining records and documents at the camp; that done, they were to murder the remaining prisoners. Most of the German prisoners who fulfilled this gruesome task were then conscripted into the German military.

On April 30 Neuengamme was officially closed.

THE FINAL DESTINATION OF the evacuation and the reason for the departure were kept secret from the prisoners. Accordingly, the survivors crammed inside the train tried desperately to peer through the narrow wooden slats of the crowded cattle cars to see where they were going. The landscape they passed on their journey northward to Neustadt and Lübeck showed few signs of war except that most villages appeared to be empty of residents. They either had fled or were hiding even though north-central Germany suffered fewer bombings than other parts of the country, as the Allies had not yet arrived.

Hannover-Stöcken, a satellite camp of Neuengamme located next to a battery factory, was one of those camps that evacuated prisoners by rail. In the scramble to enact Himmler's order that no

---

* It was approximately 60 miles to the coast from the Neuengamme concentration camp, not 105 miles. However, Rygiel initially came from another camp, which might explain the discrepancy. Or the distance may have been slightly inaccurate.

prisoner be allowed to fall into enemy hands, the commandant evacuated the camp over several frenetic days in April. He also sought to destroy all evidence of the Holocaust by removing the bodies of dead prisoners each night under the cover of darkness. The dead were burned at a nearby location or, in the final days of the evacuation, at the camp itself. Before the commandant could burn or relocate all of his prisoners, however, the U.S. 84th Infantry Division arrived at Hannover-Stöcken. Unfortunately, they arrived just days too late to save the prisoners evacuated by train. The report described unimaginable scenes of inhumanity.

Prisoners were sent from Hannover-Stöcken by rail to Bergen-Belsen. Because this camp was too full, they had to then be moved to Mieste. From there they were marched to an army camp at Gardelegen. Meanwhile, the difficult trek continued for the inmates from Hannover-Stöcken because no camp wanted them. After two days they were again moved, this time to the nearby town of Isenschnibble. Finally, not knowing what to do with so many prisoners, the frustrated camp guards turned the prisoners from Neuengamme's satellite camp over to Gerhard Thiele, the Nazi Party official in charge of the district. Thiele ordered his SS guards to take the surviving 1,038 prisoners to a large barn and force them inside. The barn was then drenched in gasoline and the doors sealed shut. A burning torch was thrown against the wall. The barn was quickly enveloped by flames. Prisoners inside screamed and tried in desperation to escape the inferno. To further ensure no survivors, the SS guards and elderly recruits from the Volkssturm fired their weapons into the burning barn. A few prisoners managed to dig under a side wall and crawl out. But most of them were shot as they ran. Somehow twenty-two of the prisoners escaped death that day.

On April 19 the first wave of prisoners from Neuengamme arrived by train in Lübeck on Germany's northern coast. Commandant Pauly had packed at least fifty prisoners from Neuengamme into each of the train's cattle cars, making it difficult for the prisoners to sit or lie down amid so many bodies. There were no toilets, water was severely rationed, and often there was no food. Within hours, the smell inside the cattle cars was overwhelming. By the end of the trip, the stench of feces, urine, and death was so overpowering that the guards riding in nearby cars became ill.

The death toll on the trains numbered in the thousands. But still they came. Over the course of the next week, more than eleven thousand additional prisoners arrived at the port in cattle wagons, trucks, or barges or on foot. Upon arrival at Lübeck, the guards made those prisoners who survived the journey unload the dead bodies of their fellow inmates. Ropes were tied around the corpses, which often numbered twenty to thirty per car, to help drag them off the trains. During the confusion at the port, one group of prisoners from Neuengamme was forced to remain in their cattle car for ten days. All of them died.

At the coastal city, the prisoners were divided into two groups. About 250 prisoners of Scandinavian ancestry were loaded into two white hospital ships on orders from Count Folke Bernadotte, who had earlier negotiated their release. They were headed to safety in Sweden; all others were taken to the port to be transferred to the *Cap Arcona* and other ships in the bay.

ONE OF THE FIRST CAMPS to evacuate north to the Baltic was Auschwitz, in Poland. The Red Army was closing in on the camp. The rushed evacuation included Auschwitz's satellite camps such as Fürstengrube, which was a coal mining camp established in 1943 near the town of Wesola, about nineteen miles from Auschwitz. Three months before the prisoners at Neuengamme set out in cattle cars and by foot, Commandant Max Schmidt ordered his detainees at Fürstengrube to line up in formation. It was January 11, 1945, a freezing morning with frost covering the ground. While the prisoners struggled to stand in the bitter cold, guards searched the barracks for anyone hiding. Satisfied that everyone was accounted for, the guards dispensed a little bread, margarine, and marmalade to the starving prisoners shivering that gray January day. Sixteen hours later the prisoners from other camps arrived, and the evacuation began. Prisoners were organized into groups of one hundred with five per row and marched out of the camp at midnight. Two of the prisoners shuffling west were Berek Jakubowicz and his brother Josek.

As soon as the death march began, one of the guards shot a prisoner and announced to the rest, "The guards will shoot anyone who doesn't keep up with us." Soon afterward, a prisoner tripped and fell to the ground. An SS guard appeared and shot him. Berek Jakubowicz remembered, "Before long so many lay dead on the road that we had to walk carefully to avoid stepping on the bodies."

The prisoners were marched throughout the night with only short breaks for rest. The destination was a city about forty-five miles away. The snow and frozen ground made walking all the more difficult, but the guards continued executing any prisoner unable to keep up. Hungry, exhausted, and frozen, Jakubowicz struggled to stay upright and keep from collapsing. He recalled wanting to give up, but his brother and friends propped him up and continued pushing him forward on the grueling journey. His deteriorating condition was apparent to the guards, who likely would have killed him had it not been for the fact that he had been the camp dentist and had treated several of the Germans. Rather than shoot him, the guards gave the dentist vodka to keep him warm and moving . . . and alive.

All the while, Commandant Schmidt rode around the columns of prisoners on his motorcycle, occasionally complaining of the slow pace of the march or ordering that one of the prisoners be shot in order to inspire the others to quicken their steps. Fifteen more prisoners were killed during this segment of the evacuation. Jakubowicz and the other prisoners hoped the guards would realize the hopelessness of the situation and run for their own lives, but they remained violent and loyal to the Nazi cause to the very end.

After several nights of walking, the survivors from Auschwitz and Fürstengrube were down to around 540. Many prisoners had fallen from exhaustion during the arduous and brutally cold journey and were shot by the guards, but the convoy finally arrived at Gleiwitz. There they observed other prisoners gathered behind a high fence rimmed in barbed wire. But Gleiwitz was only a stopping point. The following morning the prisoners were forced into nearby cattle cars without a chance to eat or drink. Over the protests of a former physician among the prisoners, many of them began scooping up snow to quench their thirst before being herded into the train, oblivious of the dangers of doing so.

Conditions were deplorable on the train. There was no place to urinate, and prisoners were forced to relieve themselves in their camp uniforms. The train ride lasted all day, during which one of the prisoners in Jakubowicz's car died. When the train finally stopped, the doors were heaved open, and the guards began tossing dead and dying prisoners out the open door. However, the prisoners in the car containing the Jakubowicz brothers and a few others were forced to wait locked inside for the remainder of the day and night. There was nothing to eat or drink, and the survivors continued to scoop up handfuls of snow near the openings and cracks of the cattle cars to nourish themselves. During the ordeal, the former physician who pleaded with his comrades not to eat snow rapidly began to unravel. The man began yelling uncontrollably for his wife and daughter. The poor soul's condition attracted an SS sergeant who shot the physician and then threw his body out of the train.

Another full day and night passed without food or water. Those trapped inside tried to console themselves with the fact that at least they were no longer marching. Enough prisoners had died or were thrown out of the train to make room for those inside to finally stretch their legs or sit down. The train jerked forward and continued down the tracks, finally arriving at Buchenwald, which greeted them with an ironic message on a large sign: *Jedem das seine* (To each his own). The guards dragged the disoriented prisoners off the trains. Their stay at Buchenwald was short-lived. After being given a small ration of bread and coffee, the survivors were marched to Mittelbau-Dora, in Nordhausen, Germany. Jakubowicz and his peers were by now reduced to skin and bones.

Jakubowicz and the other surviving prisoners arrived at the subcamp and were given a ration of bread and marmalade. That was hardly consolation for what they saw. A French survivor of the

Holocaust named Jean Mialet had once said of Mittelbau-Dora, "This is what hell must be like." He was right. Roughly thirty thousand prisoners had died at the camp. The camp was overcrowded. Wooden planks over a hole served as the prisoners' latrine. Curiously, the newly arrived prisoners were kept separate from most of the other workers at the camp. While they waited in camp, an announcement was made for anyone with skills as an electrician to come forward. The general response from the prisoners, however, was to keep quiet and look busy if a guard happened by. They were manufacturing the dreaded V-1 and V-2 rockets.

Hope came in the form of Allied warplanes that now flew overhead and the absence of any German air defenses. The temptation to look upward for the liberators was hard to suppress, but the SS guards warned their charges, "Don't you stare up there gleefully." The prisoners complied, but muttered to themselves, "Don't do a thing. Just act busy when a German comes by. The Americans are not far away, and it won't be long before they're here." The prisoners busied themselves looking busy, faking production at the V rocket factory by simply moving parts back and forth or pretending to clean them. Jakubowicz was told to unpack his dental instruments and make himself useful assisting patients. He had managed to survive another ordeal, and his dental equipment had again proved useful.

The last day at Mittelbau-Dora for Jakubowicz and the other prisoners from Auschwitz had come. No one was called to assemble for work that morning. Rather, the commandant ordered all prisoners to be marched to the Elbe River. As always, Jakubowicz grabbed his dental kit. Flatbed barges awaited to transport the inmates north. Jakubowicz recalled the mixed feelings of the prisoners. They had survived Mittelbau-Dora and knew the Americans were closing in. It seemed safer to remain at the camp rather than risk another trip, this time not by foot or train, but by rusting barge.

The prisoners were seated roughly sixty per barge, supervised by a few guards and *kapos*. They were told not to move because the overcrowded barges might tip over into the cold river. The barges were old, slow, and inefficient. Black smoke billowed out of the exhaust pipes from the loud engines. Still, the trip was much easier by boat. They had fresh air and could stretch their legs a little. The prisoners were also given a ration of bread and coffee. Encouraging signs of spring were everywhere, even if cold rains pelted the old barges.

Jakubowicz and his fellow survivors wondered about the motives of the commandant, Max Schmidt. It seemed as though he was evacuating his prisoners not so much on account of orders, but rather to keep them alive in order to justify his job. Jakubowicz suspected that the commandant worried about being transferred to the front to fight against the Americans or British, or, worse yet, the Russians. Schmidt also had to know the war was ending, and, as the commandant of Auschwitz, he would surely soon face war-crimes charges.

Berek Jakubowicz and the other inmates were marched to a farmhouse in the country not far from Neustadt and Lübeck in northern Germany. When they arrived the prisoners were finally given a little food—bread with butter and coffee. Bizarrely, the farm was Commandant Schmidt's family estate in Neu Glassau. Jakubowicz was cold and starving, so he took the risk of approaching one of the soldiers and asked if the nearby village had a dentist. "[Master Sergeant], I understand that there are no dentists in Neu Glassau? I still have dental instruments from Fürstengrube. If you permit me to go there, I could help those with dental problems. You know [sir] that I will not escape."

Surprisingly, Jakubowicz was granted permission to practice dentistry in the village. A guard escorted him to and from the village. But he worried that his luck was about to expire. Even though the village had no dentists, the residents did not come to see him. The services that had kept him alive for so long were not wanted. However, while he was at the village, Allied airplanes continued to fly overhead, and the sound of bombs exploding pierced the quiet of the farming community. The Allies were near.

The prisoners remained at the farm for several days. Then, on April 27, Max Schmidt, the commandant from Auschwitz, had

Jakubowicz brought before him with shocking news. "The director of the Swedish Red Cross, Count Folke Bernadotte, will be here tomorrow to take some of you to Sweden. But he only wants prisoners who are from the West. He won't know where any of you are from. I won't stand in your way if you tell him you are from somewhere in the West."

The dentist asked, "What will happen if I stay?" Commandant Schmidt informed his prisoner that he did not know but warned him that Max Pauly, the commandant of Neuengamme, was in charge of the final leg of their evacuation and was not to be trusted. Jakubowicz shared the surprising development with his brother and friends. They finally saw an opportunity to escape. The brothers and their friends decided to hide their Jewish and Polish heritage and try to pass themselves off as French. Jakubowicz struggled to remember the few words in French he knew and hurriedly shared them with the others. He advised his brother and friends to say, "Je viens de la France." If asked by the guards or Count Bernadotte's staff "Quelle ville?" they all agreed to answer, "De Bordeaux, monsieur."

The moment arrived. The prisoners were assembled in the usual rows of five men each. At nine thirty on the morning of April 28, four white trucks and a black limousine with a Red Cross flag flying from the front fender arrived. Three tall men wearing khaki uniforms stepped out of the limo and met with the commandant.

Jakubowicz recalled that Count Bernadotte was one of the three, but it is uncertain as to whether his recollection is accurate.* An announcement was made to the prisoners: "All western nationals step forward." They did—fifty from Belgium, France, and Holland came forward. The Americans and British had already been released, and all the Norwegians from Auschwitz were dead. No one else stepped forward, so Jakubowicz and his brother joined the Western nationals in front of the Red Cross staff. However, in the heat of the moment, other prisoners from Eastern Europe rushed forward, doubling the number of prisoners in the special line. A tense, quiet moment

---

* In all probability, it was one of Bernadotte's associates, as surviving records do not place him at the scene.

passed before the Red Cross staff allowed all who had stepped forward to get in the trucks. The ride was nerve-racking and along a bumpy road that took the prisoners to Neustadt Bay on the Baltic coast. The bluff by the Jakubowicz brothers was working.

The small caravan arrived at the sea. A Swedish freighter sat anchored close to the shoreline. Once the prisoners were unloaded from the trucks, a Red Cross official stated, "We know that not all of you are from the West. Those who are not we cannot take." No one said anything for a tense minute. The official then walked the length of the line of prisoners, looking each one in the eye. He appeared visibly upset and warned them, "As long as no one is willing to admit it, we will take you all back." Still, no one spoke.

According to Jakubowicz's recollection, the man in charge was impatient and spoke to his two companions, then said, "For the last time . . . " Another call was made for the Westerners to step forward. They did, but Jakubowicz and a few of his fellow bluffers hesitated. Some of the Western prisoners likely informed the Red Cross officials that prisoners from Eastern Europe were among the group. Jakubowicz and his fellow Poles were forced back to the trucks.

As the Western prisoners were being taken to the dock to be transferred to the Swedish ship, Jakubowicz tried to appeal to the officials. "Can't you take us? We are condemned. Look at the condition of some of these people. If you return us, they will be dead tomorrow." But the response from one of the Red Cross staffers was, "I don't have enough room on the ship." Jakubowicz continued begging, saying that he and his comrades would stand on deck. But the agreement with Heinrich Himmler was that only Western prisoners be loaded onto the Swedish ship, and SS guards were nearby watching the entire operation. A justifiably frustrated and defeated Jakubowicz recorded in his memoir years later of the man he thought was Count Bernadotte, "To this day I still don't know why he did not take us."

On April 30 two Swedish ships—the *Magdalena* and *Lillie Matthiessen*—sailed from Lübeck Bay, one carrying 223 European prisoners, the other with 225 women from Ravensbrück. They were taken to Sweden to hospitals. In separate incidents, more than 250 other prisoners from Neuengamme had been evacuated across the Baltic by the Swedish Red Cross on the ship *Westpreussen*. As for Jakubowicz, he and the other prisoners were taken by truck back to the farm where they had been before. His fate would take him to a different ship, one not headed for Sweden.

Chapter 16

FLOATING CONCENTRATION CAMPS

ALTHOUGH THE NAZI EMPIRE had crumbled by April and the fatherland was being overrun by the Allies, Germany's northern Baltic coast remained perhaps the safest place in the country. In addition to prisoners being transported to the Baltic, German civilians and important Nazi leaders fled to the coastal communities still under Nazi control, including Neustadt and Lübeck in Holstein. Unbeknownst to the Nazi commanders and prisoners arriving at the Baltic coast, a deal had been made in 1944 by C. J. Burckhardt, the president of the International Red Cross, and Allied commanders to spare as much of Lübeck Bay as possible from the bombing campaign because it could potentially serve to collect and evacuate war prisoners. Nazi officials therefore concluded that it would also be a good place to send the *Cap Arcona* and other large ships.

Nestled along the Baltic coast, the city of Lübeck functioned as a major seaport. Neustadt was a smaller, quieter community approximately eighteen miles northeast of Lübeck and thirty-one miles from the major seaport at Kiel. Brick warehouses, a small port, and fishing boats dotted the tree-lined shore. The tall spire of a church marked the center of the downtown. Had it been another time and altogether different situation, it would have been described as charming or quaint. Two bays—named for the towns—were visible from the shoreline. Neustadt Bay was about two miles wide and a bit shorter in length. It opened into Lübeck Bay, which was much larger and flowed out to the Baltic Sea.

The coast in the late winter of 1945 was abuzz with activity and anxiety. Neustadt had a naval base, which housed a submarine training school headed by Captain Albrecht Schmidt and the 3rd Submarine Division commanded by Heinrich Schmidt.* Two smaller freighters waited at the port, while two massive ocean liners were anchored not far from the dock. In town people and soldiers rushed at a frenzied pace to abandon the area, knowing that the Allies were closing in fast.

By late April the scene at the coast was one of chaos. There were far too many prisoners arriving for the number of guards, amount of food and water, and facilities available at the harbor. Given the impossible situation and lack of clear orders, the SS guards were not sure what to do, nor were they told what was happening. The only news that arrived at the coast told of Germany's dire situation, yet the guards did nothing to help any of the prisoners. As a result, some of the prisoners arriving at the coast were so weak that they died while waiting at the harbor. In this tense situation, rumors swirled among the guards and prisoners. Some suspected that Nazi leaders and soldiers would try to flee to German-held Norway to establish a final redoubt. However, the *Cap Arcona*, the largest transport ship gathered at the bay, was in no condition to set sail, and there were far too many prisoners, soldiers, and civilians in the area to fit on two large liners.

Another rumor was that Count Folke Bernadotte, operating on behalf of the Swedish Red Cross, was at the coast, trying to rescue prisoners. However, as one historian explains, "Some of the seamen on the *Cap Arcona* were told that the prisoners were to be taken out

---

* The Germans also had research facilities at the coast dedicated to developing new technology for underwater rescue, naval weaponry, and other military applications.

to sea and then collected by Swedish Red Cross ships, but this assurance was probably a means of allaying their fears." Word also
spread at the port that Heinrich Himmler was involved in secret
peace negotiations in late April. This gave rise to yet another rumor—that the prisoners were to board ships to be handed over to
the British. During the war-crimes tribunals afterward, the provincial governor of Hamburg, Karl Kaufmann, testified that the prisoners were to be taken to Sweden.

There was a more gruesome rumor. Georg-Henning Graf von
Bassewitz-Behr, head of the SS in Hamburg, who was also forced to
testify at the postwar trials, claimed the prisoners were to be killed
"in compliance with Himmler's orders." All evidence of the Holocaust, he noted, had to be eliminated. Kurt Rickert, who worked for
Bassewitz-Behr, testified at the Hamburg war-crimes trial that the
prisoners were to be loaded on the large ocean liners, and then the
ships were to be sunk by a U-boat or Luftwaffe plane. Eva Neurath,
a survivor of the death march and ordeal at the coast, testified at the
postwar trials that she was told by a police officer that the ships
were to be blown up.

THE LOADING OF PRISONERS onto the ships began on April 17. It was
announced that prisoners waiting at the port would be taken from
the docks to the two freighters and two larger ocean liners in the
bay, but the process was anything but orderly. Absent any clear mission or direct orders, the chaotic situation devolved into shouting
and threats from Kaufmann and protests from the ships' captains.

The plan was to transport the prisoners from the port to the
ships at anchor using the *Athen*, a 401-foot freighter built in 1936.
With its single massive smokestack, the *Athen* was larger than the
Thielbek, the other freighter at the port, but much smaller than the
two ocean liners at anchor, the *Deutschland* and *Cap Arcona*. However, Fritz Nobmann, the skipper of the *Athen*, refused to allow
prisoners to board his ship. After a short delay, the captain was
threatened by the SS and told he would be shot. Nobmann backed
down, and the first group of prisoners was violently herded onto

the *Athen*. Over the next several days, the freighter would make repeated trips to and from the *Cap Arcona* and the other two ships.

Another confrontation occurred later that same day when Kaufmann ordered Johann Jacobsen, the captain of the *Thielbek*, to stand by for orders to take on prisoners from the docks. He too protested. The *Thielbek*, a freighter roughly 300 feet in length that displaced 2,815 tons, was in bad shape and unprepared to accommodate even a fraction of the number of prisoners gathered at the docks. Because it was a freighter it was not designed for passengers—it had only two holds and a handful of cabins. It had also been bombed the prior summer, and the repairs, conducted at Maschinenbau-Gesellschaft shipyards in Lübeck, its home port, were unfinished when it was called back into service. Both the rudder and the steering apparatus were not fully functional; the ship had to be towed by a tugboat into its present position at the pier. Captain Jacobsen was still waiting for new motors for his ship when the loading began.

Captain Heinrich Bertram of the *Cap Arcona* was also told to prepare to accept prisoners. The famous ship was no longer the celebrated ocean liner that carried elite passengers to South America in style; nor was it the ship commissioned by Joseph Goebbels and Herbert Selpin to star in the Nazi film about the *Titanic*. It had been painted a dull gray, and much of the elegant interior had long since been removed. Like the *Thielbek*, the three-funneled ocean liner was barely seaworthy and, despite its size, was ill-prepared to take more than a few hundred prisoners. The ship was low on sanitary facilities, had little food or water, and was completely defenseless.

Captain Bertram refused to follow the orders, claiming his ship was not equipped to hold prisoners and was no longer in military service. He wrote to Hamburg-Süd, the company that owned the *Cap Arcona*, complaining about the situation. "For me it was a matter of course to refuse to accept the prisoners, since any responsible seaman knows that the risk at sea to take on human beings without absolute necessity during wartime is dangerous enough, especially such masses."

The *Cap Arcona* under construction in the Blohm + Voss shipyards in Germany, 1927

The *Cap Arcona* docked on one of her cruises

A poster advertising the *Cap Arcona*'s cruises to South America

Distinguished passengers on board the *Cap Arcona*—Ernst Rolin and some of his officers pose next to Princess Cecilia of Prussia and her son Prince Federico. Heinrich Bertram, the second officer, is on the right

Two passengers from Brazil seated on the *Cap Arcona*'s deck

Adolf Hitler, who was passionate about large ships, poses with a group of sailors aboard the warship *Deustchland (United States Holocaust Memorial Museum)*

Reich Minister for Public Enlightenment and Propaganda, Joseph Goebbels, delivers a speech during the book burning in Berlin *(National Archives and Records Administration)*

Movie buffs Adolf Hitler and Joseph Goebbels watching a film shoot

Herbert Selpin, the director of the propaganda film *Titanic*

Herbert Selpin on the set of *Titanic (Filmmuseum Berlin—Stiftung Deutsche Kinemathek)*

Herbert Selpin hanging in a jail cell in Berlin

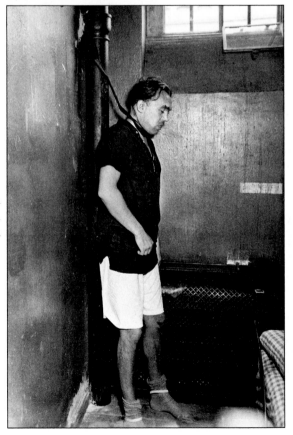

Poster (in French) for the new German film *Titanic*

Scene of the *Titanic* flooding, from the film

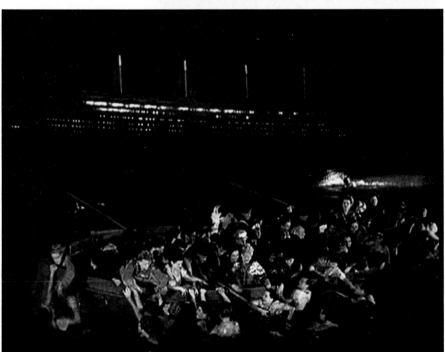

The *Titanic* sinking and lifeboats, from the film, 1943

View of a section of
the Neuengamme
concentration camp
after liberation,
1945 (*United States
Holocaust Memorial
Museum*)

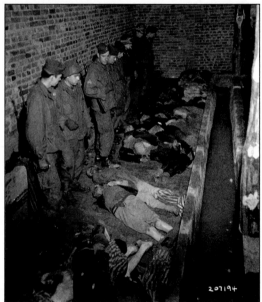

Troops with the American 82nd
Airborne Division examine
corpses found in the latrine
of one of Neuengamme's
subcamps (*National Archives
and Records Administration*)

Count Folke
Bernadotte of the
Swedish Red Cross
with a convoy of
vehicles from his
"White Buses"
campaign, 1945

The *Cap Arcona*
painted a dull
grey and rusting
in port at
Gotenhafen on
the Polish coast

Airmen with a
60-pound rocket, the
kind used to destroy
the *Cap Arcona*, 1945

Typhoon fighter-
bombers attack the
Cap Arcona, 1945

The *Cap Arcona*
on fire after the
attack, 1945

The *Cap Arcona*
capsized in
Lübeck Bay after
the attack, 1945

The marker memorializing the *Cap Arcona* disaster in Neustadt on
Germany's Baltic coast *(The Cap Arcona Museum of the Municipality Neustadt
in Holstein)*

However, on April 18, SS soldiers boarded the *Cap Arcona* and *Thielbek*, and Captains Bertram and Jacobsen, respectively, were informed that they had to accept the camp prisoners on board their ships. After the SS soldiers departed the *Thielbek*, Captain Jacobsen, with Captain Bertram at his side, issued a warning to his officers of what was about to happen. "There is no way to keep it a secret: There will be concentration camp detainees coming on board soon. Captain Bertram and I refused to take detainees on board. However, there is going to be another meeting tomorrow." Walter Felgner, the second officer on the *Thielbek*, survived the war to tell the story. He recalled that both captains remained resolutely opposed to the orders and were ordered to come ashore to meet with Karl Kaufmann.

The second meeting did not go well for the captains, but Captain Bertram did not give up. Still holding out hope that he could defy the order from Kaufmann and the SS, Bertram traveled to Hamburg to discuss the matter with Hamburg-Süd, the company that owned the *Cap Arcona*. He complained about losing command of his ship, the mission, and personnel issues.* However, any hopes Bertram had that Hamburg-Süd could intervene on his behalf were dashed. When he returned to Neustadt the next day, April 20, he and Captain Jacobsen of the *Thielbek* again met with Kaufmann, but were informed that concentration camps in the region were being evacuated and at least 10,000 more prisoners from Neuengamme were on their way to join the thousands already at the coast, and all were to be loaded onto their ships.

Kaufmann reminded Bertram and Jacobsen that he was not only the provincial governor but was also the Reichskommissar with authority over shipping. The *Cap Arcona* and *Thielbek* would be accepting thousands of prisoners whether the captains cooperated or not. Another ship, the *Deutschland*, a converted hospital ship, would likely be forced to accept prisoners as well. If the captains refused,

---

* The captain's crew had been reduced from 250 to 70, which was an amount inadequate for the number of prisoners the ship was housing or for setting sail.

Kaufmann informed them that they would be stripped of command and shot on the spot.

Captain Jacobsen again met with his officers aboard the *Thielbek*. Visibly depressed, he complained, "Starting today, I'll have no command over my own ship anymore." The *Athen* began transporting prisoners to the *Thielbek* and *Cap Arcona*.

Loading resumed on April 20. That same day another 2,500 prisoners arrived at the port. Max Pauly, the commandant of Neuengamme, had also sent his chief officer, Major Christoph-Heinz Gehrig, to Lübeck Bay to oversee the transfer of prisoners to the ships. The captains aboard the prison ships came to realize that this operation was a priority to Kaufmann and that something was about to happen. The man that Kaufmann dispatched to supervise the loading had a reputation for being especially vicious. Indeed, Gehrig had been responsible for killing the children used for the tuberculosis tests at Neuengamme and the nearby Janusz-Korczak School at Bullenhuser Damm. He remained just as ruthless in his new task, threatening to kill the captains and crew of the ships if they disobeyed his orders. And so he ordered that Captain Nobmann of the *Athen* transport the 2,500 newly arrived prisoners to the *Cap Arcona*, along with 280 guards to prevent any resistance.

But when the *Athen* arrived to tie up next to the *Cap Arcona*, the prisoners were unable to be transferred to the larger ship. Captain Bertram had again gone ashore to try to negotiate to save his ship and had given orders to First Officer Felgener to allow no prisoners on board the old liner. The *Cap Arcona* was so large and its decks so high off the water that it was logistically difficult to transfer prisoners from a smaller ship without the full cooperation of the *Cap Arcona*'s crew. Despite the complaints and threats by the SS guards on the *Athen* below, First Officer Felgener simply refused to lower the ladders and gang planks. Felgener realized the hopelessness of the situation and informed his fellow officers that it was only a matter of time before the ship would become a "floating concentration camp."

The *Athen* remained next to the large liner all night, its captain not sure what to do and leery of reporting to Kaufmann or Gehrig that he had failed in his mission. In the morning the captain gave up and sailed the freighter back to port with all twenty-five hundred of the new prisoners still aboard. A convoluted series of communications, protests, and orders then ensued. It started when Gehrig saw the *Athen* docking with the prisoners on the morning of April 21. He was furious and immediately notified Commandant Max Pauly. Together, they also reported the problem to the provincial governor and head of the Gestapo in Hamburg.

It took five days of bureaucratic bickering, but orders were eventually transmitted back to Gehrig. They stated that the loading of prisoners must proceed no matter what. Kaufmann, the governor, dispatched additional men to enforce the order and notified John Eggert, chair of the board of directors at Hamburg-Süd, reminding him that their ship was now under his control and that any further attempt to try to secure the *Cap Arcona* would not be tolerated. On orders from Kaufmann, Gehrig impounded the *Cap Arcona* on April 26.

Captain Bertram was met at the harbor by Gehrig and SS officers carrying machine guns. Bertram described the situation on April 26. "Gehrig had brought a written order to my attention for me to be shot at once if I would further refuse to take the prisoners on board. At this point it became clear to me that even my death would not prevent boarding of the prisoners, and so I informed the SS officer that I categorically declined any responsibility for my ship."

Soon afterward, the *Athen* sailed back to the *Cap Arcona* filled with prisoners, minus those who had perished during the wait. Bertram stepped aside but instructed the officers and crew of the *Cap Arcona* that they were not to mistreat any of the concentration camp prisoners who boarded the ship. The *Cap Arcona* and its sister ships were now floating concentration camps.

On board, the crews scrambled to ready the ships. Provisional toilets had to be set up on the deck of the *Thielbek*. The entire process of transferring the prisoners from the harbor to the ships was further hampered by the fact that the mariners and SS guards did not like or trust one another. The crews were outraged by what was happening to their ships and alarmed by the savagery of the SS guards toward the prisoners.

The twenty-five hundred prisoners from the *Athen* were crammed into the *Cap Arcona*'s holds and rooms. Major Gehrig informed Captain Bertram that more prisoners were coming and that he was expected to accommodate as many as seven to eight thousand of them. Bertram complained that it was impossible to accommodate that many, given his skeletal crew, lack of food and water, and general poor condition of the ship. Bertram had been making this argument for days, so Gehrig and his SS guards decided to see the conditions for themselves. What they saw shocked even them.

The ship was in deplorable condition, and the stench of human feces from the toilets that had long since ceased to function was overwhelming. Dead bodies littered the holds and had to be removed. Still, the bureaucratic-minded Nazis recorded the deaths and identities of as many prisoners as possible. One of them was Jelis Laskovs, a twenty-year-old Polish Jew, who, according to Nazi records, died on April 27 of diarrhea. The Nazi officers reluctantly agreed that the scheduled number of prisoners was too high, but also maintained that the ship must take on *some* additional prisoners. Commandant Pauly from Neuengamme sent an order that Bertram had to accept three thousand more prisoners. Bertram acquiesced, but announced that he refused to accept responsibility for what happened and attempted to leave the ship. However, the captain was stopped by Gehrig, who ordered two SS guards to detain Bertram and shoot him if he tried to leave. One of the SS troopers stuck a pistol in Bertram's chest, causing the captain to step aside, saying, "I have a wife and two children. That is the only reason why I will comply with this insane order."

From that point onward, the transfer of additional prisoners to the *Cap Arcona* continued without interference. Additional SS guards arrived on the *Cap Arcona* for sinister purposes. They began removing all life vests, life jackets, and anything else such as wooden benches that might float. These items were locked in storage, and then the guards began punching holes in the twenty-six lifeboats and landing crafts. These cruel acts were surely not lost on Captain Bertram and his crew, who likely began to figure out the mission planned for their ship.

Transferring weak and dying prisoners from one ship to another proved to be no easy task. Frustrated by the difficulty, the SS guards kicked and beat the prisoners while trying to load them onto the *Athen* and then onto the *Cap Arcona*. When the freighter tied up next to the *Cap Arcona*, flimsy ladders were thrown over the side of the tall ship, but the malnourished and weak prisoners had a difficult time trying to climb them. Those prisoners unable to climb were shot. One Polish prisoner remembered the ordeal in vivid detail. "They drove us on board the ships with shouts and blows. We climbed down steep ladders into holds. In the rush, many prisoners fell from a great height into the depths of the hold and were severely injured, suffering contusions and breaks. We could hardly move below. It was dark, cold, and damp. There were no toilets. No water. It began to stink."

Once the prisoners made it up the rope ladders and onto the *Cap Arcona*, they were gathered on the Promenade Deck, where only a few years earlier passengers boarded the ship to toasts of champagne. As the prisoners shuffled in bare feet down the halls and stairs of the ship, they glimpsed signs of the splendor of the *Cap Arcona*'s glory days that the SS guards had failed to remove—brass railings, bronze ornaments, mahogany tables, and elaborate tapestries. They were marched across Persian carpets and through the Victorian dining room, usually at the end of a cracking leather whip, and locked into crowded rooms stripped bare of any amenities.

The SS guards occupied luxury suites on the upper decks of the *Cap Arcona*. From time to time, they received another kind of visitor. Women were brought aboard by small launches. These included girlfriends among the local women and prostitutes. German prisoners were put in the first-class cabins; Poles and Czechs in the second-class cabins; French, Italian, and Dutch prisoners in the third-class rooms; and Soviet soldiers and Jews were forced into the cargo and storage holds in the deep bowels of the liner, an area known as the "banana deck" and easily containing the worst conditions on the ship. One Jewish prisoner recalled being in a supply room well below sea level that was roughly twenty-five yards long by ten yards wide, packed full of survivors from Neuengamme. There were no beds or facilities available to the prisoners. There was no place to bathe or sleep; there was no privacy.

For the prisoners in the deepest holds, there were no windows, and the hatches were kept shut, which denied the prisoners any fresh air or light. The only light they experienced was when the hatches were quickly opened during the initial days of captivity to pass down buckets with a little food and water. Those rations consisted of an inedible soup without any bowls or spoons. Much of it spilled out of the bucket and onto the urine-filled floors. Buckets were also lowered by rope to collect the feces and urine, which also spilled back out of the bucket while being pulled up to the deck. One inmate who survived recalled that when the bucket reached the hatch, "The thing tipped up, emptying its revolting contents on the heads of the prisoners who had gathered underneath for a glimpse of the open sky."

Soon, feces and urine filled the floors. Prisoners attempted with desperation to wipe the feces and urine from their bodies and find a clean spot in order to sit down, but it was impossible and they were forced to sit and sleep in human waste. The stench was so strong that the guards eventually stopped opening the hatches altogether. Either way, the ship had run out of food and water.

Throughout the ship, typhoid fever and lice spread among the prisoners, and bodies began piling up in the rooms and on deck. The conditions and smell were now so awful on board the *Cap Arcona* that most of the SS guards complained and demanded to be taken off the ship. They were replaced by about two hundred old men from the Volkssturm (men over the age of fifty-five conscripted into the home guard). Some prisoners recalled that at least the daily beatings stopped when the SS guards abandoned the ship.

The conditions on the *Thielbek* were equally abysmal. A narrow side door was used to load the prisoners, and, because the guards were in a panic, they kicked and shoved the survivors onto the ship. The prisoners were forced into a central storage area that was so crowded that it was difficult even to sit down. A large tub in the center of the open room was used as a latrine by the prisoners, but it soon overflowed onto the floors, and the prisoners, like those aboard the *Cap Arcona*, were forced to sit or stand in the waste in pitch-black darkness. Here too the screams from the dying and terrified, along with the overpowering smell, were such that the guards only rarely opened the doors.

Aboard the *Thielbek*, Captain Jacobsen sent a letter to his wife, describing the abysmal and deteriorating situation. "The dead are removed from the [holds] every morning. We had five this morning. But because [so many are dying] . . . they are being picked up by boats, to be taken ashore. . . . [P]risoners of all ages from 14 to 70 and from ministers, professors, doctors, captains, to workers—all are represented. . . . The foreigners are forced to go and remain in the [holds]; they are not allowed on deck. They are crammed in like sardines."

One of those prisoners crammed like sardines into the holds of the *Thielbek* was Frenchman Michel Hollard. One of the leaders of the French Resistance who had established the espionage ring Réseau AGIR, Hollard had played a vital role in providing the British valuable information on German military plans and the V-2 rockets. The dashing spy remembered his efforts to comfort fellow prisoners. "My friends, our turn has come to set out for the unknown. We are all afraid, and I must admit that the prospect is far from reassuring. Is not this the moment to show what sort of men we are?"

The French spy called his fellow prisoners together for a final prayer. Holding hands with one another, Hollard prayed, "Oh God, from the depths of our agony, we beseech you, whatever happens to us, protect, we implore you, our wives and children and guard them against all evil."

At the port prisoners continued to arrive by the thousands, and the *Athen* continued shuttling them to the three larger ships. A few small launches and rafts were commandeered to expedite the process and assist the *Athen*. From April 27 to 30, roughly sixty-five hundred additional prisoners, mostly from Neuengamme, were loaded onto the *Cap Arcona* and *Thielbek*. On board the *Cap Arcona*, the number of prisoners swelled, and the ship soon ran out of food, water, and medicine. Prisoners were dying in alarming numbers. Some of them were thrown overboard, while others were taken by the *Athen* and smaller launches back to the port, where they were disposed of in mass graves.

And then something happened . . .

The *Athen* made its final delivery of prisoners on April 30, bringing roughly two hundred more prisoners from the Fürstengrube concentration camp. Since being brought aboard the *Cap Arcona*, the prisoners had been trying to form a rudimentary organization to communicate with one another and lobby the crew to share their food and water. Unbeknownst to the skeletal detachment of guards still on board, this impromptu prisoner organization had also managed to lower some inmates over the sides of the ship and into the water. Led by a few British prisoners, they recruited some Soviet soldiers to try to swim to shore. However, in the cold water, the fragile prisoners perished.

The prisoner organization was, however, successful in registering their complaints about the inhumane conditions on board. Captain Bertram responded by requesting that some of the prisoners on board the overcrowded *Cap Arcona* and *Thielbek* be permitted to go back to the port. Amazingly, the officers at the harbor agreed, and around two thousand prisoners from the ships—mostly French, along with a few Belgian, Dutch, and Swiss prisoners—were taken back to the port. They could not have known, but Count Folke Bernadotte and the Swedish Red Cross were back at the port, demanding additional prisoners be released.

One of those taken off the *Thielbek* was French spy Michel Hollard. He and his comrades almost did not cooperate, for they feared the worst. But when they arrived on the top deck, they were hosed down to remove the feces and urine and then taken to the port. There they were met by the count. The detainees were transferred to the Swedish ships *Magdalena* and *Lillie Matthiessen*. On April 30 the hospital ships departed for Sweden. Hollard, aboard the *Magdalena*, had miraculously survived.

On May 1 Captain Bertram met with the prisoner organization on board the *Cap Arcona* and their leader, German actor Erwin Geschonneck, to inform them of some long-overdue good news: Hitler was dead, and the prisoners removed from the ship the previous day were rescued by the Swedish Red Cross. There was hope.

Chapter 17

IN THE BUNKER

As THE PRISON SHIPS in the Baltic were being loaded, another scene of desperation was taking place underground in the heart of Berlin. Adolf Hitler marked his fifty-sixth birthday on April 20, 1945, in the confines of his bunker, receiving devastating reports of German defeats and Allied advances on all fronts. In the South, Field Marshal Albert Kesselring was fighting a hopeless battle against the Americans, the Allies were closing in on Grand Admiral Karl Dönitz's forces in the North, and the eastern and western fronts had completely collapsed. The only good news for the German people still loyal to Hitler was the delusional statement issued to the public by Joseph Goebbels that, on his birthday, "Our Führer has not deserted us. That is our victory."

Two days later Hitler was dealt another devastating blow. The tide of the war had long since changed and the Red Army was on the march to Berlin, but Hitler had ordered a last-ditch counterattack by the Panzer Corps under General Felix Steiner in hopes of delaying the inevitable. However, General Steiner and other senior German commanders were either unable or unwilling to follow their leader's frantic and unrealistic orders.

Upon hearing the news, the führer exploded into another one of his meltdowns. For a full thirty minutes, he stormed around the conference room in his bunker, screaming and pounding his fists on the table, accusing everyone in his senior command of disloyalty and betrayal. Finally, he collapsed in exhaustion and muttered the obvious, "It's all lost, hopelessly lost." For the first time in a long time, Hitler acted with prudence—he ordered his personal papers be destroyed. Aides burned them in the garden outside the bunker, which was the same fate that awaited Hitler himself.

Berlin was being overrun. One month earlier, on March 13, bombs had destroyed Goebbels's Ministry of Propaganda, but he avoided being killed in the attack. The capital city's defenses were meager, and civil government had ceased to exist. While some older men and young boys in the home guard tried to fight, many soldiers and civilians simply fled or surrendered. The city, like the country itself, was cut in half and unable to communicate effectively or mount a viable defense. Heinrich Himmler's prediction that the Allies would eventually march through Berlin had come true. For those prisoners gathered at the port at Lübeck Bay and suffering in the crowded holds of the *Cap Arcona*, hope came in the form of Allied advances combined with crumbling Nazi defenses. The war would soon end.

DESPITE THE GRAVE SITUATION in Germany, Hitler and his loyal propagandist kept up the pretense of victory to the very end. On April 22, the day Goebbels arrived in the bunker, Hitler issued his "Proclamation to the People of Berlin," warning: "Anyone who proposes or even approves measures detrimental to our power of resistance is a traitor! He is to be shot or hanged immediately!"

In two Mercedes limousines, Goebbels had moved his wife and six children from their private home near the Brandenburg Gate to the bunker and informed Hitler that they would all remain at his side. Before leaving his office, however, Goebbels made one final radio address to the German people. In it he continued the lie he had created about Hitler, claiming, "The Führer is in Berlin and will die fighting with his troops defending the capital city." Likewise, in the final issue of the Nazi propaganda newsletter *Das Reich*, Goebbels ordered everyone, including women, children, and the elderly, to fight at all costs to the very end. Inside the bunker, however, it was apparent that the war was lost. Hitler told his senior staff to leave the city, but a few of his loyalists and secretaries refused to abandon their führer. Hitler's longtime mistress, Eva Braun, was one of those who remained, leading him to complain, "Ah, if only my generals were as brave as my women."

One of those top commanders who abandoned Hitler was Himmler, who sought to negotiate a separate surrender with the West through Count Folke Bernadotte. Hitler had received news of Himmler's actions while hunkered down in his bunker and exploded. "He raged like a madman, his face so suffused with blood as to be unrecognizable, beside himself with fury and, strange as it sounds, grief," according to one witness.

Just before midnight on April 28, Hitler also ordered one of Germany's most celebrated aces, Ritter von Greim, on a priority mission. He and another pilot were to fly to the combat zone and locate Admiral Karl Dönitz, commander of all Nazi forces in the North, where Himmler was last seen. The pilots were to instruct the admiral to have Himmler arrested and shot. The search for Himmler, however, meant that the Gestapo chief could no longer conduct negotiations with Count Folke Bernadotte to free prisoners from the concentration camps or those waiting at the coast or on ships anchored in Lübeck Bay.

Seeking an outlet for his anger, Hitler ordered that Himmler's top aide, Hermann Fegelein, also be executed. Fegelein was Eva Braun's brother-in-law by marriage. But not even the pleas of Hitler's mistress could save Fegelein from the führer's rage. Members of the secret police were dispatched to arrest him. Himmler's aide was then taken to the Chancellery garden and shot in the head.

Himmler was not the only top commander attempting to seize power and cover his own tracks at the very end. That winter Hitler's top general and Luftwaffe commander, Hermann Göring, ordered that his Berlin estate, Carinhall, be blown up. He moved his family south to his villa in Bavaria. The rotund general ordered aides to also move the fortune in art and treasures he had looted

from conquered territories. On Hitler's birthday Göring tele-
graphed his führer, wishing him well and claiming that he was
moving the Luftwaffe command south to continue the fight. It was
a boldface lie, and Hitler knew it. The telegraph also boldly indicated that if a reply was not forthcoming from Hitler by ten o'clock
in the evening, the Luftwaffe commander would assume power.

Göring had been the heir apparent to the Third Reich but was
now simply the latest commander to abandon Hitler. Although
many Nazi commanders knew the war was lost and that Hitler was
mad, few were willing to openly defy the führer, especially in such
direct ways. But as Göring was about to discover, fewer still were
willing to back the arrogant, unpopular Luftwaffe commander.

Göring had lived extravagantly, enriching his bank account and
ignoring Nazi doctrine. He also failed spectacularly in his pledge to
defend German cities from Allied aerial bombing, prompting Goebbels, on hearing the news of Göring's treasonous actions, to roar,
"Medal-jangling asses and vain, perfumed dandies don't belong in
the high command." The führer, who had long since grown suspicious of the Luftwaffe commander, agreed. "None of this is new to
me. I have always known that Hermann Göring was lazy. He let the
Luftwaffe fall apart. The man was a monumental crook. . . . He has
been a drug addict for years."

Hitler removed his number two from power and ordered SS
agents to arrest him in Bavaria. Göring was to be killed, and the
Allies nearly accomplished the task for Hitler. The next day the
Royal Air Force's powerful Lancaster bombers attacked Berghof
and the homes of Hitler and Göring. Explosions cratered Göring's
mountain villa, blowing out windows and knocking pots and pans
from the shelves. Luckily for him, his security force managed to
rush their leader out of the villa and to safety through an underground escape tunnel. Göring was now on the run for his life and
unable to command.

In the end, Hitler was unable to lead from either a logistical perspective or an emotional one. He had lost too many of his commanders and withdrew to the bowels of his bunker, saying simply,

"Do whatever you want. I'm not giving any more orders." Surviving documents suggest that Hitler continued his downward descent into madness at the very end. He had trouble sleeping, and his black eyes were described as having a glazed, disconnected appearance. He shook uncontrollably, stopped changing his clothing, and took no concern about his appearance, often sitting hunched over like a much older, defeated man. His hair grayed to the point that he was nearly unrecognizable.

Hitler still had his moments of volcanic rage. One of the final fits occurred when he sent for General Gottlob Berger, who was now functioning as the chief of the SS. When Berger arrived in the bunker, he found Hitler ranting about his commanders. "Everyone has deceived me!" he screamed. "No one has told me the truth! The armed forces have lied to me!" Berger had been summoned to the cavernous bunker to carry out orders regarding prominent political prisoners and disloyal Nazi commanders. The führer issued one of his last orders, demanding that no high-level prisoners or disloyal Nazi commanders fall into enemy hands. The command concluded with the words, "Shoot them all! Shoot them all!"

Nor did Hitler himself want to fall into the hands of Soviet troops or be tortured and paraded about by them as a trophy of war.* Knowing the end was at hand, Hitler planned his own suicide, describing to those aides remaining in the bunker exactly how his body should be destroyed. The führer explained his reasoning to Joseph Goebbels, saying, "It's the only chance to restore personal reputation. If we leave the world stage in disgrace, we'll leave for nothing. . . . Rather end the struggle in honor than continue in shame and dishonor a few months or days longer."

Traudl Junge, Hitler's personal secretary, chronicled the final hours in the bunker, recalling that the führer first tested the cyanide pills on his German shepherd Blondi. It worked. He then checked to determine that enough fuel remained to burn his body. Satisfied,

---

* This had been the fate of Benito Mussolini, the leader of fascist Italy, who was hunted down by his own people, executed, and then strung up by his feet for public display next to the corpse of his mistress.

he sat down to dictate his last will and testament to Junge. His aide Martin Bormann was made executor of his will. Hitler's personal belongings were to be given to the Nazi Party as well as to a few loyal members of his staff. The former artist made sure to include in the document that his collection of paintings was to be displayed in a gallery in his hometown of Linz.

Hitler also used the opportunity to again justify his actions and place blame for the war on his perceived enemies, including Jews. After his usual hate-filled, delusional diatribe, Hitler claimed that "history would eventually record Germany's struggle against Jews as one of the most glorious and valiant manifestations of a nation's will to existence." He predicted that Nazism would be resurrected and offered a final edict: "Above all I enjoin the government and the people to uphold the race laws to the limit and to resist mercilessly the poisoner of all nations, international Jewry."

The führer named Admiral Dönitz as head of the armed forces and state. The admiral was tall, socially stiff, and neither a politician nor close to Hitler. However, the fifty-four-year-old commander consistently proved to be highly competent. Through Hitler's many purges of senior commanders, Dönitz, the submarine hero from World War I, remained, and his voice was one of the few that carried weight inside the German Chancellery. When the Wehrmacht and Luftwaffe commanders failed time and again, Dönitz's U-boats continued to be effective, despite being outgunned by the Allied navies.

Other staffing changes were made. Himmler was replaced by Paul Giesler, the provincial governor of Munich, who would be the new minister of the interior. Karl Hanke, a fanatically loyal Nazi, was designated to take over the Gestapo. Hitler also appointed Goebbels as chancellor of Germany.

The final set of orders and drafting of the will lasted well past midnight. In the early hours of April 29, Hitler married Eva Braun, his longtime mistress, whom he met in Munich when she was only seventeen and working as a seamstress and model. Hitler had always dismissed the idea of marriage, explaining to Braun that his country and the Nazi struggle were his spouses. But in the final day of his life, Hitler rationalized that, with Germany gone, he could marry.

The thirty-three-year-old Braun wore an elegant dark silk gown and expensive Ferragamo shoes for the impromptu ceremony. Unlike Hitler, who remained in an exhausted, hunched state throughout the service, the bride was so delusional that she gushed during the mad ceremony. The couple even poured champagne. Goebbels and Martin Bormann were asked to witness the marriage, which was hastily conducted by a local government official named Walter Wagner. The strange wedding party stayed up "celebrating" until nearly five in the morning, yet their wedding "music" consisted of the sounds of Berlin being reduced to rubble. The dreaded Red Army had entered the city and was nearing the final hideout.

A short time later, Hitler awoke, ate a light lunch of spaghetti and salad with his secretaries, and announced that the end was at hand. There were formal and tearful farewells exchanged among the loyalists remaining in the bunker. Adorned in his usual attire of black pants, white shirt, and tan military jacket, Hitler shook hands with everyone in the bunker. His new bride was at his side, still wearing her black dress and carrying a bouquet of roses. The new Mrs. Hitler spoke briefly to Traudl Junge, begging her, "Please do try to get out. You may yet make your way through." She said her final good-bye: "And give Bavaria my love."

Hitler and Eva walked slowly to his study. The staff remained outside the door, giving the couple ten minutes alone. The couple consumed cyanide pills, and then a shot rang out. When they opened the door, they found the führer and his bride seated side by side on a small white and blue couch. Eva was bent over sideways, her feet tucked beneath her body; Hitler's head hung down, a hole visible in the right temple from his Walther pistol. Blood was splattered on his shirt and jacket.

It was three thirty on Monday afternoon, April 30. As per Hitler's instructions, the bodies were taken to the garden and burned.

Goebbels had finally attained the power he longed for, but the cost was too much for him to bear. Even though the führer had, in his final political testament, just named Goebbels as his heir, the propagandist never accepted the position. Rather, he wrote an amendment to Hitler's last will and testament, saying, "For the first time in my life I must categorically refuse to comply with an order from the Führer."

To the end, Goebbels remained fanatically devoted to the Nazi cause. Not long before his final day in the bunker, the Reich minister was even planning additional propaganda films, including a new breakthrough—color films. That very month Goebbels had gathered fifty top aides together at his Berlin office to encourage them not to abandon the city, war, or cause. His delusion was such that he promised them that they would all star in a great film titled "Twilight of the Gods in Berlin in 1945" that would be shown in one hundred years. "I can assure you," he pleaded, "it will be a fine and elevating picture, and for the sake of this prospect worth standing fast." Goebbels tried to rally his propagandists, begging them to "hold out now, so that a hundred years hence the audience does not hoot and whistle when you appear on the screen!" After the motivational speech and peculiar promises, most of his aides quickly fled for their lives.

Despite his convictions, or perhaps because of them, the end was difficult for Goebbels. He drafted his last letter from the bunker, writing to his wife's son from her first marriage, Harald Quandt. In it he reveals to Harald his fate. "We are now confined to the Führer's bunker in the Reich Chancellery and are fighting for our lives and our honor. God alone knows what the outcome of this battle will be. I know, however, that we shall come out of it, dead or alive, with honor and glory. I hardly think that we shall see each other again. Probably, therefore, these are the last lines you will ever receive from me." Goebbels closed by telling the young man that he was ready to make the "supreme sacrifice" in order to bring the Nazi regime to its "only possible and honorable conclusion."

Both Hitler and Goebbels wanted Magda Goebbels to escape and encouraged her to do so. Hitler even awarded Mrs. Goebbels with the Golden Party Badge he had worn for years. However, she echoed her husband's sentiments: "The world which will succeed the Führer and National-Socialism is not worth living in and for this reason I have brought the children here too."

From the underground command center where Hitler spent his final hours, Goebbels ordered a Nazi physician to administer to his six children a lethal dose of poison while they slept. He and his wife then went to the garden where Hitler's body was burned and took cyanide capsules. Goebbels had also arranged to have one of the loyal SS guards remaining at the bunker put a bullet in their heads as assurance that they would not survive. The Little Doctor who had caused so much violence and suffering was dead on May 1.

Goebbels once prophetically predicted that the Nazis would long be remembered, saying, "We shall go down in history as the greatest statesmen of all time, or the greatest criminals." True to his prediction, his final words were "When we depart, let the Earth tremble!" The propagandist's perspective that the only options were complete victory or complete destruction proved true.

RUSSIAN UNITS WERE IN control of much of Berlin and were still searching for Hitler and his senior commanders. It would take them until May 2 to discover Hitler's underground bunker and another two days beyond that before they were able to identify his charred remains in the Chancellery garden. They also found the remains of Eva Braun and the entire Goebbels family; the six children were still in their pajamas tucked into bunk beds in the bunker. Goebbels's remains and those of the others were identified by Rear Admiral Hans-Erich Voss for the Soviets.

Hitler was dead, but the war was not over. The day after the suicide, Admiral Dönitz announced the führer's death in a radio broadcast that continued the propaganda. It read: "It is reported from the Führer's Headquarters that this afternoon Führer Adolf

Hitler fell in his command post in the Reich Chancellery, fighting with his last breath for Germany against Bolshevism."

The night of his radio announcement, Dönitz met with Himmler at the ad hoc headquarters at Plön, about twenty miles from Lübeck in northern Germany and near the port where thousands of prisoners from the concentration camps were being forced onto the *Cap Arcona* and three other ships. The admiral did not arrest or kill Himmler as he had been ordered. Dönitz desperately needed intelligence and resources, and Himmler offered both. Together, they ordered German forces in Hamburg, Lübeck, and Neustadt in Holstein to continue the fight. The meeting between the admiral and the Gestapo chief also served two other functions. It would soon contribute to the fate of the prisoners aboard the ships in the Baltic, and it seemed to lend credence to the rumor that, with Nazi commanders, troops, and ships concentrated at the coast, they might attempt to evacuate across the Baltic to Norway.

A reporter with the BBC named Chester Wilmot was also in northern Germany and headed toward the Baltic. The day Hitler killed himself, Wilmot was on the radio with a report from northern Germany. "Here in the north, there's still an army to be reckoned with: an army whose fighting power Himmler may still regard as a bargaining weapon. . . . We have smashed the German Army as a whole and its Air Force; but we haven't yet broken the power or spirit of the German Navy."

That report stirred concerns about what might be happening in the Baltic. Indeed, British and Canadian forces had encountered stiff German resistance along the North Sea and Baltic, as well as at the port in Kiel. With Admiral Dönitz in charge, roughly one hundred thousand Kriegsmarine forces had been scrambled to fight on land. Ships had ferried German forces from Denmark back to the fatherland in a desperate attempt to bolster defenses. Wilmot continued his broadcast, indicating that the war was far from over along the Baltic coast. "We can't afford at this stage of the war to pause in the task. So long as there are pockets of resistance as well organized as this one, the Nazis may be encouraged to fight on elsewhere. And so here in the north, the Second Army is striking at what amounts to Himmler's last hope."

Nazi Germany still flashed its fangs, and it appeared that German resistance in Neustadt and Lübeck would be tenacious. American, British, Canadian, and Russian forces were closing in fast on the Baltic coast. The Red Army was only about thirty miles east of the bay. A final terrible battle loomed in northern Germany, and the *Cap Arcona* and thousands of concentration camp prisoners gathered on the Baltic coast would be smack in the middle of it.

Chapter 18

OPERATION RAINBOW

Many of the last evacuees to arrive at the port at Lübeck Bay came on barges that had traveled north or west to the Baltic on rivers. Several of the barges came from Stutthof, on Poland's Baltic coast, near Danzig and Gdansk. The Nazi official who had established the notorious camp was Max Pauly, who would later serve as commandant of Neuengamme. The evacuation of Stutthof began on January 25 in response to news that the Red Army was moving toward the coast. The initial evacuations were on foot and contained twenty-five thousand prisoners constituting nine huge columns. The harrowing trip through snow and freezing weather would end up taking ten days; they were given food rations for two days.

In March and April, the Soviets began bombing the area around Stutthof, and it is likely that many of the prisoners either still in the camp or on the march and in the barges died from the aerial campaign. But the bombing campaign also meant that the camp was about to be liberated.

The last prisoners to evacuate the camp did so in one cargo ship and old barges. One of these groups comprised two thousand prisoners who were ordered by Stutthof's new commandant, Paul Werner Hoppe, to board an old cargo old ship lacking food, water, or sanitation. Commandant Hoppe ordered the last of Stutthof's prisoners out of the camp on April 17, three days after Himmler's evacuation order. Nearly five thousand prisoners from the camp and nearby satellite camps were loaded onto five old barges. Three of the barges departed immediately and were towed by tugboats from Hela Peninsula, on the Vistula River. Each one was packed with around a thousand men, women, and children. Most were Jews, but one of the barges held some Norwegians. The conditions on the industrial barges were crowded and miserable. Like the cargo ship, they lacked adequate supplies of food or water, facilities for relieving oneself, or areas to sleep. The barges were open on top but contained a deep hold, ideal for carrying rocks, coal, or equipment—but not people.

Many of the prisoners, already weak and sick, heads shaved and wearing old camp garments, died during the journey to Lübeck Bay. The old barges were so severely overcrowded and unseaworthy that the dead had to be thrown overboard. Two Jewish women on one of the barges could take the inhumane treatment no longer; they tied themselves together and jumped overboard in an act of joint suicide.

The smell of death was too overpowering for the guards topside, who decided that the weakest among the living should also be thrown overboard. It would lighten the barges. The SS guards asked for volunteers among the prisoners to complete the gruesome task, and a group of Ukrainian men agreed to do so. An eyewitness who survived the journey described the scene: "They picked out some people from among us, whom they threw overboard. Those selected were undressed, dragged up a steep iron ladder, and thrown through the hatch into the sea."

Eventually, however, it then became too much of a problem for the guards to descend into the reeking holds to fetch the dead or to lower the ladder for the Ukrainians. The prisoners, reduced to skin and bones, were too weak to help lift the dead out of the deep holds. And so the dead bodies began to pile up in the barges.

Not long afterward, the convoy of barges spotted British tanks and soldiers along the coast, headed toward Lübeck, which momentarily provided hope for the prisoners but created a panic among the guards. After spotting the Allies on the shoreline, the crew of one of the tugboats decided to try to save their own lives. They purposely sank one of the three barges, killing every prisoner aboard, and then steamed away from the scene. The other two barges were ordered to change course and make their way to the bay.

The captain of one of the other tugboats could take the inhumanity no longer and, on May 2 as they neared the coastline, ordered the rope to the barge cut in order to set it free. It was the barge carrying Norwegians, who had been law enforcement officials who had run afoul of the occupying Nazis. The police officers on the barge raised a makeshift sail and managed to bring it ashore near town. Fortunately, they were able to hide until the British army arrived the next day to liberate the town and rescue them.

Others were not so lucky. The third barge was towed into port on May 2, but as the prisoners were being unloaded they were beaten by the SS guards. Some were pushed into the frigid water and left to drown; others were lined up and shot by the sailors and a few naval cadets from the nearby U-boat base. A British officer whose unit arrived at the coast that same day described a gruesome scene. "The beaches for a good few hundred yards were covered with bodies. . . . These people had been mown down by machine guns. . . . The children had been clubbed to death and judging by the shape of their wounds, rifle butts had been used."

The last of the inmates from Stutthof aboard the remaining two barges—*Vaterland* and *Wolfgang*—arrived on the evening of May 2. They were traveling a few hours behind the initial three barges. These two last barges had been towed by the tugboats *Bussard* and *Adler*, respectively, and each one was trailed by a few small launches carrying more dying prisoners. One of the barges was towed to the *Cap Arcona*, the other to the *Thielbek*, whereupon they were tied up to the larger ships. The guards from the barges boarded the two larger ships anchored in the bay, but Captains Bertram and Jacobsen, despite the constant threats of death, refused to permit any additional prisoners on their ships.

The Nazi guards on board the *Cap Arcona* simply cut the lines to the barge and let it drift away. On board the *Thielbek*, the crew watched as the situation on the old barge turned chaotic. As Walter Felgner, one of the officers on the ship, recalled, "The prisoners began panicking, because the guards had left [the barge to board the *Thielbek*]. . . . The prisoners thought they would drown. On Captain Jacobsen's orders, we set them adrift, and we told the prisoners to stay calm because the wind was blowing them towards the shore. . . . But as they drifted, guards . . . shot at them." Perhaps hearing the gunshots from the *Thielbek*, the guards on board the *Cap Arcona* also started firing down into the floating barge with their rifles and machine guns, killing some of the prisoners.

In the predawn hours of May 3, the barges ran aground on the shallow sandbar by a small peninsula at Pelzerhaken, near the port. The prisoners somehow managed to climb out of the holds and, under cover of darkness, began swimming toward the shore. An account by a survivor named Saba Feninger describes the tense scene. "With the first light of dawn, we could already see that we were close to shore, and we also saw figures in uniform. Even though we thought 'Hitler is dead, it's the end of the war,' we came [ashore] where there were Germans again."

Fininger and the other prisoners tried in desperation to escape from the Nazi soldiers. Fortunately for her, she was pulled to shore by some of the prisoners and managed to get into a rowboat to hide. However, others were not so fortunate. She remembered, "Those who couldn't get up quickly enough, those whose legs were swollen [or] who were too weak stayed below deck." They attempted to hide, but "the Germans came up with machine guns and machine gunned everyone who was on the barge. . . . And that was not the end." A few of the prisoners who had made it ashore were "pushed into the sea next to the barge. They were pushed into the water and machine gunned. The water turned red."

Tragically, cadets from the nearby U-boat training base, a few older men conscripted for home defense at the end of the war, and young boys from town belonging to the Hitler Youth were nearby, searching for escaped prisoners. One of the very few prisoners to survive the ordeal was only fourteen and described the events. "The sick and weak were first to disembark. I was one who disembarked early. I remember being put down by a tree, where I was able to witness the other people getting off the boat. Then suddenly, out of nowhere, the guards reappeared, yelling and screaming that no one gave orders to disembark. They started shooting at people still on deck, waiting to go down the makeshift gangplank. Hundreds were killed like that."

Other prisoners were shipped from the port in nearby Kiel, just west of the towns of Neustadt and Lübeck. Many of these ships were hit by Allied bombers who mistook them for troop transports in the final days of the war. One such ship carried hundreds and perhaps thousands of prisoners from camps in north-central Germany. While en route to Kiel the ship was hit by two Allied air attacks, killing many of the prisoners. The ship, however, managed to limp into the harbor at Kiel, where it dropped anchor. While sitting in the harbor on May 2, a third Allied air attack targeted the port. The ship was hit multiple times, caught fire, and sank while at anchor. Only thirty-three of the prisoners on board survived.

On the foggy mornings of May 2 and 3, more prisoners were transported to the ships anchored in Lübeck Bay on small launches and rafts. One of those prisoners recalled being on a launch with about thirty other inmates and seeing through the thick fog the hulking ship at anchor. Large letters on the back of the ship identified it as *CAP ARCONA*. From the decks high above, a voice was heard through a bullhorn: "Are you bringing more prisoners? I can't take them. I have over four thousand already on board. I have no more room."

Another voice from above yelled out: "We are overloaded. Why don't you try the *Thielbek* or the *Deutschland*?" But the guards on the launch said their orders were to unload the prisoners on the *Cap Arcona*. The bullhorn again sounded: "I am the captain of this ship, and I will not take them. That is final." The SS guards gave up and went back ashore in the launch. However, they returned with another threat to kill the captain. Roughly five hundred additional prisoners were brought to the *Cap Arcona* and forced into the crowded holds.

Captain Nobmann aboard the *Athen* had also refused to accept prisoners on May 2. He then made a very fateful decision to sail his floating concentration camp from Lübeck Bay to the port at the smaller Neustadt Bay. It is possible he received an order to do so, or perhaps he was hoping to unload his detainees. Nobmann's decision to dock at the pier in Neustadt would ultimately save many lives aboard the *Athen*. Not far away, over the protests of Captain Jacobsen, the *Thielbek* was ordered to be towed out of the dock by a tugboat on the afternoon of May 2. This action would also prove to be fateful, but in another way.

Another order was given on the afternoon of May 2 to transport fuel to the *Cap Arcona*, anchored about two miles offshore. Even though there were severe fuel shortages in Germany and the threat of Allied air attacks in the southern Baltic, a tanker was sent from Kiel filled with one hundred tons of fuel. The *Cap Arcona*'s engines had ceased to work, so the only reason fuel would be pumped into its tanks was to make the liner more flammable.

Amid the flurry of rumors throughout the Nazi command and along the Baltic coast, a new order from the supreme command of the Kriegsmarine was given. The reports arrived on the coast on May 2. The order, code-named Operation Rainbow, was to begin scuttling all German warships. It would be accomplished by having naval commanders self-sink their crafts.

There was a precedent for the desperate decree. The armistice that ended World War I on November 11, 1918, included severe war reparations for Germany. As the belligerent and losing nation, Germany's ships were confiscated by the victorious countries as part of the terms of surrender.* The British decided to sail German ships to

---

* It was uncertain at the time of the treaty whether the German navy would be held only temporarily by the victors or if the forfeiture of their ships would be permanent. The United States proposed that the remaining German fleet be interned at a neutral port for the time being. Spain and Norway were approached as possible harbors for the belligerent fleet, but they both declined to participate in the arrangement.

Scotland. Only skeleton crews of German sailors would be permitted on the ships, and they would be supervised by the Royal Navy. However, while awaiting the final terms of the peace treaty, German commanders decided not to let their warships fall into enemy hands. Admiral Ludwig von Reuter ordered his fleet to be quickly scuttled and, on June 21, 1919, the action took place at Scapa Flow, the Royal Navy base where the German fleet was being held. The British intervened, but they were too late. The British were able to save only 22 of the 74 German ships.

With World War II all but over in May 1945, some Nazi commanders shared the views of their predecessors in World War I: they did not wish to again hand over their navy to the Allies. The remnants of the once-powerful Kriegsmarine would be scuttled, and the Allies would be denied the fruits of war. Most of the German navy was already lost; only a few warships such as the *Prinz Eugen*, which was sheltered in German-occupied Copenhagen, remained, along with roughly 470 U-boats, 170 of which were still fully operational and hidden in the deep fjords of occupied Norway.

The scuttling began the day before the order arrived on the Baltic coast when three U-boats were sunk at Warnemünde. On May 2 more than 30 U-boats were destroyed at Travemünde, near Lübeck Bay. On May 3 39 U-boats were exploded at Kiel, and on May 4 a few more were destroyed at Kiel and Hamburg. Other warships and support craft were sunk in early May as well.

Ironically, the scuttling order was released prematurely, most likely on account of a complete breakdown in communications in the Nazis' chain of command. The decision had been under consideration since April and was not the only leak or conflicting command that plagued the Nazis in the final days of the war. The official order to scuttle ships was not given by Admiral Dönitz until the morning of May 5. Dönitz countermanded his order only eight minutes later so that he could continue negotiations with the Allies for surrender. It was too late. Ships were being scuttled by their captains for at least four days.

The countermanding order from Dönitz also stated that all U-boats were to stand down from combat operations. Nevertheless, another 87 of them were sunk by their commanders, including 64 on the Baltic Sea, either because they did not receive the communiqué from Dönitz or because they refused to surrender their ships.*

Most of the ships and commanders had heard preliminary reports of the scuttle order and were faced with a difficult decision: Follow the order, wait and confirm the order, or save their ships by disobeying the order? Loyalties to the Nazi regime versus a postwar Germany were at stake. Likewise, questions remained as to whether civilian ships such as the *Cap Arcona* and three other "floating concentration camps" in Lübeck Bay were "military" ships and therefore subject to the scuttling order. They had been conscripted by the military to serve a military operation, so their fate seemed sealed along with that of the concentration camp prisoners being loaded onto them. However, the scuttle order did not include instructions about the prisoners on board; that matter would be decided by individual officers at the site.

The senior Nazi official in the region was Karl Kaufmann, the provincial governor of Hamburg and commissioner of ships. His jurisdiction included Neustadt in Holstein and Lübeck. It was Kaufmann who ordered that the *Cap Arcona* and other ships be brought to the port and the prisoners be loaded on them. During a war-crimes tribunal a year later, Kaufmann denied he gave the order and claimed the prisoners were to be sent to Sweden. But the testimony of others contradicted his account.

The other senior Nazi officer in the region was Count Georg-Henning Graf von Bassewitz-Behr, the Gestapo chief in Hamburg, officer in charge of all prisoners of war in and around Hamburg, and man responsible for the Nazi "werewolf" force in April 1945. The latter operation was designed to disrupt Allied advances through northern Germany by guerrilla operations. At the same postwar trial, Bassewitz-Behr contradicted Kaufmann by claiming the

---

* When Germany surrendered unconditionally not long afterward, roughly 150 U-boats still remained either at sea or in port. All but 4 surrendered. Two fled to Argentina and 2 to Portugal, both neutral ports at the time.

inmates were scheduled to be killed, most likely by scuttling the ships with the prisoners on board.*

Whatever Kaufmann's and Bassewitz-Behr's plans involved, a potential problem presented itself on April 29. Amid the loading of prisoners, news arrived at the port that the British 11th Armoured Division and other units were not far away. Intelligence reports estimated that the Allies could be in Lübeck as early as May 1. Kaufmann and Bassewitz-Behr thus began moving prisoners to the port at Neustadt, a short distance away. In a rush, they loaded the prisoners onto any available truck and forced others to march along the shoreline. The transfer of as many of these remaining prisoners to the *Cap Arcona* and other ships in the bay occurred with much haste. Kaufmann likely intended to scuttle the ships with the prisoners on board as soon as possible and before the British arrived.

Captain Bertram had heard about the pending order to scuttle ships from aides to Governor Kaufmann, but he also knew that Red Cross hospital ships were taking prisoners to Sweden. Bertram did not know what to make of the conflicting details regarding the fate of his ship, but he expected the worst. Likewise, the Hamburg-Süd executives had also been told of Kaufmann's scuttling order for their ship and others, but they believed such a decision would never happen, especially for ocean liners and commercial ships.

The captains and crew of all four prison ships in the bay were uncertain of their ships' fate. Bertram decided to try one last time to save his ship, the prisoners in his charge, and himself. He contacted Admiral Konrad Engelhardt, the head of naval transport, with a request that he intervene to stop Kaufmann from sending more prisoners to his ship and from scuttling the liner. Admiral Engelhardt complied by dispatching a captain named Rössing to meet with Kaufmann about his plans for the ship. The meeting produced no results. The Hamburg-Süd company also lodged protests, hoping to save their investment, a ship that had once been the jewel of

---

* For a full discussion of the motives for putting prisoners on the ships and whether the Nazis intended to sink them, see Appendix I.

their South American cruises. They were far less interested in saving the prisoners on their ship.

News arrived along the coast that the celebrated British general Bernard Montgomery was at the head of an army closing in on the Baltic. And they were in a hurry, eager to deny the Soviet Union access to northern Germany. The British took Hamburg with hardly a shot fired. The campaign, however, had been aided by intensive Allied bombing that had destroyed half of Hamburg's homes and killed roughly forty-three thousand people, mostly civilians.

In advance of Montgomery's main force were British Special Forces from the 6th Commando, 1st Special Service Brigade, under Brigadier General Derek Mills-Roberts, and tanks from the 7th and 11th Armoured Divisions, led by Major-General George P. B. Roberts. These advance units were already in northern Germany, having driven through France and Belgium, and were now within mere miles of Neustadt and Lübeck.*

On May 2 British tanks had liberated much of nearby Holstein and Mecklenburg, in northern Germany. That same day the British Second Army finally reached the towns along the bay. Tanks from the 7th and 11th Armoured Divisions entered the city of Neustadt at four thirty that afternoon and reached the market district in the center of the city thirty minutes later. The British commanders asked to see the mayor, chief of police, and any local military commanders. After questioning them about defenses and troop strength in and around the city, the British demanded the unconditional surrender of Neustadt. The German authorities agreed at six o'clock. Their only condition was a request by the chief physician at the local hospital, a Dr. Longo, and Professor D. Redeker that the liberators allow the local hospital to treat any wounded German soldiers and civilians. The British agreed.

Concurrently, Major General Alwin Wolz, the military commander in charge of the Hamburg region, which included the two coastal cities, also agreed to surrender. It would have been a bloody

---

* Some of these units were a part of the heroic army that had defeated the skilled German commander Erwin Rommel in the North African campaign earlier in the war.

street-by-street fight and one that the Germans could not possibly have won. General Wolz was but one of many Nazi commanders who ignored their now-deceased führer's order that they defend every inch of German soil to the last person. Moreover, even though the Volkssturm had established defenses throughout the two cities, they were outmanned and outgunned, and many of the older men who composed the home guard had lost their appetite for war. Indeed, many of the German soldiers had spent the first days of May scrambling to get out of uniform and procure new identities for themselves. Several of those still in uniform were only too happy to surrender to the British.

Knowing the British were nearing the city, the SS guards in the coastal towns had been attempting to relocate all the prisoners remaining at the port onto the ships or to a stadium in Neustadt. Even though the fighting had largely ended on May 2 with the surrender by the city's mayor and military commander, the guards ordered a final large group of prisoners into the stadium on the morning of May 3. The plan was to execute all of them. As the prisoners were being lined up to be shot, however, British tanks appeared at the stadium. The Nazis surrendered, and the surviving prisoners' lives were saved.

The British now controlled Neustadt. Word of Adolf Hitler's suicide and the arrival of the Soviets in Berlin had finally reached the town and ships floating nearby in the bay, causing much rejoicing among the prisoners. Welcome sights and sounds of warplanes from the Royal Air Force flying overhead also emboldened the survivors. Those on or near the top decks of the *Cap Arcona* even waved to the liberating pilots. The good news managed to spread through the prison population trapped in the foul holds below.

Small launches had taken many of the SS guards off the *Cap Arcona* on May 1 and 2. Finally free of SS officers on his ship, Captain Bertram dispatched his second officer and a cabin boy named Franz Wolff in the captain's personal launch. They were assigned to take dead inmates off the ship and back to Neustadt for burial, a task usually completed by SS guards from the port. Bertram also sent his two crew members ashore to notify the British that there were thousands of prisoners on his ship, to request lifeboats to remove the prisoners, and to obtain a boat large enough to carry his crew off the *Cap Arcona*. While the second officer went about his business, the cabin boy had also approached Nazi officials not yet captured by the British with a request that they send lifeboats to the *Cap Arcona*. It was denied. The officer and young Wolff returned around one thirty that afternoon with a small cutter named the *Störtebeker*.

That same morning, Admiral Dönitz dispatched his chief aide, Admiral Hans Georg von Friedeburg, to Lüneburg to meet with the commander of Allied ground forces, Field Marshal Bernard Montgomery, to discuss an armistice. The talks concluded on May 4 when Montgomery accepted the surrender of German forces in the northern part of the country.

However, while the talks were occurring on May 3, orders arrived back at Lübeck Bay that none of the prisoners remaining along the coast be allowed to survive. Presumably, the orders came from Karl Kaufmann, the provincial governor. The ships in the Baltic were to be scuttled immediately with the prisoners still on board. Events were unfolding rapidly.

Chapter 19

DEATH FROM ABOVE

ALTHOUGH THE WEATHER REMAINED chilly, the signs of spring were everywhere. Soft buds had returned to tree branches, and the frozen ground under foot had given way to fields of velvety new grass. The date was May 3, 1945, and the long and terrible war was in its final fitful throes. Peace was inevitable, and negotiations were under way throughout the region.

As the dawn sun struggled to warm the frigid waters of the Baltic Sea, a thick fog rolled in across Germany's northern coast, followed by a light rain. It seemed to be a typical spring morning, except, of course, for the presence of the British army and floating concentration camps anchored off shore. Not far away, near the Elbe River in the west, the tranquillity of the early hour was interrupted by the roar of airplane engines. The engines that coughed and sputtered to life that morning belonged to Hawker Typhoon Mark 1B fighter-bombers involved in large-scale operations against German shipping on the Baltic.

The Typhoon pilots of the Royal Air Force stationed at air bases at Ahlhorn, Celle, Hustadt, and Plantlünne in German territory were rustled from bed around four o'clock that morning. Mechanics were already on the tarmac, preparing the warplanes for major antishipping strikes along Germany's northern coast from Kiel Bay to Neustadt Bay on the Baltic Sea. This morning it was the 83rd Group of the Second Tactical Air Force that received the mission. Six squadrons would be involved, supported by a few planes from the 84th Group assigned to the 83rd in order to supplement the loss of planes from previous missions. By five o'clock the pilots were given their mission orders, targets, and a weather report, which indicated a light drizzle and low clouds along the southern Baltic.

Before being taken in jeeps out to the runways, the Typhoon pilots received an update indicating that Red Cross ships might be operating in the Baltic and that "they are not—repeat—not to be attacked." However, the pilots were also issued RAF Operation Orders 71 and 73, which instructed them to "destroy the concentration of enemy shipping in L Bay west of Poel Island and northwards to the border of the security zone. The reconnoitering shows a high concentration of ships in the bay of Lübeck, which is generally moving northbound. While the enemy is in possession of all of its war- and cargo-vessels, there is no ship of His Majesty in this area to stop them."

What was not clear in the reports was how the pilots were to differentiate between enemy ships and Red Cross vessels. While an experienced pilot would have little difficulty identifying such ships, the flyers taking off that morning included many young men who had only recently earned their wings. They also had to contend with overcast skies and showers. Moreover, this mission was different from those of the previous weeks. According to Martin Rumbold, a Typhoon squadron leader, one RAF intelligence report, issued just days prior to the mission, warned that "Nazi leaders wanted to move to set off to Norway. That was the last country, besides Denmark, they had under control. From there they wanted to continue the fight."

The Nazis had invaded Norway on April 8, 1940, and, although they were met by determined resistance, quickly overran the Norwegian defenders.* Norway remained a priority for the Nazis at

---

* Dubbed Operation Weserüburg by the German military, the Nazis sought additional naval bases and access to the rich deposits of ores in the region. Seizing Norway also preempted the Allies from establishing bases there, and the blond-haired, blue-eyed Norwegians fit the racist Nazi ideal for the Germanic empire.

the end of the war. In German-occupied Norway, they could rendezvous with units of the Wehrmacht garrisoned there, and the country's deep, protected fjords provided natural shelter for their dreaded U-boats. Therefore, the concern among some Allied planners was that high-ranking Nazis would flee northward to organize a final redoubt. The task of dislodging the Nazis from Norway would likely be a long and bloody affair. As such, it was best to destroy any transport ships before they set sail.

Other reports suggested that ships were seen traveling north, which might have been taken as proof positive of a Nazi redeployment to Norway. Even though the war was ending, not all German commanders and units were surrendering. Opposition was still ferocious in many areas, and Allied reconnaissance planes had observed trucks and military units on the move throughout northern Germany. At nearby Kiel, a large port with a naval base, hundreds of vessels were spotted, including warships and submarines. Such signs reminded Allied military planners of another, similar, effort by the Nazis. After Field Marshal Erwin Rommel's defeat in the spring of 1943 in the North African theater of the war, the Germans evacuated armies north into Italy for another stand.

The Second Tactical Air Force's raid on shipping in the Baltic was, in part, designed to deny the Third Reich the ability to transfer troops to Norway or any other locations. Before taking off, Captain Rumbold informed the seven pilots operating in his air group, "Aerial images show the spread of enemy ship movement out of the bays in Schleswig-Holstein. The objective is to destroy the gathering of ships during the whole day in the area west of Poel Island." When the RAF pilots took off that morning, they were primed to destroy any and all German ships.

Recalled another squadron leader in response to the concerns about the Nazis fleeing to Norway, "We were on 'readiness' when we were told by Operations that a very large ship loaded with SS troops was leaving to continue the fight from Norway and had to be sunk." He admitted, though, "We were not too happy, as the war was obviously ending and we were experiencing SS flak."

Despite these reports, Count Folke Bernadotte and Major Hans Arnoldsson of the Swedish Red Cross notified the British command in northern Germany that there were prisoners from the concentration camps aboard some of the ships at Neustadt and Lübeck Bays. Whether the messages were transmitted to the RAF pilots leading the bombing mission against ships in the Baltic that day is uncertain.

THE BRITISH WERE AWARE of the importance of the Baltic to Germany, and their aircrews had fitted some of the Typhoons with a deadly payload of eight high-explosive 60-pound rockets, each roughly the size of a grown man; others carried 500- and 1,000-pound bombs. Each Typhoon was also brimming with four 20-mm cannons capable of knocking an airplane out of the sky, shredding a truck on the ground, or cutting a person in half with ease.

These formidable single-engine warplanes had wreaked havoc on German tanks and trains in the closing months of the war, earning for them the nickname "Terrifying Fighters." It was said that, at the mere mention of the term, Nazi soldiers would look skyward in fear. By the end of the war, the Typhoon Mark 1B fighter-bombers were some of the most effective weapons in the Allied arsenal. Manufactured by the Hawker Company in England and nicknamed "Tiffy," the warplane was first flown on May 27, 1941. At nearly thirty-two feet in length, with a wingspan in excess of forty-one feet, Tiffies were large, heavy planes. Powered by a single 24-cylinder, 2,189-horsepower engine, the seven-ton planes could reach speeds of 412 miles per hour and could cruise comfortably at an altitude of nineteen thousand feet.

But the Typhoon was a tough plane to fly on account of its weight, which limited agility. In fact, early in the war Typhoons were more likely to be lost to malfunctions than to enemy fire. Pierre Clostermann, a member of the Free French Army flying with the British, recalled that they "overheated very quickly" and were "treacherous" to fly. "The amount of noise," he complained, "seemed five times as great as in a Spitfire." They were even difficult for pilots to enter, with the cockpit six feet above the ground. Clostermann described the arduous task. "You have to get your fingers in the hollows which are covered by metal plates on spring hinges." Having done that, the ground crew would help "hoist" the pilot into the cockpit. Clostermann and his fellow pilots referred to the planes as "monsters," on account of both their difficulty and their deadliness.

Nevertheless, the RAF did not give up on the warplane, and after several rounds of reengineering the Typhoon finally proved effective. Too heavy and lumbering for air-to-air combat, the Tiffies proved to be perfect for low-altitude bombing missions. In this capacity, they wreaked havoc on German trains, trucks, and ships. Such was the case in northern Germany and the Baltic, where Typhoons flew more than a thousand sorties in the spring of 1945 alone, leaving behind a path of destruction.

The Second Tactical Air Force, 83rd Group, was assigned the task of eliminating the remaining assets of the Third Reich—most notably ships. The mission was tasked to several Typhoon squadrons flying out of newly seized German air bases near the Baltic, but months of vicious fighting had left the Second Tactical at less than full strength. Only six squadrons were assigned to the Baltic. Each of the squadrons normally flew twelve Typhoons, organized into two teams of six planes. By May 1945 most of the squadrons were flying only eight planes.

As a result, when they took off on the morning of May 3, the squadrons assigned to the bombing mission—the 184th, 193rd, 197th, 198th, 263rd, and 609th—were unable to form full flying patterns. But some of the men of the Typhoon squadrons of the Second Tactical Air Force were battle-tested, worthy fighters, many of them having been in the war since 1943 and many having served at the landing at Normandy and during the liberation of France. The squadrons would prove to be as ferocious and deadly as the war mottoes each squadron adopted: "To command the air and earth," "We cleave the sky," "By his claws the lion is known."

The Typhoons raced down the old Luftwaffe runways and headed toward Lübeck Bay and Neustadt Bay in the Northeast. As the squadrons entered the bays on the southern Baltic coast, they were met by low, heavy cloud cover, making it difficult to spot enemy ships in the water without flying very low. The pilots had to drop to below two thousand feet, but such low-altitude flying put them at risk of any antiaircraft defenses. In the gray, rainy skies they could barely see one another, so the decision was made to delay the mission. The British pilots exhaled and flew back to their bases, where the planes were refueled and put on standby. They would not have to wait long.

By noon weather reports indicated that the clouds that had covered the southern Baltic all morning had largely dissipated. The bombing mission against German shipping was back on. Refueled, the Typhoons set off once again for Neustadt and Lübeck Bays. Four squadrons from the 83rd Group led the initial attack. As per protocol, they followed the contours of the German coastline to their targets in the Baltic. The 184th was based at Hustadt, the 198th at Plantlünne, and both the 197th and 263rd at Ahlhorn, meaning they had roughly 90 to 130 miles to cover.

The mission to attack the ships in the bays was witnessed by Don Saunders, one of the RAF pilots who flew support for the Typhoons assigned to attack the ships in the bays. He noted, "We had extra fuel this time to stay in the air longer." It was a good thing because they encountered Luftwaffe warplanes. After downing a few of the enemy warplanes, the pilot "reported our victories and rose to a height of 11,000 feet," whereupon they escorted the Typhoons to the target. Saunders described what happened next:

> We now had to take over the fighter cover for the attacking formations. I saw a formation of 8 planes at starboard. Mackie agreed, "Yes, those are Typhoons." They approached a big ship, which was underneath us, in the middle of the bay, which I assumed would be the bay of Kiel, which I know today, was actually the Bay of Lübeck. Even a big ship appears to be small from a height of 11,000 feet. It was the *Cap Arcona*. The Typhoons were heading straight towards the ship. Each machine had 8 rockets underneath their wings.

As the RAF pilots dipped below the light cloud cover en route to their targets, what they saw that morning seemed to match the reports suggesting the Nazis were headed to Norway. One of the Typhoon pilots, Peter West, reported: "We flew over the coast of Lübeck Bay. It was unbelievable how many ships were anchored there. Until that day, we had seen hardly any. Now suddenly we saw ships of every kind—transport, patrol boats. I can remember seeing a long line of submarines, one behind the other." Pierre Clostermann described seeing "in every bight, in every estuary, along the beaches, were moored entire fleets of Blohm + Voss . . . boats."

Sure enough, there were merchant, fishing, and military ships along Germany's northern coastline, and a lot of them. The pilots also observed U-boats docked near a submarine training base by Neustadt. They knew that, because German mines blocked the entrance to the Baltic, there were no American or British ships nearby to stop a planned Nazi escape to Norway. It was up to the Typhoons to deny the Nazis an escape route and thus bring the war to an end.

The pilots were likely both very concerned and intent on inflicting total destruction on the enemy. In the two months leading up to the attack, members of the 83rd Group had suffered serious losses. The Germans were still putting up a fight. Pierre Clostermann recalled that in two earlier missions, they lost six pilots. His squadron was down to just eleven pilots and sixteen warplanes. And they were flying three missions a day. "We couldn't possibly keep it up," worried Clostermann. Indeed, many of the Typhoons and support planes in the mission were "riddled" with bullets and flak. One had "a hole two feet across in his tail fin." Clostermann's own plane had two holes the size of "fists" in the fuselage. But they were also inflicting massive damage on Germany, destroying numerous trucks, locomotives, and ships on nearly every mission. The pilots also expected to encounter German planes and fire from antiaircraft batteries on the ground, something they endured "everywhere, even in the most unexpected places," throughout Germany.

Flying in tight formation in order to protect themselves from any blind spots above, below, and behind the planes, the Typhoons came in low and fast, dropping from ten thousand to about three thousand feet over the bays. To their relief, the pilots encountered minimal fire from antiaircraft batteries at the port. The only thing that greeted the Tiffies that morning was a very light rain. On May 3 the skies belonged to the RAF Typhoons.

Fortunately, the ships in the bays, much like the towns of Lübeck and Neustadt, were largely defenseless. British ground forces had already pacified much of the area. The Luftwaffe had been destroyed, and only a handful of planes were scrambled to intercept the Typhoons. Likewise, only a few antiaircraft batteries were still operational and managed to shoot down only one RAF bomber that day—a Typhoon piloted by L. S. Brookes, who was able to make an emergency landing near Blauer Abel and Wintershagen.

There were four major synchronized Typhoon strikes from the 83rd Group. All ships in the waters were possible targets, but the main focus of the RAF pilots was on the two largest ships—the *Cap Arcona* and *Deutschland*. Given their size, these ships posed the greatest threat because they were capable of transporting thousands of German soldiers. But the pilots could not know that the *Cap Arcona* did not even have flak guns on board. Like the *Athen* and *Thielbek*, it also had little in terms of exterior markings to indicate it transported prisoners. Captain Heinrich Bertram had attempted to light up the *Cap Arcona* in order to mark it as a hospital ship, but the SS guards on board disallowed it. The crew of the *Deutschland* started to paint a red cross on one of the ship's large funnels but ran out of paint.

The first strike, launched from Hustadt just after the noon hour by the 184th Squadron, consisted of four Typhoons led by Lieutenant D. L. Stevenson. Their target was the *Deutschland*. The massive liner was converted to function as a hospital ship, but some of the wounded German soldiers it had been carrying were sent ashore on April 20 to make room for prisoners from the concentration camps. The crew had been reduced from 220 to 80 and was supplemented on April 30 when a naval surgeon and 25 nurses boarded the ship.

At roughly two thirty that afternoon, the four Typhoons roared into the bay and attacked the *Deutschland*. The red cross that had been painted on one of the funnels failed to fend off the attack. The Typhoons struck from the opposite direction and never saw the marking. Swooping down out of the sky, they dove toward the flat waters of the protected bay, launching all thirty-two of their rockets into the ship below. The RAF pilots found their marks; all but one rocket exploded. The tranquil waters of the bay erupted into high waterspouts and deep concussions from the bombs exploding. In Neustadt sirens sprang to life. The ships were close enough to the shore for villagers and those survivors still gathered at the harbor to see the flames and hear the sounds of explosions and creaking of steel. Some eyewitnesses at the dock even reported hearing the cries of the dying on the old liner.

The result was that the *Deutschland*'s superstructure was ripped apart, causing an enormous fire to erupt midship. The operation lasted one hour and ten minutes. Don Saunders, the RAF pilot who flew cover on the mission, recorded with pride that he "destroyed two mechanical transports on the ground, one locomotive and one truck." He also shot down two German planes.

When the first wave of attacks ended, the captain of the *Deutschland* desperately ordered his chief engineer, Adolf Kolster, to sew white sheets together and fly the flag of surrender atop the ship. It did not work. The British attacked again at 3:55 p.m. with more rockets and bombs. They need not have bothered. The ship was finished.

From the bridge of the *Cap Arcona*, Captain Bertram watched the attack with binoculars, counting his blessings that his ship was not targeted. "They must know that we have prisoners on here," he reasoned. He nonetheless ordered his crew to quickly hoist a white flag and tried to communicate with the other ships, telling them to cease firing their flak guns. Bertram was joined by a few SS officers sent by Karl Kaufmann to supervise the prisoners; they now desperately tried to raise a white sheet above the ship. The efforts were futile.

Soon after the initial air strikes commenced, the cloud cover thinned. This allowed the subsequent waves of planes arriving around midafternoon to fly in from higher altitudes. One of them was the 198th Squadron, whose nine Typhoons had flown out of Plantlünne at 2:00 p.m. The squadron flew over the bay at an elevation of roughly ten thousand feet. The *Cap Arcona* sat utterly defenseless at anchor in the bay below them, making an inviting target for the young pilots. The Typhoons from the 198th headed directly toward the enormous ship, floating at coordinates 54 degrees, 03′23″ north, and 10 degrees, 50′22″ east in the southern Baltic.

The Typhoons of the 198th were led by Captain Johnny R. Baldwin, arguably the most famous and accomplished Typhoon pilot of the war. With a wave of brown curls and a neatly trimmed mustache framing his handsome face, Baldwin looked the part. A hero with multiple Distinguished Flying Crosses and sixteen and a half confirmed kills, he was a legend among RAF pilots. Baldwin reached his quotient of five enemy kills to earn the status of "ace" in record time, and his accomplishments also included shooting down three German planes when defending London from the Luftwaffe bombings in January 1943, reaching the rank of captain at age twenty-six, and surviving a direct hit to his plane that caused serious burns to his body before he bailed out from the skies over England.

Baldwin's heroics continued when, in August 1943, he volunteered to fly the first long-range strikes across the English Channel that hit Nazi targets in France. The dashing Typhoon pilot also conducted daring raids in July 1944 in France against the forces of the famed general Erwin Rommel. It was even Baldwin who was credited with striking Rommel's motorcade, causing serious injuries to the "Desert Fox."*

In the midafternoon of May 3, 1945, with the end of the war at hand, Commander Johnny Baldwin flew in the lead with eight

---

* Not long after this attack, while Rommel was recuperating, Hitler discovered his celebrated general's complicity in a plot to assassinate him. In a savage twist, Hitler ordered that Germany's national hero be eliminated, but quietly because of a possible backlash from the German people. Rommel, however, was given the option of committing suicide, which he did by swallowing cyanide in exchange for his family's immunity. Rommel was given a hero's funeral in Germany.

other young pilots.* Baldwin ordered four of the warplanes to veer off and head to the *Thielbek*, anchored roughly a half mile from the *Cap Arcona*. The *Thielbek* opened fire with its antiaircraft flak guns. During the attack one of the warplanes flown by P. W. Millard was struck by the antiaircraft fire and disappeared into the clouds. The defenses, however, proved inadequate. At least thirty rockets found their mark, many hitting below the waterline, ripping gaping holes into the sides of the ship. Explosions rocked the old freighter while fires erupted belowdecks, burning most of the prisoners who were now trapped deep in the flaming holds.

The ship was just under three miles off shore and sinking fast when Captain Jacobsen ordered his officers and crew off its decks. Several of them tried to help the prisoners belowdecks, constituting one of the few acts of humanity by German soldiers, sailors, or townsfolk that day. But the ship listed at a forty-five-degree angle, causing large cargo containers to break loose from their grips and careen across the tilting deck. Many of the ship's crew and guards were crushed. The captain, along with his first officer and first engineer, were among those killed.

Efforts to save the prisoners belowdecks were abandoned. The freighter's lifeboats, like those of the *Cap Arcona*, had been punched with holes by the SS guards and were of no use. The *Thielbek*, which had been flying a white flag, sank only fifteen to twenty minutes after the first rockets exploded on deck. Only a few of the sailors and guards managed to make it into the water. Only fifty of the approximately twenty-eight hundred prisoners on board survived the ordeal. Most died while still in the hold either from smoke inhalation from the raging fires or by drowning in the frigid water that rushed in and filled the lower decks of the ship.

Captain Baldwin then ordered the other four planes from the 198th Squadron to follow him. They dove fast and low on the *Cap Arcona*. No smoke billowed from its large stacks, indicating it was still at anchor in the bay. The target was locked, and the Typhoons

---

* Baldwin's team included G. S. Chalmers, P. D. Cross, R. A. Gillam, B. G. Kirk, F. B. Lawless, P. W. Millard, J. E. Scoon, and W. R. Wardle.

released their rockets on the defenseless liner. All of them found their mark, the first rockets striking the large gray liner directly between the first and second smokestacks atop the ship. The next barrage hit the third funnel and sports deck. Ensuing attacks struck the side of the hull. The *Cap Arcona* shuddered violently. The concussion of each strike caused windows to explode. Glass flew about the ship, while the wood, rugs, and draperies on the old liner caught fire. In minutes, the entire ship was ablaze.

The Typhoon attacks continued, and spouts of water and gray funnels of smoke from the explosions shot high into the air in every direction. In the bowels of the ship, prisoners had no chance. Locked in holds below the waterline, many were incinerated when the first rockets tore into the hull. Others drowned as the sea rushed into the lower decks. Still others were crushed when hot steel, furnishings, and shrapnel flew through the belly of the massive liner.

The *Cap Arcona* was struck by forty rockets, several of which pierced the hull and exploded inside. There were no lifeboats, no pumping system to deal with the water pouring through gaping holes in the ship, and no operable firefighting system. Some of the prisoners trapped belowdecks managed to scramble up ladders, but many fell. Those who made it out of the holds and into hallways were engulfed in flames. From the bow to the stern, the once-grand ship was now a fireball.

One of the few prisoners who made it out of the locked rooms was Heinrich Mehringer, a German. Mehringer was in a cabin on C deck, which contained luxury rooms. By not being below the waterline, he was able to escape. Like the other prisoners, he was weak and slowly starving to death. He described the fight for his life. "People rushed out of the cabins. Prisoners were in the passageways, their clothes on fire. We threw covers over them. A Frenchman came up the companionway, his clothes were also burning. He stammered 'Water everywhere! Everything gone!' Then he collapsed. Beneath our cabins the fire must already have been raging—the cries stopped suddenly. The floor was very hot. . . . [E]veryone beneath us was dead and burnt."

As Mehringer ran down the hallway, the flames below the floor were so hot that he remembered, "My back and head were burning, but because of my agitation I did not feel the fire." At the end of the hallway near the exit, many of the prisoners were gathered, trying to get out of the narrow portal. Frantic, they fought and tried to climb over one another. At that moment, Mehringer climbed on the shoulders of the people in front of him. He helped a friend up as well. Holding onto a pipe overhead, he recalled, "We ran for our lives on the heads of our comrades as if on a pavement. The people beneath us were standing so close together that we could not fall through." Mehringer and a friend managed to climb out of the hallway. Everyone else behind them burned to death.

Prisoners on the ship were jumping overboard, desperately trying to escape the roaring fires and explosions, which were so violent that Mehringer recalled the ship "shuddering as if hit by an earthquake." The small transport ship that brought crew to and from the *Cap Arcona* was still tied to the liner. Miraculously, around fifty of the prisoners managed to lower themselves down to the transport and escaped.

Amid the panic on board, Captain Bertram ordered his crew to try to access the lifesaving equipment that had been locked away. A few vests and flotation devices were found, and some of the crew who were not killed in the explosions managed to save themselves. But the Typhoons circled and came in for another assault. It was just as violent. Another huge eruption belowdecks rocked the entire ship. It was likely that a boiler or the engine room caught fire and exploded. The *Cap Arcona* was engulfed in an inferno of flames and slowly began to sink.

A Typhoon piloted by J. E. Scoon had engine problems during the attack and had to force-land nearby, but he survived the incident and was rescued by British forces. P. W. Millard, whose plane was hit in the attack on the *Thielbek*, managed to fly his damaged Typhoon back to the air base at Plantlünne at 3:10 that afternoon. A few minutes later, the remainder of the planes arrived. It was another successful and devastating attack.

Chapter 20

WAVES

Two ADDITIONAL WAVES OF bombing attacks commenced that afternoon, coming from the RAF's 193rd, 197th, and 263rd Squadrons. Some of these warplanes carried not rockets but massive 500- and 1,000-pound bombs strapped to the underside of each plane.

Beginning at roughly 4 o'clock, nine Typhoons from the 263rd Squadron at Ahlhorn air base, near Oldenburg, swept down from the skies, coming in from higher elevations because the clouds had largely dissipated by the late afternoon. Many of the ships below them were already inoperable, with telltale signs of smoke billowing into the sky from the burning hulks. Some of the sailors on the *Deutschland* were frantically waving white sheets in a sign of surrender; others scrambled down into the lifeboats that the captain had ordered dispersed. However, the Typhoons led by twenty-three-year-old Martin Trevor Scott Rumbold were determined to inflict complete destruction on the enemy.

The *Deutschland* was listing some thirty degrees to the starboard and was already ablaze from the earlier attacks. But the second wave of Typhoons from the 263rd dropped low and hugged the surface of the bay, firing a deadly series of rocket salvos. The *Deutschland*'s captain, Carl Steincke, was on the bridge when the first rockets hit the ship. One of them went directly into the bridge, killing Captain Steincke instantly. Already aflame and sinking, the *Deutschland* shuddered from additional explosions. Other smaller ships in the bays were also hit before the squadron flew back up into the clouds. They left behind a grisly site; more ships were on fire, capsized, or sinking, dead bodies littered the water, and a few survivors were desperately trying to swim or cling to debris in the chilly Baltic.

At 4:15, another wave of Typhoons comprising the 193rd and 197th attacked. Even though the *Cap Arcona*, *Deutschland*, and *Thielbek* were already destroyed, the RAF pilots from the 197th, led by their squadron commander, K. J. Harding, zeroed in on the three larger ships, striking from the east. The 193rd hit the *Deutschland*, while the eight Typhoons from the 197th flew over the *Cap Arcona*, dropping sixteen heavy bombs. All but one hit the sinking wreck. Huge explosions reverberated across the bay, rocking the liner forcefully from side to side, gouging additional gaping holes out of the steel hull, and sending bodies high into the air like human sparks floating on a fire's updraft. The concussions from each of the large bombs were so powerful that they were felt in the nearby towns.

John Attenborough, a British soldier who saw the follow-up attack by the Typhoons, described them as "looking like wasps around a honey jar" as they repeatedly struck the *Cap Arcona*. Even before the RAF strike, Attenborough observed that the two liners were "smoking" and "turning turtle," a reference to their capsizing.

As if things could not have been worse for the desperate prisoners trapped on the *Cap Arcona*, the small detachment of Nazi guards that remained on the ship tried to prevent their charges from escaping, even placing their own lives in danger to do so. They barred doors shut, refused to unlock the storage areas containing flotation devices, and even took the time amid the attack to shoot at those prisoners who made it onto the deck or into the water. Heinrich Mehringer, the German prisoner from the upper decks who managed to run on top of the shoulders and heads of his fellow inmates, remembered the scene as he and others attempted to escape. "At the stairs, humans were jammed together. Shots were ringing out.

An SS man [was] standing at the top, shooting with two guns into the desperate, pushing prisoners. . . . He had hardly emptied his magazines when the angry crowd ran over him."

Crew members and prisoners desperately clamored over the sides of the ship to escape the flames, dropping from the high railings the distance into the sea below. But the water offered no escape. Many of the people in the water were caught in the powerful whirlpool of the sinking liner and were sucked below the waves, while others succumbed to hypothermia in the frigid sea.

Berek Jakubowicz, the Polish dentist whose occupation helped him to survive Auschwitz, remembered the explosions shaking the ship violently and sending prisoners careening across the room. He and others raced to the door where they had been held captive, but it was locked. The room was filling with smoke, and some of the weaker prisoners began choking. Frantically pounding on the door, they screamed for deliverance. A few prisoners broke a wooden shelf in the room and used a large piece of it to try to pry the door open, but it snapped and the door remained shut. With the ship listing, others lost their balance and fell. The single lightbulb in the room went out, and the room was cast into complete darkness and smoke.

Suddenly, the door opened. A prisoner escaping down the hallway had heard their screams and stopped to open it. Jakubowicz and the others poured out into the hallway and ran for their lives. He momentarily lost his brother, Josek, but soon found him, and they ran together to the stairs. However, flames were filling the stairwell. When the prisoners turned around, one of them yelled that he knew the way out. All followed him, backtracking through three other corridors, which were also now filling with smoke. Along the way, some of the prisoners collapsed, but Jakubowicz and a few others made it to a grand dining room that opened to one of the decks midship. But it too was in flames.

They turned and tried to go back through the corridors from which they had come, but there was too much smoke. Jakubowicz remembered the hallways being so hot that he and fellow prisoners had to close their eyes and cover their faces. Their hair was even singed from the heat and fires in adjacent hallways. The ship was listing even farther, making it very difficult to stand upright, much less walk or run. Just when there seemed to be no more options and death seemed certain, they miraculously found a shaft by a bathroom. It was nearly twenty yards long and three yards wide. The prisoners yelled up the shaft, and faces of fellow prisoners appeared above them. It was a way out.

A rope was lowered down, and they attempted to climb up the narrow shaft. But in the chaos, the desperate prisoners climbed atop one another and grabbed at the person on the rope, who fell backward and landed on top of the others. Jakubowicz jumped up and grabbed the rope and then climbed atop his brother's shoulders. As he was beginning his ascent, however, other prisoners reached up and pulled both Jakubowicz and his brother down. With most of his fellow prisoners on the floor trying to stand back up, he quickly tried again; this time he was able to climb up the rope. From above, hands reached down and pulled him out of the shaft. His brother followed, and Jakubowicz pulled him the rest of the way up and out of the dark vent. It was not a minute too soon. As Josek Jakubowicz pulled his legs out of the shaft, fire consumed the floor below them and shot up the vent, incinerating the rest of the prisoners from their group.

The brothers had managed to make it onto the deck.

Another Polish prisoner, Bogdan Suchowiak from Posen, had a similar ordeal. Suchowiak was in a dark, dank hold with hundreds of other prisoners. It had four doors accessible by tall steel ladders. When the bombs hit, the room began to fill with smoke, and the prisoners panicked. They clamored atop one another to try to climb the ladders. Before the attack the guards would have shot or kicked the prisoners back down into the holds, but the guards had fled. Suchowiak managed to climb one of the tall ladders. Many of the other prisoners were too weak to follow. However, the doors above were locked. But another prisoner escaping the ship had stopped at just the right moment to open the door above Suchowiak's ladder. As he climbed upward, prisoners above them opened other doors and passed ropes down into the holds. Unfortunately, most of the prisoners in the holds were too sick or weak to climb, and the large room soon filled with smoke. The *Cap Arcona* suddenly lurched and was listing even more precariously, sending the prisoners rolling across the floor. Suchowiak could also feel the heat from the flames throughout the burning vessel. He gained his footing and raced out of the hold and up to the top decks. Those behind him died from the flames or asphyxiation.

Quite possibly several hundred prisoners as well as crew members and guards from the three large prisoner transports may have made it into the water during and after the Typhoon attacks that afternoon. There is no way of determining an exact number, but eyewitness accounts—including reports from the RAF pilots—describe people struggling in the water. Henry Bawnik, one of the last prisoners to board the crowded ship and one of the few who survived the ordeal, remembered prisoners yelling to remove all their clothing before attempting to get in the water and swim. Many men and women began climbing down to the water, but he could not swim, so he hung on tightly to a rope. Bawnik estimated that there were three to five hundred prisoners around him getting into the water. The prisoners, already starving and near death from their long ordeal before arriving at the Baltic, and further weakened from days without food or water in dark, crowded rooms in the ships, had little chance of swimming or clinging to debris in the frigid sea. The temperature in the Baltic that day was only forty-six degrees Fahrenheit.

Those who made it into the water were dealt yet another cruel hand. As they struggled to swim, they heard the unmistakable high-pitched sound of the Typhoons above them, circling and diving back toward the water. After finishing their initial bombing runs, several of the Typhoons swooped down to strafe the survivors. They even attacked the rescue boats in the water. The sea danced with the deadly fire from the rapid-fire guns jutting from the wings of the warplanes. In wave after wave, the screaming Typhoons opened up with their lethal 20mm cannons at the bodies in the water, unaware that most were not enemy combatants. Witnesses described the water turning red.*

In an interview conducted years after the tragedy, Allan Wyse, one of the RAF airmen involved in that fateful mission, described what happened as a casualty of war. "We used our cannon fire at the chaps in the water. Poor chaps. . . . They were bailing out of ships, hoping to be safe in the sea, away from the bombs, and it was our dastardly job to make sure they weren't safe, and we just shot them up with 20-mm cannons in the water. Horrible thing but we were told to do it and we did it. That's war."

When the *Cap Arcona*'s crew members tried to lower the few boats not punctured by the guards, the systems failed because the ropes and gears used to operate the cranes had burned or melted in the roaring fire. One of the boats they managed to lower to the water sank as soon as it was dropped. Some crew members successfully lowered another boat to the water and escaped the devastation when they were picked up by a German trawler in the bay. A few other German boats took to the bay to rescue survivors. Roughly sixteen sailors from the *Cap Arcona* and just over four hundred SS guards—including most of the female guards—were picked up. However, the guards forbade the local fishermen and mariners from rescuing any prisoners. Those struggling in the water wearing striped uniforms were violently shoved back into the water.

Captain Bertram had waited until the ship was already sinking before climbing down the *Cap Arcona*'s thick anchor chain and into the water. He was picked up only minutes later by a small motorized launch. Knowing there was little he could do to save his ship or those on board, he watched helplessly as his ship slowly sank. Bertram made it ashore and survived the ordeal.

Major Gehrig, the SS officer dispatched by Commandant Max Pauly to force Captain Bertram to accept more prisoners on board his ship, met with a different end. Heinze Schön, one of the prisoners who survived the sinking to tell his story, recalled seeing

---

* Just a few rounds of the 20mm cannons, each one the size of a tube of toothpaste, were capable of cutting a person in two.

Gehrig get into the first lifeboat launched. Ironically, it had earlier been punctured by his own SS guards in order to prevent the prisoners from escaping. Compromised, the lifeboat sank. Gehrig held onto the side of the boat for a short time, but then sank beneath the waves.

As the Cap Arcona was burning and slowly sinking, more prisoners somehow made it to the top decks. They also continued to jump off the railing . . . and drown in the cold waters below. A group of prisoners on deck managed to launch three small lifeboats that were damaged by the guards but still floated. Two of the boats were unseaworthy and, as more and more prisoners climbed aboard, became severely overcrowded. They both capsized just minutes later. Most of the prisoners in them drowned. A few, however, were able to swim to the third lifeboat and held onto the sides. But it too was overcrowded, and with so many people in the water grasping for the sides of the boat and trying to climb aboard, it too overturned.

Berek Jakubowicz had survived Auschwitz and the death march to the Baltic. He was now struggling to survive a sinking ship. He managed to make it out of his room on the Cap Arcona and recalled seeing the Deutschland listing and burning nearby. He watched prisoners from both large liners jump overboard, only to be sucked under the water by the powerful whirlpool. The Cap Arcona was listing severely to one side, and the deck was wet, making it nearly impossible for him to stand. Explosions deep within the ship continued to rock the deck and knocked him off his feet. To his horror, Jakubowicz watched the RAF Typhoons circle back around and begin strafing the prisoners struggling in the water. The planes passed so close to the ship and so low that he could even see the pilots.

Jakubowicz and his brother had a difficult decision to make—stay on the deck or jump into the water. As they clutched the railing with their arms and legs, the fires below them continued. The deck was so hot it felt as if it could bake them alive. The brothers realized help was not coming, but they waited until the Typhoons stopped their strafing runs, remaining on the railings from around three to four in the afternoon. Finally, they watched as one of the prisoners, David Kot, tied a rope to the ship's railing and lowered himself down to the water.

"Come on down! The rope is strong," Kot yelled. Jakubowicz tried to get his brother to climb down the rope, but Josek could not swim and refused. Berek pleaded that the inferno on board was growing closer and the warplanes might return and attack the ship again. To stay meant certain death. But Josek refused and said, "[Berek], you go. Perhaps you'll get help for us out there. I will stay here and wait." With a heavy heart, Berek Jakubowicz bid his brother farewell and good luck and climbed down the rope into the cold water below.

Other prisoners jumped onto the rope and attempted to follow. "No more! The rope will tear," Kot and Jakubowicz yelled. About five more prisoners began down the rope, which frayed under the strain. Finally, it tore, sending all of them into the water with a great splash. In the water the prisoners bobbed near the sinking ship. One by one, however, they lost their battles and slid under the waves. David Kot was thrashing about but unable to keep afloat and soon succumbed as well. The old shoes and camp jacket felt heavy in the water, so Jakubowicz stripped off his clothing. Down to his underwear and undershirt, he began to swim. He felt the suction of the ship pulling him backward and knew he was no match for the powerful whirlpool, so he let the force pull him back to the ship, where he managed to grab onto the sides. Working his way hand over hand, Jakubowicz crawled back to the stern.

It was then that Jakubowicz spotted a large piece of floating wood. He removed his underwear and shirt and swam with his remaining energy to it. Holding onto the wood, he kicked forcefully toward the shore but was too weak to make it such a great distance. As Jakubowicz tired, however, a small boat about fifteen feet in length was motoring nearby, filled with naked prisoners. Jakubo-wicz waved a hand and yelled frantically. But a voice cried back from the boat, "We can't take anyone. We have no more room! We are full."

Jakubowicz did not give up. He kicked with all his might toward the boat. As he did, another voice on the boat hollered, "It's Berek, the dentist. Let's try to take him." Hands reached into the water and pulled him up and into the boat. Jakubowicz was the last to be allowed into the crowded craft, which was piloted by a local German fisherman whose skin was deeply suntanned and whose name he and the other prisoners never learned. He and the other naked, shivering prisoners were taken to land. But they were not yet free. They worried about being captured or shot by Nazi troops still patrolling the area.

Fortunately, the fisherman did not turn them over to the soldiers at the port. Rather, he pointed them to a local bakery near the coastline and, without saying a word, turned his small boat around to look for other survivors. As the survivors crept quietly through the town, avoiding Nazi soldiers, a local man appeared, and they pleaded with him to send help for the prisoners still in the water and trapped on the ship. The man claimed he could do nothing, but did show them the location of the bakery. He then nervously fled.

Jakubowicz and his fellow prisoners found the bakery and broke through the door. Inside they used empty burlap bags as blankets to try to warm themselves. There was no food in the bakery, but there was water. More important, it was quiet, safe, and warm. The prisoners hunkered down for the evening, letting themselves fall asleep despite their worry about being discovered.

Throughout the evening more prisoners arrived and sneaked into the bakery. One of them informed Jakubowicz that, when he abandoned ship, he had seen Josek still holding onto the ship. The news that Josek was still alive was comforting, but, exhausted, Jakubowicz soon drifted off to sleep. At around dawn a civilian arrived at the bakery and told the prisoners to come outside and get into two trucks. Eyes widened at the request. Were they being arrested? But the man said that he would take them to a hospital now controlled by the British. Cold, tired, naked, and hungry, they shuffled out the door and into the truck. Out in the bay, the *Cap Arcona* was still visible. It had rolled over, but because of its size the big liner still loomed above the waterline of the shallow bay like a beached whale. As they drove to the town, they saw bodies strewn about on the beach. Some had been shot by Nazis waiting on the beach; others died in the water and had washed ashore. The prisoners finally relaxed when they saw British tanks on the road.

The British soldiers at the hospital were friendly and, with their fingers, flashed the prisoners a "V" for victory. At the local hospital, a nurse helped Jakubowicz locate his brother, who had survived. Although their parents and a sister did not survive the camps, Berek Jakubowicz and his brother managed to survive concentration camps at Steineck, Gutenbrunn, Auschwitz, Fürstengrube, Buchenwald, and Mittelbau-Dora. He recalled the incredible ordeal: "I survived Auschwitz because I was young and had completed a year of dental training. I had a few professional tools with me as a result of my mother's begging me to take them along when I was deported." The forceps, syringe, and extractor Jakubowicz carried with him were in demand by the Nazi guards and officers at the camps. As a result, "With these tools and the one year of instruction I had received before the Germans invaded our country, I was able to be helpful." The prisoner performed extractions and treated gum disease for both inmates and guards. He therefore became known as "the dentist of Auschwitz."

Jakubowicz was lucky. Heinrich Schmidt, the garrison commander in Neustadt, had given orders that no prisoners from the ships were to be rescued. Most of the German boats that finally sailed through the bay refused to pick up prisoners in the water. They saved only German sailors and guards. Bogdan Suchowiak, the other Polish prisoner who, like Jakubowicz, made it out of the holds and onto the top deck, remembered his predicament. "It was clear to me that if we did not jump overboard immediately we would all be drown[ed] into the deep by the suction of the sinking ship. I undressed to my shirt and let myself down slowly on a rope. The water was damned cold. I clung to a wooden plank."

Suchowiak and several other prisoners made it into the water together. He was the only one to survive. The others died of hypothermia, drowned immediately, or were gunned down in the Typhoon strafing attacks. Suchowiak felt too weak to swim the long distance to shore, but willed himself to stay afloat in the cold water. Numb and close to death, he was finally rescued a few hours later by a German minesweeper.

Suchowiak swam toward the German ship, but heard an officer on board giving orders to the crew, "Don't pick up any prisoners, only SS personnel and sailors." Fortunately, Suchowiak spoke German and yelled for help in the language. The Nazi sailors picked him up, but some of them were not pleased with the decision to rescue someone who was obviously a prisoner. While they openly debated his fate, he sneaked into a bunk and hid. Of the ordeal, he recalled that "I covered myself with everything I could find. Two Soviet prisoners followed my example. The bunk collapsed. A sailor came in and ranted at us. Then one reported to him that we were foreigners. The sailor drew a bayonet. I ran up to the deck and hid myself in a hawser locker. The boat was moving very quickly. A sailor found me and shouted 'Get lost!' and pushed me and sent me overboard." Fortunately, the minesweeper was close enough to the coast that Suchowiak was able to swim the remaining distance.

Another survivor was Witold Rygiel who, like Jakubowicz and Suchowiak, was a Pole. He was part of a forced march of roughly fourteen thousand prisoners to the Baltic. Rygiel suffered from appendicitis the entire march. As a boy Rygiel had joined the Polish Resistance and functioned as an intelligence gatherer, following and reporting the movements of the Gestapo in and around his town. Rygiel disrupted Nazi military operations in Poland by flattening the tires of German vehicles, pouring sugar into their gas tanks, and cutting communications cables. The Gestapo finally caught Rygiel, who was taken with twenty of his fellow resistance fighters to Auschwitz in southern Poland.

Rygiel remembered the camp as unimaginably horrific. "You were actually not supposed to survive three months at Auschwitz. We did hard physical work, sometimes throwing sand from one place to another for sixteen hours a day with minimal food, to exhaust us to death. I was the only one of our group to survive." But he survived. Rygiel was then sent to Neuengamme to work in a munitions factory. He did what he needed to do to keep alive, but continued his efforts to disrupt Nazi war efforts by sabotaging some of the ordinance he was supposed to make.

Rygiel and the other prisoners drew strength from the awareness that the war was nearly over, remembering that "there were links to the outside and secret radios. We knew the movements of the armies and could observe the British and American airplanes bombing Hamburg almost every day. Sometimes we were made to go to Hamburg to clear the houses and the burned corpses of the people."

Rygiel also survived the death march from Neuengamme to the Baltic. At the coast he was forced onto the *Thielbek*, which floated in sight of the *Cap Arcona*. The conditions on board nauseated Rygiel and his fellow prisoners. Like the experiences of other prisoners, they barely had room to sit down, and there were no beds and very little food or water. Rygiel was on the *Thielbek* when it was attacked and burst into flames, and he remembered being sent careening across the floor when the freighter listed severely to one side. Nearby, he saw guards, crew members, and prisoners crushed when the smokestacks and debris broke loose and slid violently across the ship.

Rygiel had a choice to make: remain on the ship and hope that it would not sink, or jump into the water and swim. He chose the latter: "It was so horribly unexpected and strange. You didn't have time to think. I jumped down between two steel ropes, that's what saved my life. When the bombing was over the ship sank in about 15 minutes. I removed my clothing and started to swim. It took two-and-a-half hours to reach shore."

Somehow, the Polish saboteur managed to avoid the remaining Nazis on the shore and was soon rescued. He was taken to a Red Cross hospital in Sweden. But there were other prisoners still struggling on the ships, in the water, and at the port.

CURTAIN CALL

Chapter 21

FINAL ACT

THE ATTACKS ON THE *Cap Arcona* and other ships on May 3 are all the more tragic because British forces had largely secured the area the day before the Typhoon strikes. British units first arrived in Lübeck from the Herrenbrücke Bridge on May 2 and soon thereafter made it into Neustadt, moving into position on the outskirts of town at approximately four that afternoon.

The team from the 30th Assault Force was the advance unit, clearing the way for the main liberating force and providing forward-looking intelligence.* After liberating the nearby towns of Süsel and Wintershagen, the British established temporary headquarters in Lübeck, approximately twelve miles from Neustadt, to launch their mission to secure Germany's north-central coastline.

One of the lead tanks in the column that arrived at the Baltic coast had a commander who had been on the beaches of Normandy during the D-Day operation and had gone on to liberate towns throughout France. But unlike in Belgium and France where people ran into the streets to cheer and hug the liberators, the reception in these coastal communities was quite different.

---

* One of the 30th Assault Force's founders and leaders was Commander Ian Fleming, who would go on after the war to write the hugely successful James Bond series, which was based in part on his wartime experiences in intelligence and espionage.

What residents remained in town tried to stay out of view. Only a few people waved flags, but their faces remained subdued with fear. Others were on the move, leaving the towns on foot, on bicycles, or by any means possible.

British forces continued along the coast to the bays where the *Cap Arcona* and other ships were anchored and areas that were among the last to be liberated. Coming to a crest on the hill overlooking the Baltic, they were able to see the ships. The commander recalled the fighting on the ground, in the water, and in the air. "In the harbor several submarines could clearly be seen and as the tanks deployed, three RAF Typhoons went in to attack them. Anti-aircraft fire opened up from the U-boats and other shipping in the Bay. The squadron including myself joined in the fun, opening up on all the vessels we could see."

The tanks from the 11th Armoured succeeded in sinking a few of the submarines at the U-boat base, which prevented the Nazis from scuttling the ships in the bay. Another target for the British was the *Athen*, which was docked in port. The old freighter had been outfitted with flak guns, which fired on the Typhoons. However, the British tanks destroyed the rear flak guns, causing the remainder of the gunners on the ship to abandon ship. The British units were, however, too late to save most of the prisoners on the ships.

Several old barges that had transported prisoners to the coast sat idly in the harbor on May 3, waiting to unload their cargo of concentration camp prisoners. But before the prisoners could be shuttled out to the larger ships at anchor in the bay, the Typhoons attacked. Like their fellow inmates trapped on the large ships, many of the prisoners in the barges were unable to escape the rusting coffins because of the high walls and lack of ladders leading up and out of the deep holds. They were caught in the aerial attacks and the skirmishes on shore between British forces arriving at Neustadt and the sparse German resistance. The barges took direct hits from the gunfire and were pelted by flying debris.

Remarkably, most of the prisoners trapped in the barges docked at the port survived these attacks. However, as the Typhoon bombing runs were ending, a small band of Nazis encountered two of the barges and attacked. It is not known which units were responsible—presumably either cadets from the nearby U-boat training school or the remnants of the SS guards assigned to the prison transports and ships. The prisoners piled deep into the open holds of the barges had no chance. The British later found the two barges littered with corpses inside; the evidence suggested they had all recently been shot from above.

Other Nazi units patrolled the beaches that afternoon searching for any prisoners from the ships that might have made it ashore. A few hundred of them managed to do so. Tragically, they were met by sailors and cadets from the U-boat base who fired into the water. A group of young boys from the Hitler Youth joined the melee, attacking the naked, weak prisoners struggling to crawl out of the water. Groups of survivors who made it onto the beaches were lined up and shot by firing squads. At one section of the beach, the Nazi soldiers shot so many of the prisoners in the water that they ran out of ammunition. That did not stop them; the soldiers simply turned the butts of their guns into weapons and clubbed the hapless prisoners to death. The British later found the bodies of several children on the beaches with their skulls crushed from these blows.

The few prisoners from the *Cap Arcona* made it to shore and survived because they arrived later in the afternoon, after British units either drove the Nazis off the beaches or had killed them. The 15th Scottish Division, for instance, happened upon SS guards and naval cadets in the act of attacking prisoners on the beach. The Scots made quick work out of the Nazis, killing every one of them and saving a few of the prisoners. Elsewhere, the final remnants of the SS guards at last gave up, but not before killing as many prisoners as possible. One of the British officers described the poetic justice that occurred. "The Germans who saw that the tables had turned stopped firing and ran to our soldiers to seek protection. Many displaced persons, who were about to be shot, wanted to avenge their executioners and encircle them. It was the first time that [the commandos] did not hurry to intervene."

Among the survivors saved by the liberating army was Bogdan Suchowiak, the Polish prisoner who had endured fifty-seven months in a concentration camp ever since his village in Poland was overrun by the Nazis in 1939. He also endured the ordeal aboard the *Cap Arcona* and had managed to make it into the water and to the beach. Suchowiak was on his knees praying when he heard a German voice scream out from behind him, "Bandit, do as you are told or else I shoot!" There stood a young boy roughly sixteen years old dressed in the attire of the cadets from the naval training school and holding a gun in an awkward manner. A few other nervous cadets were nearby.

Suchowiak and about fifteen other prisoners were captured on the beach by the cadets and marched to a nearby building. The boys shoved and hit the exhausted prisoners with their weapons until they arrived at the building. The prisoners were lined up, and Suchowiak expected to be shot. He remembered what happened next. "After a long time, a navy truck arrived. We were ordered to climb in—in the distance we could hear machine-gun fire. Suddenly the truck stopped. We were afraid we were going to be executed. Someone opened the rear door of the truck. I did not believe my eyes. In the middle of a group of German soldiers stood a British captain—a German infantry major was saluting him." The cadets surrendered immediately, and Suchowiak and his comrades were rescued.

THE FEW GERMAN TROOPS, SS guards, and sailors and cadets from the U-boat base in town were severely outgunned by the formidable ground troops of the 159th Infantry Brigade, 15th Scottish Division, and 1st Special Services Brigade, with its elite units such as the 6th Commando and 30th Assault Force. The British also had more than one hundred tanks from the 11th Armoured Division.

Still, it was not until May 4, the day after the air attacks, before all German forces in the area finally surrendered and Lübeck and Neustadt were fully secured. The gruesome task before the British now involved documenting what had happened on May 3 at the coast. When soldiers boarded the *Athen,* one of them described what he saw. "We discovered that the cargo consisted of some 6,000* prisoners who were being transported to Norway. They were . . . emaciated and half naked, hardly human in appearance. They were of every nationality; many were Jews, many were political prisoners, and one group who struggled to maintain a form of military order, when eventually they reached the shore, were survivors of Maquis† prisoners from the occupied countries, in particular, from Norway." Even the British units who liberated the coast believed the prisoners were being evacuated to Norway, presumably to avoid their falling into the hands of the liberators in order that they be used as bargaining chips in postwar negotiations.

The report by the British colonel H. G. Sheen went on to note that the prisoners "were packed so tightly in the holds that it was difficult for them to lie down, and they had been without any food whatever for 12 days, and without water for a week." The colonel summed up the mood of his men, saying, "But the place will be memorable to us for the Unit's first—and most salutary—experience . . . of German methods of dealing with 'difficult' prisoners."

The British also noted, "The German guards had fled that afternoon, giving themselves time as they went to shoot such of the prisoners as had been stowed on deck, whose bodies were floating in the harbor when we arrived." The grisly scenes had another result. They incensed the soldiers at the port. Said one of them, "I am glad to report that at any rate, two of the SS guards from the *Athen* fell into our hands, and were summarily executed."

The British commander of the liberating force was the highly decorated brigadier general Derek Mills-Roberts. The general, who had come up through the ranks of Britain's Special Forces and now led the commandos of the 1st Special Services Brigade, documented the carnage. "When we reached Neustadt we saw several sunken ships in the bay and on one of the headlands many corpses of displaced persons were found: they had been dragged ashore from the

* The actual number of prisoners was probably closer to two thousand.

† The Maquis is another name for the French Resistance.

ships and butchered. When the place looked [that it was about to be] overrun by the Allies, these wretched people had been shot by the SS captors." But the tough general remembered one scene in particular that had a different ending. He described it as follows: "When 6 Commando, which was in the lead, arrived on top of the hill, this massacre was still taking place, and the Germans, seeing that the tables had been turned, ceased fire and ran toward the new arrivals for protection. A crowd of displaced persons waiting to be butchered immediately turned on their late captors and swallowed them up—it was about the only time in the war that 6 Commando could not raise a gallop to save a situation."

Mills-Roberts had seen the work of the Nazis when he liberated Bergen-Belsen, but the tough general was shocked when he came upon the destruction at the Baltic coast. The following atrocity was especially difficult for him to process. "We found a hastily filled-in grave and a number of corpses lying on the edge of the sea. All these people (and there were women and children amongst them) had been shot in the head at close quarters and in many cases had had their heads battered in. Some of them were roped together round the neck and ankles."

As the British units secured the beaches, they discovered other gruesome crimes. The general chronicled one of them: "In a barge which had drifted ashore were many more in a similar condition, and amongst them we found a girl who was still alive. She had been overlooked earlier in the day as she was huddled up under a blanket against two dead bodies. She was uninjured except for a bad bruise on one hand, but was so weak from starvation that she could hardly talk. She died in the hospital some three weeks later."

The sight of dead children on the beaches with their skulls bashed in sent Mills-Roberts into a fit of anger. He demanded to see the senior Nazi officer on the coast, Field Marshal Erhard Milch, who had been captured by British soldiers in Lübeck. Perhaps by reflex, when Milch met General Mills-Roberts he snapped a crisp "Sieg Heil" salute. This prompted the British general to grab Milch's baton and break it violently over the Nazi commander's head. General Mills-Roberts ordered his men to take Milch to the beaches and barges to see the work of his Nazi soldiers. On the day after the attack, a Colonel Christopher led the Nazi commander to the site of the slaughter and reported: "When I arrived on the scene of this outrage with Field Marshal Erhard Milch on the 4th of May, I saw about 100 bodies, old men, women, and children lying on the beach having been shot in the face at very close range." Milch broke down in sobs when he saw what his soldiers had done.

Over the next two days, both communities resembled apocalyptic nightmares: the stench of concentration camps was everywhere, refugees shuffled through town looking for food and water, lines of people hurried out of town, dead bodies littered the beaches, and in the bay numerous ships burned. Even the battle-hardened British soldiers were shocked at what they saw. Some of the soldiers described it as what they imagined hell looked like. One of them came across the body of a little girl he estimated to be about seven who was still clutching the hand of a woman beside her. They were dead on the beach, water lapping up against their bodies. It was presumed that they were mother and daughter. Both bodies wore black-and-white-striped wool garments from the concentration camps.

ONCE THE REMAINING GERMAN resistance had been neutralized, the British set about attempting to feed and clothe the prisoners. The sheer number of inmates in town was staggering, and desperate prisoners continued to arrive at the hospital in Neustadt, which served as the temporary British headquarters. In response, the British also commandeered the barracks at the U-boat base as a second hospital. General Mills-Roberts summed it up as follows: "Into the square, at first a trickle then a stream then a flood, there staggered the emaciated half-naked remnants of a huge number of political prisoners, the survivors of the two large ships still blazing in the bay. Some, unable to walk, sank to the ground, while others tried to drink from the puddles in the road."

The tank crews and British commandos provided biscuits and water from their military rations, but the amount of prisoners was such that it was simply not enough. The British then ordered the town's residents to prepare meals and turn over food for the survivors; restaurants in town were ordered to cook whatever food remained in their pantries. However, some of the prisoners were so malnourished that when they ate, they consumed too much food initially and either became very ill or died. The British also decided to confiscate food, clothing, and medicine from German soldiers and distribute it to the prisoners, many of whom were still naked or wearing torn, wet uniforms from the camps. The situation was so dire that, more than once, British officers had to fire shots in the air to restore order to the process.

The liberators also had to contend with the grim necessity of burying thousands of dead prisoners. Hundreds of corpses were found on the beaches, hundreds more in the barges, and hundreds more found murdered throughout Neustadt and Lübeck. General Mills-Roberts had roughly twenty-five hundred German soldiers and sailors in custody and ordered them to dig graves for the dead.

One of the British commandos remembered it as being a particularly difficult situation. "Under instructions not to retaliate, we called out the Germans to bring their spades and shovels to bury the corpses. When they saw the handiwork of their compatriots they assumed that they were called out to dig their own graves and to be shot in retaliation, and some tried to run away. In the end, they dug the graves to bury Himmler's victims. While they dug into the night, they could see on the horizon lights from explosions and fighting as Russian artillery and tanks approached from the east."

It was impossible to try to identify all the bodies on the beach and account for all those killed by firing squads in town. The British decided to bury all of the prisoners quickly and in unmarked mass graves.

By seven on the evening of May 3, the British finally had the entire towns of Lübeck and Neustadt, the harbors, and the coast under control. It was then that they finally sent boats out to rescue any survivors still aboard the ocean liners and freighters smoldering and laying partially submerged in the bay. Amid the cold rain that began in the late afternoon, confiscated tugboats, fishing boats, and assorted other craft headed to the *Cap Arcona*, navigating the bodies that floated in the water.

One of the prisoners rescued was Henry Bawnik, one of the last to board the *Cap Arcona* and the man who held onto a rope leading from the sinking hulk into the frigid waters of the Baltic. Bawnik had survived the camps at Auschwitz, Mittelbau-Dora, and Furstengrube as well as the difficult journey to the Baltic coast. A passing tugboat picked him up. Bawnik grimly asked which camp he was to be taken to, but to his delight the man on the tugboat answered, "There are no more concentration camps for you. The English are in town."

The senior German naval commander in Neustadt, Captain Heinrich Schmidt, informed investigators after the war that "during the attack all available vessels were put into action by me. There were approximately six to eight small vessels. . . . [A]pproximately 200 humans were rescued." Schmidt's version of the tragic incident was, however, a distortion of the truth. They did not rescue prisoners, only SS guards and German crew members.

There were, however, a few righteous responses from Germans. One act of selflessness occurred at four that afternoon when Wolff, the cabin boy from the *Cap Arcona*, managed to secure a tugboat whose captain had been shot by the British. He sailed tugboat *AKTIV* back to the ship and picked up survivors and then proceeded to rescue additional survivors from the waters of the bay. He was joined by a few local Germans. Two of them were Fritz Hallerstede and his brother-in-law, Hans Frolich, who sailed their fishing boat around the bay and to the *Cap Arcona*. In an act of compassion, they were able to pull eighteen survivors from the water and sinking ships.

Throughout the afternoon and evening, the *Cap Arcona* occasionally groaned and exploded as the boilers and engine rooms succumbed to the flames. The old liner slowly began to roll over. Anywhere from 100 to 450 prisoners were still hanging onto the ship in hopes of being rescued. They had remained in that condition through the entire afternoon, somehow managing to scramble along the massive liner's decks, side, and bottom without falling into the water while the ship rolled over. They also survived the scalding heat from the fire in the ship's interior, although several suffered severe burns from sitting on the partially sunken hull.

To the relief of the few prisoners on the *Cap Arcona*, a small motorboat appeared on the water around sunset. One of the survivors who spotted the rescue boat was Heinrich Mehringer, the German who managed to escape from his cabin. He recalled his survival: "We were aft and had to run along the hot hull towards the bow. The surface was so hot that we had to lay planks one in front of the other, taking the lead one and putting it in front so that we could walk over them."

The delay in the rescue ended up saving Mehringer's life. Most of his fellow prisoners who made it into the water and onto the beach were shot by the Nazis on the shoreline. Mehringer and his comrades scrambled down into the water and were pulled into a boat captained by a local fisherman. They were taken to the pier guarded by two British tanks. The British seemed preoccupied with securing the port, and Mehringer did not speak a word of English. He needed to find warm clothing and shelter, so he walked in what he described as a state of "delirium" to some nearby homes, which looked unoccupied from the outside. However, when the prisoners tried to enter the homes, they were turned away by fearful residents.

One German woman finally pointed him in the direction of the U-boat base, which was now occupied by British soldiers. When Mehringer arrived, a British soldier came and took him inside to a room. He found warm blankets, remembering, "I made myself a thick lair and sank into my heavenly bed."

The American 161st Tactical Reconnaissance Squadron flew over Neustadt Bay soon after the attacks. They photographed the carnage. Surviving images showed three large ships—the *Deutschland*,

Thielbek, and *Cap Arcona*—still smoldering and countless bodies in the water. In just over an hour, thousands of men, women, and children, the lion's share of them survivors of concentration camps in the area including Neuengamme, lost their lives. Only a small number survived. The *Athen* alone escaped the carnage inflicted on its sister ships thanks to the decision by the captain to sail back to Neustadt Harbor before the first wave of attacks. Although the *Athen* was hit by some cannon fire from the warplanes and armored units, it did not sink, sparing the lives of roughly two thousand prisoners stuck in the ship's holds.

Most of the survivors from the *Athen* had made it off the ship and hid at the wharf. A few remained on board in whatever section of the ship was not burning. The British quickly pulled the remaining prisoners out of the old freighter and had tugboats tow it away from the harbor in the event the ship's boilers exploded. Around one mile north of the bay, the ship went aground near Pelzerhaken, a peninsula jutting out into the Baltic. Soon thereafter, flames aboard the *Athen* finally reached the engine room, and the ship detonated in a great blast heard and felt back on the harbor and in town.

The Typhoon pilots returned to their bases in the late afternoon of May 3 with the satisfaction that the mission in the southern Baltic was a success. The RAF report offered a bureaucratic description of the mission. "All aircraft carrying bombs or R/P* were diverted to deal solely with the large concentrations of shipping making their way from Lübeck, Kiel and Schleswig in the general direction of Norway. . . . Full results will doubtless show that a very satisfactory score was achieved."

Indeed, the RAF inflicted massive destruction, sinking more than two dozen ships and damaging more than one hundred others. The toll included two liners, two tankers, a freighter, two U-boat tenders, nine destroyers, ten minesweepers, and numerous tugboats, fishing boats, and other vessels. They suffered only minor casualties and no loss of life. In total, the British Second Tactical Air

---

* R/P was an abbreviation for rocket-propelled missiles.

Force flew 117 sorties that day, using dozens of rockets, a score of bombs, and thousands of rounds from deadly 20mm guns.

One of the Typhoon pilots, unaware of the actual target of their attacks, offered a chilling assessment of the day. "In what can only be described as 'brilliant attacks,' 9 aircraft of the 198 Squadron destroyed a 12,000 ton ship and a 1,500 ton cargo ship. . . . The 12,000 tonner, when left, is reported to have been burning from stem to stern. . . . From observation of the balers-out from them, and from the circumstances, it may be assumed that many Huns have found the Baltic very cold today."

Chapter 22

AFTERMATH

THE *CAP ARCONA* BURNED all afternoon on May 3. Despite the sheer number of rockets, bombs, and cannon fire from the Typhoons, the old ocean liner managed to remain afloat after the attacks, although the list on deck became more pronounced as the afternoon wore on. At approximately four thirty, the fire had finally reached the ship's fuel tanks, and an enormous explosion reverberated through the bay and town, launching steel and debris high into the sky. The *Cap Arcona* shuddered from the blast, and black smoke puffed through the decks, soon enveloping the entire ship. The prisoners remaining on the ship were sent hurtling across the decks as the old liner lurched sharply to the side. Many of them were knocked overboard into the sea below. Shortly thereafter, the steel creaked and groaned loudly one last time, and it rolled over and sank.

However, with a beam of eighty-four feet, the liner was much deeper than the fifty-foot depth of the bay, leaving the enormous hull of the capsized ship partially exposed on the flat sea, a grim reminder of the events of that day. Only a few hundred yards away, the superstructure of the *Thielbek* was also visible in the sea, leaning to the starboard. Much smaller than the *Cap Arcona*, it was nonetheless too large to drift completely below the water. The *Deutschland* would join its sister ships at approximately six thirty, when it too sank partially below the waterline.

The tranquillity that marked the hours before twilight belied the gruesome event that had just transpired. Corpses floated around the wrecks and littered the beach. The harbor and a few buildings in town still smoldered from fires. Bricks and debris lined the streets, while grim-faced residents slowly emerged from their hiding to take stock of the shocking events. Bodies from the three ships continued to wash ashore for weeks and were collected and buried in a single mass grave at Neustadt. Periodically, for the next twenty-five years, there were reports of human remains still drifting ashore on the currents of the southern Baltic. In 1971 a twelve-year-old boy was playing in the sand on Neustadt's beach when he discovered the remains of a man's skeleton that had washed ashore. Authorities believe this was the last remaining victim of the May 3 attacks.

The *Thielbek* was refloated four years later, in late 1949 and early 1950. During the effort, salvage crews discovered forty-nine skeletons still on board the old freighter. Both curious residents from the area and individuals who had lost loved ones in the tragic attacks came out to see the old ship be raised. The remains were taken to the cemetery in Neustadt and buried alongside the victims of the *Cap Arcona*.

The *Thielbek* was repaired and returned to service by the Knöhr and Burchard Shipping Company with a new name: the SS *Reinbek*, named for a transport ship sunk by an Allied torpedo in 1939. It was sold in 1961 and sailed under a Panamanian flag as the SS *Magdalene*, ironically a similar name used by one of Count Bernadotte's hospital ships that rescued concentration camp survivors. A few years later, it was again renamed, this time as the *Old Warrior*, before being scrapped in 1974 in Split, in former Yugoslavia.

The *Athen*, the only one of the four large ships to survive the Typhoon attacks, was purchased by the Soviet Union. After the necessary repairs, it was renamed the *General Brusilow*. On May 27, 1947, the former freighter was given to the Polish government and later renamed the *Warynski*. It sailed for another quarter century, traveling from Poland to Hamburg and even to Buenos Aires on the route sailed by the *Cap Arcona* during its prewar glory days. In 1973 the old ship was finally taken out of service and used as a floating warehouse in Stettin. In the end, it was ingloriously renamed *NP-ZPS8*.

The *Deutschland* remains at the bottom of the bay of Neustadt. Scuba divers occasionally visit the wreck site and, over the years, have found artifacts and bones in the holds.

The *Cap Arcona* remained partially submerged, resting on its side after the attacks and smoldering for days. After the war divers visited the wreck and salvaged a number of artifacts from the ship. The capsized ocean liner eventually drifted ashore and was photographed extensively by the Rolls-Royce Company. The company was interested in the wreck because it was testing the effectiveness of one of the products from its defense industry line. Ironically, before and during the war, Rolls-Royce had manufactured the very rockets that were fired at the *Cap Arcona*.

Stuck in the sand near Neustadt, the beached hulk was purchased by shipping companies in 1949, dismantled, and taken away. A few scraps of metal and parts ended up being used to build other ships, a humbling end to a remarkable but tragic life.

IT IS NO EASY MATTER to estimate the death toll from the attack on the *Cap Arcona* or on all of the ships in the southern Baltic on May 3, 1945. The survivors hid throughout the town, others ran, and most had no identification other than a number tattooed on their arms. They also comprised many nationalities and spoke different languages. What is known is that from January 1945 until the very end of the war, they came—by foot, on barges, or in cattle cars—to the Baltic coast by the thousands. The Nazis, usually meticulous in their documentation, were forced to evacuate the camps with much haste. The sense of urgency caused by approaching Allied armies therefore precluded them from recording with accuracy the numbers of prisoners sent north. The number was in the tens of thousands. However, there was no time to count how many prisoners died while en route, but it is safe to say that thousands perished during the grueling journey. Hundreds, if not thousands, more died while waiting at the harbor and while aboard the ships during the days spent locked in rooms and holds without food or water.

Nearly all of the estimated 1,998 on the *Athen* survived because the ship docked just before the aerial attack. It is uncertain how many people perished on board the *Deutschland*. However, it is likely that at least several hundred, if not several thousand, additional prisoners, wounded soldiers, and German medical personnel staffing the converted hospital ship were lost in the attacks. Based on the sparse evidence that survived history, the U.S. Holocaust Memorial Museum estimates that at least 2,500 prisoners perished on the *Thielbek* and roughly 4,500 prisoners died on the *Cap Arcona* as a direct result of the attacks on May 3. These seem to be very conservative estimates; it is possible those lost on the *Cap Arcona* number well in excess of 5,000.

The total fatalities on all the prisoner ships and at the port that day were likely in the range 8,000–10,000. Obviously, there is no consensus, and we will never know the final loss. These estimates constitute only those lost in and around Neustadt in the closing days of April and first three days of May. This figure does not include the German soldiers and sailors killed when the British liberated the area or the countless prisoners who died while being transported or marched to the coast. Moreover, for weeks to come, bodies of the victims washed ashore. A report commissioned by the U.S. military after the war concluded that from May 1945 through the end of July, a total of 253 bodies washed up on the beaches near Neustadt. Over the next two months, another 474 bodies came ashore. It therefore seems likely that the total loss from the march north *and* the attacks in the bay was much higher.

There are verifiable reports that some of the guards and sailors managed to survive the attacks on the ships. Whereas the survival rate by the prisoners was very low, especially for those stuck in the lower decks—nearly all of whom died—the survival rate among prison guards on the *Cap Arcona* was much higher. It appears that around 80 percent of the guards and crew survived. Most of the guards from the *Cap Arcona* had abandoned ship before the attacks, and several of those remaining on board until May 3 survived, amounting to about 490 out of a total of 600 ship's personnel. This number includes 16 of the 70 crew members and 20 of the 24 female SS guards who were on board. Captain Heinrich Bertram and his second officer also survived the attacks and the sinking of their ship.

It was a different matter on the *Thielbek*, which sank very quickly. Roughly 200 of the Nazi guards and all 11 sailors on board went down with the ship. Only a handful of guards managed to survive after they boarded a lifeboat.

Only about 350 prisoners aboard the *Cap Arcona* and only around 50 of those on the *Thielbek* survived the ordeal. Those lost that day on the *Cap Arcona* and its sister ships represented at least twenty-five nationalities.* None of the handful of Americans on the old liner survived the attacks. The *Cap Arcona* disaster at the end of the Holocaust claimed more than three times as many people as did the loss of the *Titanic* and remains one of the world's worst maritime disasters, the worst instance of friendly fire, and one of history's bloodiest and most tragic episodes.

THE DAY AFTER THE devastating air attack in the southern Baltic that killed many prisoners from Neuengamme, the notorious concentration camp was liberated by the British. But they were too late. Commandant Max Pauly had already marched and shipped the prison population north; those remaining at the camp were killed just days earlier. Sadly, about 17,000 prisoners were killed or died in the two months prior to the arrival of British forces. Even the most battle-hardened soldiers had trouble grasping the extensiveness of the horrors at the camp. Evidence suggests that prisoners were shot, hanged, gassed, and given lethal injections. But that is only a part of Neuengamme's notorious legacy.

---

* The prisoners who perished on the *Cap Arcona* included Americans, Belarussians, Belgians, Canadians, Czechs, Danes, Dutch, Estonians, Finns, French, Germans, Greeks, Hungarians, Italians, Latvians, Lithuanians, Luxembourgers, Norwegians, Poles, Romanians, Russians, Spaniards, Swiss, Ukrainians, and Yugoslavs.

From 1939 to the end of the war, more than 106,000 prisoners were incarcerated at Neuengamme. More than half of them would not survive the nightmare. The U.S. Holocaust Memorial Museum estimates that approximately 50,000 prisoners died there and at Neuengamme's many satellite camps, most from the inhumane living conditions that included a lack of sanitation, health care, and nutrition. Those who perished at the hellacious facility represented twenty-eight nationalities.* Thousands of Jews, alleged prostitutes and homosexuals, Gypsies, and Jehovah's Witnesses also died at Neuengamme.

Surviving records have made it possible to identify roughly 42,900 of the camp's prisoners. The list includes several prominent inmates: Rein Boomsma, a Dutch soccer player and colonel in the Netherlands army; Claude Bourdet, a noted French writer and politician; Emil Burian, a talented Czech journalist, musician, playwright, and poet; Ernst Goldenbaum, a German politician; Michel Hollard, a French colonel and heroic leader of the French Resistance; Henry Wilhelm Kristiansen, a Norwegian newspaper editor and politician; Léonel de Moustier, a French politician; David Rousset, a French writer; Kurt Schumacher, a German politician; and Johann Trollmann, a successful German boxer. Another casualty of Neuengamme was Fritz Pfeffer, a German Jew who happened to live at the home where Anne Frank hid. All were innocent; nearly all died.

The commandant of Neuengamme, Max Pauly, was captured at the end of the war and detained by the British army. Beginning on March 16, 1946, he and sixteen of his camp officials, SS guards, and staff were tried at the Neuengamme war-crimes trials in the Curiohaus in Hamburg. The former warden was pronounced guilty of many charges and hanged at Hamelin Prison. He was thirty-nine years old. Several of his officers, guards, and physicians were also found guilty of an array of crimes against humanity and sentenced to death on October 8, 1946.

---

* Among those who died at Neuengamme were 34,350 Soviets (mostly soldiers), 16,900 Poles, 11,500 French, 9,200 Germans, 6,950 Dutch, 4,800 Belgians, and 4,800 Danes.

After the end of the war, the occupying British army used Neuengamme as a displaced-persons facility for Russian Jews unable or unwilling to return home and a detention center for captured members of the SS and other Nazi prisoners. Neuengamme was given a new name: Civil Internment Camp Number 6. It was eventually closed by the British army on August 13, 1948. The City of Hamburg then converted it into a prison. In 1989 the city began transferring prisoners from the site and finally closed the prison in 2004.

Thousands of photos have been collected from Neuengamme from private collections and from international archives. These collections reveal and preserve the struggles of those who died and those who somehow survived the camp, including scenes of torture and day-to-day work. Many of the photos had to be smuggled out before the camp was destroyed. Other images came from Josef Schmitt, a German photographer who was assigned by the Gestapo to photograph the camp in 1943. After the war, Schmitt turned over approximately one hundred photos to the British military. In the year 2011, they were part of an exhibit at the town hall in Hamburg titled *In the Focus*.

The first memorial to those who suffered and died was established in 1953 at the site of the former camp's garden. In 1965 and 1981, ceremonies were held on the grounds of what had been Neuengamme. In 2005 a new memorial and museum were opened, and a memorial was dedicated at the Bullenhuser Damm School, where a group of children were the subject of Nazi medical experiments. Several of the original buildings of the camp remained until 2006.

THE "HOLOCAUST SURVIVORS AND Victims Database," housed in the archives of the U.S. Holocaust Memorial Museum, lists the names of some of those killed in the bombing of the *Cap Arcona* and other ships. It contains 1,020 names. Partial information exists for other inmates. The names were gathered from reports and prisoner identification numbers; most of them were Belgian, Dutch, French,

German, and Polish laborers from Neuengamme. A few of those identified were sent to the *Cap Arcona* from Buchenwald and Stutthof. Despite the work of researchers to identify the victims, the museum notes that "most of the prisoners that died that day could not be identified."

Although only a few people survived the *Cap Arcona*, several of them went on to live distinguished lives. Berek Jakubowicz changed his name to Benjamin Jacobs when he emigrated to the United States after the war. His brother, Josek (who changed his name to Joseph), also moved to the United States. Their parents and sister, however, were lost in the Holocaust. Thanks to his dentistry kit and a year of dental training, the man known as "the dentist of Auschwitz" was able to escape death in the concentration camps. Once in the United States, Jacobs did not pursue a career in dentistry, but the business he opened prospered and he later penned his memoirs. He died on January 30, 2004.

Like Benjamin Jacobs, Szmuel Piwnik was Polish and just thirteen when his country was invaded by the Nazis. He managed to survive a Jewish ghetto in his hometown of Bedzin and was later transferred to Auschwitz and the mining camp at Furstengrube. He survived all three as well as the death march to the Baltic coast and sinking of the *Cap Arcona*. Piwnik wrote that there was simply no way to survive the brutal conditions and Nazi violence, but he survived all of them. Piwnik lost his entire family to the Nazis and wrestled his entire life with the emotional scars from the Holocaust.

After the war he fought in the struggle to establish the state of Israel and then moved to London, where he changed his birth name to Samuel Pivnik and enjoyed a successful career as an art dealer. In 2012 he published his memoir, where he described the Nazis as having "no value whatsoever of human life." As of 2016, he was still living.

Francis Akos was born on March 30, 1922, in Budapest, Hungary. A gifted musician, he attended a music academy and graduated in 1941, becoming the concertmaster for a Jewish community cultural center in the city. He was drafted in 1943 and, while on leave in Budapest, was captured and sent by train to Neuengamme. He too survived the brutal conditions at the camp, the death march, and both the sinking of the *Cap Arcona* and the Nazi attacks on the beach. Akos came to the United States, where he enjoyed an acclaimed career as a violinist and assistant concertmaster for the Chicago Symphony. As of 2016, he was still living.

Like Jacobs and Pivnik, Henry Bawnik was also Polish. He survived several concentration camps and the brutal evacuation to the Baltic. Bawnik made it to the United States, married, and had three daughters. In 1959 he moved to Buffalo, where he opened a dry-cleaning business. His story went untold for decades until a friend noticed the blue tattooed number on Bawnik's arm. At the urging of his friend and grandson, who is a writer, Bawnik finally revealed the details of his life. As of 2016, he was still sharing his incredible story.

Witold Rygiel was also Polish and just thirteen years old when the Nazis invaded his hometown of Warsaw. He too survived the concentration camps, death march to the Baltic, and detainment on the *Thielbek*. After an extended rehabilitation in a Red Cross hospital in Sweden after the war, Rygiel returned to Poland in 1947. He attended medical school and became a pediatric orthopedic surgeon. In 1963 he and his wife, a professor of pediatrics, moved to Canada and lectured at McGill University. The Rygiels opened a hospital for children in Hamilton, Ontario, in 1968. After a very successful career, he retired to Arizona.

In 2010 another Polish survivor, Janusz Franckl, an electrical engineer living in Argentina, was visiting Warsaw and encountered someone who knew Witold Rygiel. The person informed Franckl that Rygiel had moved to Arizona. Franckl wrote to Rygiel, and, amazingly, the two reunited after sixty-five years. They had been sent to Neuengamme in 1943, and Franckl, aged sixteen, and Rygiel, aged fifteen, became bunkmates during their incarceration. Franckl still remembered their struggle together at Neuengamme. "We were sharing a tough life. We were treated like animals and would sometimes return to the block covered in blood but we helped each other as much as we could. We became close friends and that helped us through that time we had no idea would ever end. We believed it would be over but it would be a long time away."

After their reunion Rygiel began thinking about revisiting the scene of so much devastation in 1945. On the occasion of the sixty-fourth anniversary of the sinking of the *Cap Arcona*, the then eighty-three-year-old said, "I think this is my last opportunity to tell my story . . . of one of the greatest tragedies at sea." He shared his amazing story with those in attendance at the anniversary commemoration. The two friends were still living in 2016.

Another one of the few to survive Neuengamme, the death march to the Baltic, and the bombing of the *Cap Arcona* was Erwin Geschonneck. The debonair German actor was born in East Prussia on December 27, 1906, to a working-class family. To pursue his passion for acting, the young boy moved to Berlin and began performing in theater groups that staged avant-garde productions. When Adolf Hitler rose to power in 1933, Geschonneck fled Nazi Germany for the Soviet Union. While living in Odessa, he worked in a German-language theater but was expelled in 1938 and moved to Czechoslovakia. In 1939 the Germans invaded Czechoslovakia, and Geschonneck was caught and arrested by the SS in Prague. He was taken to Sachsenhausen, then to Dachau, and ultimately to Neuengamme. There he witnessed the Jewish children being subjected to vicious medical experiments at Bullenhuser Damm.

After the war Gerschonneck became one of East Germany's best-known actors, starring in many films and on the stage and serving as vice president of the East German Film and Television Federation. The actor received numerous awards for his work and continued working until very late in life. As one of the few survivors of the sinking of the *Cap Arcona*, Gerschonneck was the subject of the televised program *Der Mann von der* Cap Arcona (The man of the *Cap Arcona*) in 1982, a riveting telling of the tragedy and of the German actor's life story. Late in life, he devoted two years to the production of the documentary *The Fall of the* Cap Arcona.

Geschonneck lived an extraordinary life, dying in March 2008 at the age of 101.

KARL KAUFMANN, THE PROVINCIAL governor of the Hamburg region who ordered the ocean liners and freighters into the bays of the southern Baltic, forced the captains to accommodate thousands of prisoners, and enacted the plan to sink the ships with the prisoners on board, was arrested by the British soon after the war ended. Like Commandant Max Pauly, he was placed on trial at the Hamburg war-crimes trials in 1946. Kaufmann was tried on numerous war crimes, but denied that there ever was an order to kill the survivors of the concentration camps or that the ships were to be scuttled. Instead, he claimed that the prisoners were to be sent to Sweden by ship.

Even though little evidence existed to substantiate Kaufmann's claims and his comments ran contrary to the testimony of other Nazi officials, the bloodthirsty governor escaped a death sentence. Kaufmann was sent to prison but was released because of poor health. When new evidence of Kaufmann's complicity in the tragic events at the end of the war later surfaced, he was rearrested but was again released. Shockingly, a book published in 1947 by Kurt Detlev Möller titled *Das Letzte Kapitel* (The Last Chapter) even called Kaufmann "the good Gauleiter" and spoke of him as the "rescuer of Hamburg." The governor lived a long life and died comfortably at home on December 4, 1969, in his hometown of Hamburg.

Kaufmann's accomplice in the plan to kill the prisoners by scuttling the ships was Count Georg-Henning Graf von Bassewitz-Behr, who was in charge of the Gestapo in Hamburg. He too was tried during the Hamburg war-crimes trials but escaped justice. However, the count was captured by the Soviets and incarcerated. He allegedly died on January 31, 1949, while in a Soviet prison in Magadan in eastern Siberia.

An investigation into the death of Herbert Selpin, the director of the Nazi *Titanic* propaganda film, was commissioned in August 1947. The trial was inconclusive. During the trial Walter

Zerlett-Olfenius, the scriptwriter who turned Selpin over to Goebbels, was brought to court as a witness. The photographs and reports ordered by Goebbels were introduced as posthumous evidence at the trial. Zerlett neither denied nor regretted his actions and was ultimately given a five-year sentence with hard labor for his complicity in the death of his former friend. Additionally, half the former scriptwriter's assets were confiscated, including his property. In 1949, however, the sentence was revoked after an appeal.

After being freed from his prison in Berlin, Zerlett moved to Rosshaupten in Bavaria, where he lived out the remainder of his life with his wife, Eva Tinschmann, a former actress. Zerlett never again worked in the film industry. However, back in 1942 when the film was finally completed, Zerlett was able to screen the finished product of his former friend's masterpiece. However, his thoughts about the film remain unknown. He died on April 18, 1975, taking many secrets to the grave with him.

Questions remain about the motives of Herbert Selpin before his death. Given Selpin's rash behavior on the set of his film and his defiance in front of Joseph Goebbels and the Gestapo when summoned to Berlin, it is possible that, rather than being simply despondent or drunk, the director may have ingeniously used his film on the *Titanic* to critique the Third Reich and Hitler. Perhaps he intended the film as a mirror to be held up by the German people and their leaders. Some evidence for such a hypothesis may exist in the script. Petersen, the first officer and hero of the film who happened to be German, was ordered by his superiors not to question orders, yet he did so repeatedly. The antagonist, Bruce Ismay, the owner of the White Star Line, listened to no one, was fanatically devoted to his vision, and ultimately doomed his passengers to a tragic fate. Could these characters have been planted in the film by Selpin in order to criticize Hitler? If this was indeed Selpin's intention, it might explain his defiant death wish in the closing hours of his life during the meeting with Goebbels.

Two of the führer's top officials—Hermann Göring, the Luftwaffe commander, and Heinrich Himmler, head of the SS—were on the run in the final days of the war, attempting to seize power for themselves, conduct a separate surrender, or negotiate for their own lives. Göring was caught by the Allies at the end of the war but, while awaiting trial at Nuremberg, managed to obtain a cyanide capsule and commit suicide. Himmler adopted a disguise as a police officer named Heinrich Hitzinger but was captured by Soviet soldiers on May 20. The soldiers who initially stopped him did not recognize their prisoner and handed him over to the British. When Himmler was sent to a British detention camp at Lüneburg, he informed the captors of his true identity. Perhaps Himmler thought he could negotiate his way out of the predicament but was informed that he would stand trial. On May 23 the loyal Nazi bit down on a cyanide capsule hidden in his mouth. Minutes later he was dead.

Joseph Goebbels, the Nazi propagandist, had committed suicide in Hitler's bunker only hours after his führer. With many of the top Nazis either dead, captured, disloyal, or on the run, in the final days leadership of the failed cause fell to Admiral Karl Dönitz, the head of the Kriegsmarine. It was he who ordered that military operations be ceased; he surrendered only one week after Hitler's death. At the postwar trials, Dönitz was convicted as a war criminal and sentenced to the infamous Spandau Prison. However, he was released in 1956 and lived in relative anonymity in northern Germany. Late in life Dönitz wrote his memoir, *Ten Years and Twenty Days*, where he never apologized for the horrors of the Nazis and boasted of his role in leading the largest successful evacuation in the war, Operation Hannibal, the naval evacuation that moved German refugees across the Baltic and away from the approaching Red Army. The naval commander died on Christmas Eve 1980 at the advanced age of eighty-nine in the town of Aumühle, only minutes away from where the *Cap Arcona* sank.

Johnny R. Baldwin, the British RAF ace who served with great distinction in the Second World War but led the terrible Typhoon attack on the *Cap Arcona* and other ships, survived the war. His military service included combat missions in Egypt and Iraq. During the Korean War, he flew alongside the U.S. Air Force. However, after flying several sorties in a short period of time, Baldwin failed to return from a mission on March 15, 1952. The weather was bad that day, but the details of his demise remain unknown. The greatest Typhoon pilot and one of Britain's heroes of World War II was listed as missing in action.

Whereas many of the Nazis directly involved in the tragic events leading to the *Cap Arcona* disaster avoided imprisonment or punishment, the one who tried to prevent it was found guilty. Captain Heinrich Bertram, the skipper of the *Cap Arcona*, was sentenced to prison at the postwar trials for allowing too many prisoners onto his ship. However, when evidence later surfaced of Bertram's repeated efforts to oppose the forced loading of prisoners on his ship, he was released from prison after serving eighteen months.

Count Folke Bernadotte of Sweden rescued an estimated thirty thousand concentration camp prisoners, earning for him the honored nickname "the prince of peace." When hostilities ended on May 8, 1945, he ordered his white buses to return to Germany, where they continued the task of rescuing survivors. An additional ten thousand individuals who were assigned to "displaced persons" camps (often at the former concentration camps) were liberated by the count.

In honor of his service to humanity during the war, Bernadotte was a very popular choice in 1948 to serve as the mediator representing the new United Nations in the Arab-Israeli conflict. Millions of Jews were killed during the war, and countless hundreds of thousands more were rendered homeless and detained behind barbed wire in displaced-persons camps. Many wanted to relocate to Israel, the historical homeland of their faith. Although the British government was not supportive of a mass migration of Jews to Palestine and Transjordan and the establishment of the modern state of Israel, the American president, Harry Truman, championed the cause. Truman ordered that food, medicine, and clothing be provided for those suffering in the displaced-persons camps, supported displaced Jews traveling to Israel, and was, on May 14, 1948, the first world leader to recognize Israel. Truman also secured lucrative loan guarantees and other forms of assistance for the fledgling state.

However, from 1947 through the first two years of statehood, Jews living in Israel found themselves under attack by their Arab neighbors, culminating in a full-fledged war in 1948 and 1949. Into this fray Bernadotte waded, dispatched by the United Nations to serve as a broker of a peace agreement and a partition between Jews and Palestinians in the region. But things went horribly wrong.

Bernadotte submitted his initial report on June 28, 1948, advocating a homeland for both Jews and Palestinians. He recommended that Palestine and Transjordan be organized as "a Union, comprising two Members, one Arab and one Jewish." The count described the challenge as follows: "In putting forward any proposal for the solution of the Palestine problem, one must bear in mind the aspirations of the Jews, the political difficulties and differences of opinion of the Arab leaders, the strategic interests of Great Britain, the financial commitment of the United States and the Soviet Union, the outcome of the war, and finally the authority and prestige of the United Nations."

One of the organizations in opposition to Bernadotte's two-state solution was Lehi, a conservative Zionist group. Lehi's leaders had split from the Irgun, the paramilitary Zionist organization that had been fighting for a Jewish homeland. Even though the Irgun had been effective in combating Arab attacks and strident in its defense of Jews and Jewish lands, Lehi's leaders believed the Irgun was not doing enough. Lehi's leaders also opposed the British Mandate in Palestine and, shockingly during World War II, even attempted to align with the Nazis. They later began assassinating British police officers and diplomats in Palestine.

On September 17, 1948, while traveling in the Katamon neighborhood in Jerusalem, Bernadotte's motorcade was ambushed by assassins from a splinter group of Lehi known as the "Stern Gang." While Lehi militia members shot out the tires of UN vehicles, one of their members, Yehoshua Cohen, opened the door to Bernadotte's car and, with a Tommy gun, shot him in the chest at close range. The attack also killed Colonel André Serot, a French UN observer who also happened to be in the car. Although Lehi initially denied responsibility for the attack, they later claimed credit for killing Bernadotte.*

Bernadotte's body was taken back to Sweden and given a state burial. In Israel a forest was named in the slain diplomat's honor. In 1995 Shimon Peres, leader of the Labor Party in Israel, spoke at a ceremony to remember Bernadotte's contributions to the Jewish people.

ON MAY 4, 1945, ALLIED and Axis leaders met at Lüneburg Heath in Northwest Germany. Field Marshal Bernard Montgomery, representing the Allied Expeditionary Force, accepted the surrender of Admiral Hans-Georg von Friedeburg of all Nazi forces in northern Germany and Scandinavia. It was only one day after thousands of concentration camp survivors lost their lives on board the *Cap Arcona* and other ships.

On May 7 the British military organized a small memorial service for the victims of the Typhoon attacks. An honor guard fired rifles, while women and children from Neustadt arrived at the coast carrying bouquets of flowers. Those who had survived the tragic incident were helped from the hospital to the memorial service, wearing borrowed and baggy military uniforms, some British, some German. Flowers were placed at the mass grave, and a final salute was fired over the Baltic. That same day at a schoolhouse in Rheims, France, General Alfred Jodl, the chief of operations staff for the Nazi command, and Major Wilhelm Oxenius, a Luftwaffe officer, joined Admiral von Friedeburg to surrender to the Allies. The document marking the unconditional surrender of all German forces was finalized at one minute past midnight on May 8. The long and terrible war was over. On May 23 Admiral von Friedeburg committed suicide by ingesting poison.

---

* The day after Bernadotte's murder, the United Nations condemned the killing as "a cowardly act." Three days after the attack, Israeli prime minister David Ben-Gurion labeled Lehi a terrorist organization.

The end of any war is a time marked by a mixture of relief, mournful reflection, and jubilation. This was especially true at the end of World War II, a long and terrible conflict in which at least fifteen million soldiers and at least forty-five million civilians were killed and countless millions more were wounded and displaced. It is an impossible task to even attempt to estimate the costs in terms of the loss of property and suffering that resulted from this conflict, the bloodiest in history.

Yet because the sinking of the *Cap Arcona* occurred on May 3, 1945, just days after Hitler's death and only four before leaders met to formalize Germany's unconditional surrender, the loss was overshadowed by these other developments. Surrounded by such pivotal, long-awaited events, the tragedy of the *Cap Arcona* was quickly forgotten. Indeed, when the war concluded and the VE Day celebrations began on both sides of the Atlantic, there was little interest among the Allies, some in the Jewish community, or the world's press in investigating or reliving the horrors that occurred at the bitter end of the war. Readers wanted good news. The Germans did not want to draw further attention to their atrocities, nor were the British interested in having their role in this embarrassing tragedy soil the victory celebrations and postwar reconstruction effort. The emphasis after the war was quickly consumed by such formidable tasks as defeating the Japanese in the Pacific, the Nuremberg Trials, the Marshall Plan, and the Cold War.

And so history chose to record the spontaneous celebrations when news of Hitler's suicide and Germany's capitulation were announced rather than the sinking of an ocean liner in the Baltic, a sea that had been the graveyard to so many ships.

TODAY, THE CEMETERY AT the Neustadt promenade and memorials at Lübeck Bay, Neuengamme, and nearby Pelzerhaken where so many bodies washed ashore commemorate the bloody affair of May 3, 1945. The small stone monument that now enshrines the dead does so not with names but with a list of the roughly twenty-five countries of the prisoners who perished on the *Cap Arcona*. In

German and English, the marker reads: "Erected to the memory of the men and women of the Jewish faith who died under the evil oppression of Nazi Germany. Those buried in this place died on and after the day of liberation, May 3, 1945."

In 2010 an event was held at the memorial to mark the sixty-fifth anniversary of the loss. It was attended by eighty-five survivors from Neuengamme and the *Cap Arcona*, representing eleven countries. The anniversary also attracted children, grandchildren, and other family members of survivors. One of them commented, "The onus will then lie on us to tell their stories . . . that a human life should never go unrecognized and their deaths should never be forgotten."

APPENDIX I

WHY DID THE NAZIS LOAD PRISONERS ON THE SHIP?

QUESTIONS REMAIN ABOUT WHETHER the Nazis intended to scuttle the ships in order to deny the Allies the spoils of war and if they intended to simultaneously liquidate evidence of the Holocaust. However, the answer seems straightforward. The Nazis showed repeatedly that they were capable of the most fanatical and inhumane actions imaginable, so it is not hard to imagine them concocting such a scheme. A regime that built concentration camps, murdered millions of innocent people, and forced prisoners on a long death march was certainly more than capable of planning to load ships with prisoners and then order them sunk. Evidence that the Nazis planned to scuttle the ships is apparent in the fact that they were crammed to capacity with prisoners, stripped of emergency equipment and life jackets, inadequately crewed, defenseless even though the Allies were closing in, and denied adequate supplies of food, water, and medicine necessary if they were to set sail. The *Cap Arcona*, like its sister ships, was going nowhere.

The Nazis also ordered that the *Cap Arcona* be filled with fuel, even though its engines were likely incapable of sailing even a short distance. The only reason to haul scarce fuel across the Baltic when it was desperately needed for the defense of Germany would have been to make the *Cap Arcona* more flammable. Nor were any of the other ships in the Baltic that day suited for transporting prisoners— the *Athen* and *Thielbek* were old freighters, not passenger ships, and the *Deutschland* was never registered as a hospital ship—and they all needed repairs.

One of the *Cap Arcona* survivors, Henry Blumenfeld, recalled hearing that he and his fellow prisoners were being taken to the ship and that it would be moved deeper into the bay before being sunk. While crammed into an overcrowded room, he also watched Allied planes dropping leaflets that he believed told Germans to surrender. Rather than surrender, however, some of the SS guards on the ship began firing at the planes.

Some of the crew members on the *Cap Arcona* were told that the prisoners would be taken out to sea and then transferred to Red Cross ships, presumably from Sweden. Yet no Swedish source has ever confirmed such a rumor, even though Count Bernadotte was rescuing prisoners at the dock. At the same time, no written documentation of a specific order to transport or free the prisoners has ever emerged, whereas there were submarines based in Neustadt ready to sink the ships. It must also be remembered that Hitler had ordered that all evidence of the Holocaust be liquidated and that Himmler decreed that no prisoner was to fall into enemy hands.

Harry Cymerint, one of the prisoners who survived the sinking on the *Cap Arcona*, remembered that, when he was being taken out to board the ship, the German guards informed him that he would be taken to Sweden. Yet he noticed that all the SS guards on the *Cap Arcona* "ran away." Cymerint twice cheated death; earlier, he was being marched to Auschwitz for extermination, but the rapid approach of the Allies forced the group of prisoners to which he belonged to be sent instead to the Baltic coast.

As was mentioned earlier, it appears that the orders to sail the ships to the bays and then load thousands of prisoners on them were given by Karl Kaufmann, the provincial governor in Hamburg. However, he and Count Georg-Henning Bassewitz-Behr, the SS chief in Hamburg, may have been acting on orders from Himmler. At the war-crimes tribunal in 1946, Bassewitz-Behr maintained that the prisoners were to be killed "in compliance with Himmler's orders" and presumably by scuttling the ships with them on board. Kaufmann then tried to blame the death march and entire affair on Bassewitz-Behr.

The testimony of Kaufmann and Bassewitz-Behr during the Hamburg war-crimes tribunal is interesting, frustrating, and bizarre. Both Nazis were questioned by Kurt Wessel, the defense lawyer for Max Pauly, the commandant of Neuengamme, against whom the two Nazi officials were called to testify. It reads, in part, as follows:

WESSEL: "Do you know how the evacuation of Neuengamme was executed?"

KAUFMANN: "Yes."

Wessel: "Was it intended to hand out the detainees of the camp to the Allies at first?"

KAUFMANN: "I don't know about that."

WESSEL: "How did it happen?"

Kaufmann: "In the beginning and in the middle of March, Count Bassewitz-Behr came to see me on a daily basis to tell me that there were a high amount of prisoners of war and refugees in his area, due to the advancement of battle lines in the East and West."

WESSEL: "Did you give any orders in this regard?"

KAUFMANN: "I couldn't issue orders."

WESSEL: "Who gave the orders to bring the detainees to the ships?"

KAUFMANN: "I can't say that. What I can say, however, is that Bassewitz-Behr tried to get ships for them."

WESSEL: "Were the ships supposed to stay in the Bay of Lübeck or were they supposed to bring them to Sweden?"

KAUFMANN: "If there would've been any sign that the ships were supposed to stay in the Bay of Lübeck, I wouldn't have helped to obtain them."

WESSEL: "You are trying to say, first of all, that you obtained the ships and secondly that you were suggesting they would be used to bring the detainees to Sweden?"

KAUFMANN: "Yes, certainly."

WESSEL: "Do you know, or did you know about an order of a higher SS officer that detainees of concentration camps weren't supposed to fall into the Allies' hands?"

KAUFMANN: "No."

Kaufmann then continued to attempt to avoid responsibility for the incidents and deaths.

LATER, BASSEWITZ-BEHR was summoned as a witness.

WESSEL: "What orders did you issue?"

BASSEWITZ-BEHR: "It was determined at the conference that it wasn't advisable to stay in the camp in the current situation, due to the lack of security for the inhabitants of Hamburg. Thus, the minister of defense proposed to bring them on the ship."

WESSEL: "Who gave the order to bring these people on the ships?"

BASSEWITZ-BEHR: "I did."

WESSEL: "Was there an order that all detainees of concentration camps weren't supposed to fall into the hands of the Allies under no circumstances?"

BASSEWITZ-BEHR: "Yes."

WESSEL: "Who ordered that?"

BASSEWITZ-BEHR: "It came from Himmler."

WESSEL: "What did this mean?"

BASSEWITZ-BEHR: "It meant that no detainee was supposed to fall into the hands of the enemy."

WESSEL: "If there was no chance of evacuating the detainees, what was supposed to happen with them?"

BASSEWITZ-BEHR: "According to the order, they were supposed to be killed."

Kurt Rickert, an aide to Bassewitz-Behr, also testified at the Hamburg tribunal, saying it was his understanding that the ships were to be sunk by submarines or possibly by the Luftwaffe. Further evidence came from the testimony of Eva Neurath, who was in Neustadt the day of the attack and whose husband survived the ordeal. She stated that a police officer told her the ships were full of convicts and were to be blown up.

Indeed, there is no evidence beyond the claims of a few Nazi leaders after the war (all of whom were interested in saving their own lives) that they ever intended to relocate the prisoners or send them to freedom somewhere in Scandinavia. Rather, it seems such a scenario was based on the rumor that the Nazis were preparing to transport their remaining troops to establish a final redoubt in Norway. But the Nazis seem not to have been serious about the planned evacuation and Scandinavian redoubt. Both Heinrich Himmler and Admiral Karl Dönitz were in the Neustadt area in the final days of the war, but they did not attempt to get to Norway and no mass evacuation ever took place.

On January 31, 1947, Heinrich Bertram, the captain of the *Cap Arcona*, provided a formal statement of the incident in Hamburg. He was reporting to the board of Hamburg–South America Steamship Company, the peacetime owners and operators of the ship. It read:

On February 27, 1945, I took over the command of the 28,000-metric-ton passenger ship *Cap Arcona*, by the order of the Hamburg–South America Line, in agreement with the Navy Department.

From the captain of the *Athen* I learned that the transportation of about twelve thousand prisoners from Lübeck had begun. Most of them were destined to be loaded on the *Cap Arcona*. For me it was a matter of course to refuse to accept the prisoners, since any responsible seaman knows that the risk at sea of taking on human beings without absolute necessity during wartime is dangerous enough, especially such masses.

On Thursday, April 26, the SS officer, Sturmbannführer Gehrig, who was in charge of transport, appeared, accompanied by an advisory merchant marine captain and an executive commando, consisting of soldiers armed with machine guns. Gehrig had brought a written order to my attention that called for me to be shot at once if I further refused to take the prisoners on board.

At this point it became clear to me that even my death would not prevent the boarding of the prisoners, and so I informed the SS officer that I categorically renounced any responsibility for my ship.

Gehrig proceeded to order the transfer of the prisoners from the *Athen* to the *Cap Arcona*. Additional transports arrived from Lübeck, so that on April 28, 1945, I had a total of about 6,500 prisoners on board in spite of the statement of the merchant officer that the ship was capable of holding a limit of 2,500.

On Sunday, the twenty-ninth of April, I drove to Hamburg to request release from the order to scuttle the ship in case the enemy approached. In Hamburg I was told that Count Bernadotte had just declared that he would take all prisoners except German nationals. Swedish ships were already on their way, and I should speedily return to Neustadt.

It is worth mentioning that on Monday, April 30, 1945, the *Athen* took 2,000 German prisoners on board that were not supposed to go to Sweden, so that at the time of the sinking of the *Cap Arcona*, only about 4,500 prisoners were on board.

If there are any doubts as to the Nazis' intentions to scuttle the ships, they come from the fact that the ships were anchored too close to shore. The depth of the bay where the ships were anchored was too shallow for them to sink. Deeper waters would have allowed the ships to sink to the bottom, thus eliminating the evidence of what had happened. There were also Nazi guards and sailors still on the ships when they were attacked. Of course, it is likely the Nazis planned to shuttle the guards and crew members off the ships before sinking them in deeper waters. The Germans knew British forces were closing in on Neustadt in Holstein and Lübeck, but in the chaos of war they may have assumed they had more time before the British attacks commenced.

APPENDIX II

DID THE RAF KNOW ABOUT THE *CAP ARCONA*?

MANY QUESTIONS REMAIN ABOUT why the Royal Air Force attacked the ships in the southern Baltic on May 3, 1945, and whether they knew that the liners and freighters were carrying concentration camp survivors. In June 1945, one month after the attack in Neustadt and the war in Europe ended, at the request of the British Bombing Survey Unit and Coastal Command, specialists were brought together to assess the attacks on German shipping. This included the attacks on the *Cap Arcona*. Rather bureaucratically, the report read: "The objective of the visit was to examine the damage caused to ships by bomb, mine, rocket projectile and cannon, and to obtain as much information as possible from examination and interrogation as to the efficiency of the weapons and tactics employed. Forty-two ships were examined as detailed in the report."

The result of the study was that neither the RAF pilots nor the ground forces that liberated Neustadt and Lübeck knew about the prisoners at the port or on the ships. The lack of knowledge, however, does not mean that the British command had not been alerted as to what was happening in the bays. War-crimes inquiries were conducted on the Nazi atrocities at Neuengamme and found evidence that the British had been warned about the prisoners being sent to the Baltic coast and loaded onto the ships. One of the witnesses was the intelligence officer for the RAF's 83rd Group, which led the strikes on the ships. The officer admitted that, on May 2, they received a message that the ships in the bays had prisoners on board. The report read: "Although there was ample time to warn the pilots of the planes who attacked these ships on the following day, by some oversight the message was never passed on."

One British pilot who flew reconnaissance over the bays later stated that he knew what was happening on the ships. Typhoon squadron leader Laurence Stark was the first to fly over the bays and spot the *Cap Arcona*. He recorded his observations and thoughts. "I attacked a little motor vessel, which was moving out of Lübeck this morning, when I discovered three big ships, which anchored in the bay. They didn't seem in steam, and because the war was coming to an end and there was a shortage of shipping space, I reported my discoveries to Intelligence, so they would be spared from attack. Later, I was surprised that another squadron received the order to attack them."

Another bit of compelling evidence comes from F. G. Parson, who served as adjutant to General Sir Evelyn Barker, commander of the British 8th Corps. He noted the following after the war: "Two Hamburg-America ships . . . were used as prisons for the unfortunate detainees of the concentration camps. The British reconnoitering knew about it and warned everyone, but those ships have been attacked by some RAF Typhoons regardless."

Also, in the year 2000, historian Wilhelm Lange discovered additional evidence of reports by the British military affirming that Red Cross personnel had indeed informed the British command about the prison ships and that the information was passed along the day before the attacks. One of the reports, filed by Major Noel Till in June 1945, read:

The Intelligence Officer with 83 Group RAF has admitted on two occasions; first to Lt. H. F. Ansell of this Team (when it was confirmed by a Wing Commander present), and on a second occasion to the Investigating Officer when he was accompanied by Lt. H. F. Ansell that a message was received on 2 May 1945 that these ships were loaded with KZ (konzentrationslager [concentration camp]) prisoners but that, although there should have been enough time to warn the pilots of the planes who attacked these ships on the following day, by some oversight the message was never passed on.

Another RAF report revealed intelligence that warned of the situation at the bays. "On the ground the roads were packed with transport of all kinds and with thousands of pedestrians. The scene resembled the Falaise Gap of August 1944 but with an important difference. Among the fugitive troops and civilians were many Allied prisoners of war and displaced persons who had broken out of the labor camps."

So too in the days leading up to the attacks were many of the prisoners on the ships and in port rescued by Count Folke Bernadotte and the Swedish Red Cross. There is evidence that the Swedish Red Cross contacted British intelligence about what was happening in the bays. Likewise, an International Red Cross official named P. de Blonay and Major Hans Arnoldsson of the Swedish Red Cross met with the British commanders when they entered the towns of Neustadt and Lübeck on May 2. The men claimed they notified Major-General George P. B. Roberts, commander of the armored divisions, and Brigadier General Derek Mills-Roberts, who led the 1st Special Brigade that liberated the area the day prior to the sinking of the *Cap Arcona*, that prisoners from concentration camps were on board the ships. De Blonay estimated that there were seven to eight thousand prisoners on the ships. Both the Swiss and the Swedish Red Crosses claimed to have encouraged the RAF not to attack these targets. The Dutch Institute of War Documentation also has records showing the government of Sweden warned Britain about the prisoners being on board the ships.

Perhaps, once again, the answer lies in the rumors circulating about a planned final Nazi redoubt in Norway. The RAF pilots had also heard the rumors and were eager to thwart the plan by destroying all German ships capable of transporting forces north across the Baltic. An RAF report from May 2 indicates the concern: "Ships of all kinds were pressed into service by the enemy and large convoys began to assemble in the expansive bays of Lübeck and Kiel. It appears that they were preparing to make a dash to Norway from where perhaps they might continue the struggle."

The RAF 83rd Group echoed these sentiments in their own report, warning, "A considerable amount of shipping was seen moving up the Baltic shores from inland lakes and other movement out into the Baltic. . . . It was believed German ships were assembling to transfer troops to the garrison in Norway so as to continue the war from that country."

David H. G. Ince, one of the RAF pilots who attacked the ships in the bays, stated that it was sometimes difficult to distinguish military from civilian ships because the Germans were "masters of camouflage" in such regards. Ince also noted that he wanted to strike the ships in order to prevent the Nazi from escaping to establish a "northern redoubt." Yet he too admitted, "We were aware that these ships were prison ships," because he had heard reports. The pilot summed up the dilemma as follows: "We were briefed to attack a legitimate target . . . [but] there could have been an element of overkill." He was also concerned about the intelligence provided to the pilots, saying, "The information may have been highly erroneous."

Pierre Clostermann, a pilot from the Free French Army flying with the British that day, offers another perspective, that of a seasoned pilot who had faced death and skilled Nazi flyers for years. Clostermann said that by the time of the attack on the *Cap Arcona*, many pilots had died. Those still flying "risked being roasted alive, trapped under the blazing remains of a Spitfire, or seeing the earth surge up before them when, imprisoned in the narrow metal coffin of a cockpit with its hood jammed, you count the four, three, two, seconds left for you to live." The pilots who struck the *Cap Arcona* that day had been flying three missions a day for months on end and, until the very end, were facing a steady barrage of flak.* Everyone involved in the attacks was eager to see the war over. As Clostermann admitted, "We had a very clear feeling that we were on the last lap."

Even if the RAF pilots were concerned about a Nazi redeployment to Norway, the individuals lining the decks of the old freighters and liners that were still sitting at anchor were wearing the unmistakable clothing of prisoners. Even though the skies were overcast that day, a few survivors reported being able to see the pilots during the attack. One of them, Witold Rygiel, recalled the event: "We were quite excited that this was the end of the war. About 3 p.m., several of the British planes flew low and circled the ships, low enough to see we were prisoners by our striped clothes and we waved white flags. They knew who we were. I could even see the face of one pilot in the cockpit."

The evidence was strong enough to prompt de Blonay and the Red Cross to file a grievance in Geneva against the British:

> In view of the grievance which was found to be held by some of the survivors of this disaster at the bombing of these ships by Allied planes, it is strongly urged that an official inquiry be held by the responsible authorities into this failure to pass vital information, as it is understood that no such inquiry has taken place. It is felt that such an inquiry would go a long way to redress present grievances. The contents of the above paragraph do not in any way affect the responsibility of the German authorities for placing these prisoners on board these ships.

Indeed, even though several of the RAF pilots were quite young and it is very difficult to second-guess decisions made in the heat of battle, it is hard to imagine that the British did not know what was happening along the coast. A photographic reconnaissance unit flew over the port cities and photographed them. The British

---

* Flak is exploded shells that are shot at an enemy aircraft from large guns on the ground. The term comes from the German *Fliegerabwehrkanone*, which translates as "pilot warding-off cannon."

gathered intelligence from spies within Germany and organized resistance groups within German-occupied territories and also intercepted and decoded Nazi communications. Thousands of prisoners had, for weeks, been marched or transported by train or barge to the Baltic, and several ships had congregated there. The May 3 attack was a very large operation—one involving 200 aircraft that sank 23 ships and damaged 115 more. Significant intelligence and planning went into an operation of that size.

The evidence has even prompted a theory that the ships were purposely placed in the bay in order to "lure the British air force into bombing them and killing the prisoners on board." However, it appears that the tragedy was the result of human error and miscommunication.

THE RAF NEVER TOLD THEIR pilots that they mistakenly attacked ships carrying prisoners. It took many years before the surviving pilots learned the truth about what really happened that day. One of the pilots was Don Saunders, who was only twenty-one when he attacked the ships in Neustadt Bay. He did not discover what really happened in 1945 until the year 1981.

Martin Trevor Scott Rumbold was another one of the pilots. Rumbold was only twenty-two years old when he flew his Typhoon to Neustadt Bay but had flown missions in Sicily and participated in the Allied invasion at Normandy. When new rocket technology was developed for the weapons fired from the Typhoon bombers, Rumbold was one of the first pilots to volunteer to be trained to use them. After the attack on May 3, 1945, he recorded in his logbook: "Abortive shipping strike, flying time 1.30 hours, 8 60 lb. rockets fired—landed B 150. . . . Flying time 1.20 hours—Good fire going after attack." It was a full thirty-seven years later that the winner of the Distinguished Flying Cross discovered that he and his squadron had attacked thousands of prisoners.

Bob Kutner was also twenty-one years old during the attack. He was part of the British ground units liberating the beach at Lübeck Bay. Kutner arrived to see hundreds of bodies washed up on the shore, a sight so dramatic that he and his comrades referred to it as the "Nazi Beach of Blood." From the beach he also observed the RAF pilots bombing the *Cap Arcona* and, while completing his sweep of the beach, watched it burning in the bay. When he was eighty-one, Kutner learned that the British National Lottery was planning to help fund a commemoration of the sixtieth anniversary of the end of the war. As a veteran he applied for funds from the lottery and was given 525 pounds to cover the expense of visiting Germany for the anniversary commemoration. As he recalled:

> And I'd always thought that one day maybe I would go back to that beach where we had seen so much. It was such a pretty place, with painted beach huts. I'm sure it was lovely in peacetime but there was so much going on when we were there. We had set up a camp, interviewing German prisoners of war, but it was the bodies washing up on the beach that stuck in my mind. At the time we were curious about what had happened and we were told the British had sunk the ship but not much else. . . . All I had known before was that the British had sunk a ship after being misled by the Germans in some way. But these poor souls were crammed on to the ships until the captains insisted they could take no more. It seems the intention was to sail them out to sea and scuttle them, killing everyone on board.

Ironically, Kutner was Jewish and had been born in Germany, but his family fled to England when Hitler came to power. When the war started, he joined the army as an intelligence officer and was later promoted to the rank of sergeant, where he used his language skills to interrogate German prisoners along the Baltic. He recalled the feelings of "euphoria" felt by his fellow soldiers after the victory on May 3, 1945, and attributed his ignorance of the full details of the tragedy to the fact that it was overshadowed by the end of the fighting just days later.

At the same time, the Allied command actively squelched word of any atrocities committed by the "good guys" at the end of the war. However, the postwar report by the British military noted the responsibility of the British RAF for the attacks at the end of the war, stating, "Primary responsibility for this great loss of life must fall on the British RAF personnel who failed to pass information to the pilots concerning the message they had received concerning the presence of KZ prisoners of war on board the ships."

As of this writing, however, the British government has yet to make a formal apology for the disaster. Rather, mindful of the grave mistakes made, the British government ordered the records from the RAF's flight operations and postwar investigations to be sealed for one hundred years. They did not make the documents available to the survivors of the disaster on the southern Baltic or to the family members of those killed on May 3, 1945.

Fortunately, under their "Thirty Year Rule," the British did declassify documents in 1975, which are now available in the National Archive at Kew in London. The Freedom of Information Act in Britain went into effect in 2005, and, under it, the British Air Historical Branch, Imperial War Museum, Ministry of Defence, and National Archives have stated that there are no records that still remain sealed. Yet as documents have been made available and as evidence has surfaced over the past several years about the disaster, most of the survivors and their children are no longer around to discover the details of what happened. Even so, as history attempts to put together the full story, we will not have the complete story.

Nevertheless, it would be problematic to lay blame for the disaster at the feet of the young RAF pilots. The Allies had paid an enormously high price to win the war, and almost anything was deemed acceptable in the context of total war, especially when compared to the unthinkable atrocities committed by the Nazis and Japanese. Indeed, many of the Nazis at the Baltic coast devoted the last actions of their lives not to repentance and humanity—saving the prisoners or surrendering to the British—but to killing those who survived the sinking of the ships. Ultimate responsibility is with the Nazis.

Baltic Sea area, Germany

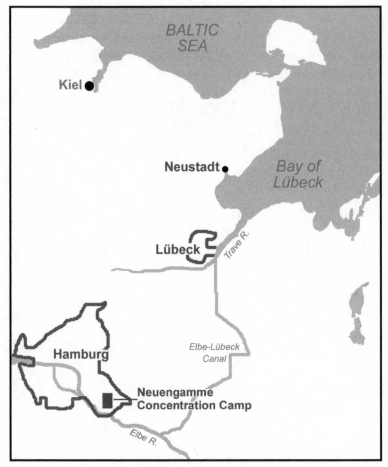

Hamburg-Neustadt area, Germany

NOTES

Introduction: History's Secrets

What we do not know about the past: Former librarian of Congress Daniel J. Boorstin discusses the loss of books and other documents from history in *Hidden History: Exploring Our Past*.

Estimates on the loss of life during the Holocaust and World War II: Several organizations provide documented estimates on the number of victims and survivors of the Holocaust and also offer databases and registries, oral histories, and records. Two in particular are the USC Shoah Foundation at the University of Southern California in Los Angeles (sfi.usc.edu) and the U.S. Holocaust Memorial Museum in Washington, DC, through their Holocaust Survivors and Victims Resource Center (www.ushmm.org).

Sources on the *Cap Arcona* tragedy: See, for example, the documentary films *Der Fall* Cap Arcona and *Nazi* Titanic as well as *The* Cap Arcona *Case Documentary*. The museum at the site of the disaster: the *Cap Arcona* Museum of the Municipality Neustadt in Holstein at Kremper Strabe 32, 23730, Neustadt in Holstein.

A reporter at an anniversary event: Robert J. White-Harvey, "The Friendly Fires of Hell," *Jerusalem Post*, April 18, 2007, www.jpost.com/servlet/satellite?cid=1176 152828674&pagename=jpost%2fjparticle%2fshowfull.

The quote by Benjamin Jacobs: Benjamin Jacobs and Eugene Pool, *The 100-Year Secret: Britain's Hidden World War II Massacre*.

Chapter 1. A Bold Idea

For information on the end of World War I: See "World War I Ended with Treaty of Versailles." Germany's loss of ships: Alison Smale, "Militarism and Humiliation Cast Shadow on Germany," *New York Times*, August 3, 2014, A11.

The *Cap Trafalgar* and the great ocean liners: See Daniel Othfors and Henrik Ljongström, "Ship Histories."

For information on the company's history and ships: See "History of Hamburg-Süd" on the Hamburg-Süd Group website, www.hamburg-sued.com.

For information on Blohm + Voss: See www.blohmvoss.com. The company was listed until 1955 with an ampersand (+ and &). Blohm + Voss and Hamburg-Süd's losses during the war: Matthias Gretrzschel, "Die Kunst, Schiffe Zu Bauen," *Hamburger Abendblatt* (Germany), May 29, 2012. The *Wilhelm Gustloff*: "Greatest Maritime Disasters."

For information on the "Strength Through Joy" program: See "Strength Through Joy" at the History Learning Site, England, www.historylearningsite.co.uk /strength_through_joy.htm.

Blohm + Voss's labor camp: "Neuengamme," Jewish Virtual Library. See also "Neuengamme: 1938–1945 Timeline," U.S. Holocaust Memorial Museum.

CHAPTER 2. THE QUEEN OF THE ATLANTIC

"Out of the waves": See Heinze Schön, *Die* Cap Arcona—*Katastrophe: Eine Dokumentation Nach Augenzeugen—Berichten*, 26; and David Stafford, *Endgame, 1945: The Missing Final Chapter of World War II*, 293. For the specs on the *Cap Arcona*, see Mark Weber, "The 1945 Sinkings of the *Cap Arcona* and the *Thielbek*"; the ship's operator was Hamburg–South America Steamship Company. The launch of the *Cap Arcona* in 1927: See Cap Arcona *Case Documentary*.

Amenities and passengers on the ship: See "The Story Behind the Song: Lili Marlene," *Telegraph* (UK), www.telegraph.co.uk/culture/music/35619461/the-story -behind-the-song-lili-marlene.html. Officers on the ship: Schön, *Die* Cap Arcona, 99, 105. Decline in travel after 1936: Ibid., 107. Information on the ship's itineraries, menus, and recreational amenities can be found in the captain's logbooks, sailing itineraries, and deck plans. This information was obtained from Hamburg-Süd, Hamburg, Germany. Other accounts are available in Hablame de Barcos, hadebarcos .blogspot.com.

CHAPTER 3. AN URGENT MESSAGE

Leisure vacations on the "Strength Through Joy" program: Schön, *Die* Cap Arcona, 108.

The number of ships, tonnage, and total travelers on the *Cap Arcona*: Cap Arcona *Case Documentary*. See also Jim Kalafus, "The *Cap Arcona*: Gallery of a Lovely— Doomed Liner."

The ship's final voyage in 1939: Schön, *Die* Cap Arcona, 116. Only two passengers booked a return trip to Germany: Ibid., 115. Important radio message on August 25, 1939: Ibid., 112. "Special Orders for the Event": *Titanic* Historical Society. Code QWA 7 provided the war order.

"What will happen to my ship": Schön, *Die* Cap Arcona, 115, 118. Wartime issues facing the ship: Peter A. Huchthausen, *Shadow Voyage: The Extraordinary Wartime Escape of the Legendary SS* Bremen. Transfer of the *Cap Arcona* to Coastal Control: Schön, *Die* Cap Arcona, 124; see also Huchthausen, *Shadow Voyage*. Commodore Niejahr dying in 1942 and Captain Seeger voted off ship: Schön, *Die* Cap Arcona, 124.

Cap Arcona captain's logbooks for 1940 and 1941 are held by Hamburg-Süd.

Chapter 4. Rewriting History

The discovery of the Goebbels diary: Louis P. Lochner, ed., *The Goebbels Diaries, 1942–1943*, v, viii. Triple-spacing the diary: Ibid., 3–4.

"Hatred of Jews": See Cap Arcona *Case Documentary*"; see also *Nazi Titanic*.

Goebbels's nickname and calling others vulgar nicknames: Lochner, *Goebbels Diaries*, ix. Goebbels's childhood and psyche: A good psychological study of Goebbels is Roger Manvell and Heinrich Fraenkel, *Dr. Goebbels: His Life and Death*. For general information on Goebbels, see ibid. Goebbels's poor health leading to military rejection and internal anger: Lochner, *Goebbels Diaries*, 3–5. Goebbels's education and literary pursuits: See the Jewish Virtual Library article "Joseph Goebbels." See also Tom Clark, "The Nazi Wrote a Novel: *Michael*," *Los Angeles Times*, October 25, 1987, articles.latimes.com/1987–10–25/books/bk-16.

"Dr. Goebbels was gifted": Adolf Hitler's speeches have been organized by the World Future Fund in Alexandria, VA. They are organized by topic and chronologically by year. See "Some Key Speeches of Adolf Hitler" at www.worldfuturefund. org. Goebbels and Hitler's relationship and Goebbels's quote "As long as he lives": Lochner, *Goebbels Diaries*; see the letter from March 19, 1942, 6. Womanizing and marriage: Magda Goebbels had been married before to an industrialist named Quandt and had a son named Harald Quandt with her first husband. Goebbels's quotes on Hitler: The items were written on June 14, 1926, and November 23, 1925, respectively; see Lochner, *Goebbels Diaries*. Goebbels's self-image and Hitler as well as quote: Ibid., letter written on April 19, 1926.

Goebbels's forging myth of führer: See the letters in Hugh Trevor-Roper, ed., *The Diaries of Joseph Goebbels: Final Entries, 1945*, xv; and Lochner, *Goebbels Diaries*, 23; see also the two diary entries from October 15 and August 12, 1925.

For an overview of the war against the Jews, the Nuremberg Laws, and Kristallnacht, see "Culture in the Third Reich," *Holocaust Encyclopedia*, U.S. Holocaust Memorial Museum, www.ushmm.org/wlc/en/article.php?module1. USM Books in Rapid City, SD, is an excellent source for old photos and documents showing the Nazi Party Days events, with descriptions and facts; see the "Nazi Party Days Photo Book," available at usmbooks.com/reichsparteig.nuremberg. See also "A History of World War Two and Nazi Germany: Joseph Goebbels" at the History of

Nazi Germany blog for a good historical overview of the events, historyofnazi germany.blogspot.com/joseph-goebbels-biography. Gripping personal accounts of Kristallnacht can be found in Uta Gerhardt and Thomas Karlauf, *The Night of Broken Glass: Eyewitness Accounts of Kristallnacht*. See also Cap Arcona *Case Documentary*.

Chapter 5. Hollywood on the Rhine

Private movie screenings quote "saw propaganda as a political weapon": Dr. Steve Luckert of the U.S. Holocaust Memorial Museum is quoted in the documentary *Nazi* Titanic. The quote "For the Nazis, film was" is also from Luckert.

The movie *Der ewige Jude* was directed by Fritz Hippler and produced by Deutsche Filmherstellungs und Verwetungs, Berlin, Germany, 1940. The movie *Jud Süss* was directed by Veit Harlan and produced by Terra Film, Berlin, Germany, 1940. A useful source for the overall Nazi film and propaganda efforts is Felix Moeller, *The Film Minister: Goebbels and the Cinema in the Third Reich*. Dr. Klaus Lankheit of the German Institute for Contemporary History in Munich is quoted in the documentary *Nazi* Titanic.

For information on Goebbels realizing Jews were successful in Hollywood and the quote "Sheer Hell," which is by Dr. Klaus Lankheit of the German Institute for Contemporary History in Munich, see the documentary *Nazi* Titanic. Goebbels's quote "I have received statistics": Lochner, *Goebbels Diary*, 183; the entry was written on April 24, 1942. Goebbels studying American films and quote "The fact of the matter": Ibid., 142; the entry was written on February 27, 1942.

Goebbels changing his approach to filmmaking: Ibid., 220; the entry was written on May 19, 1942. Nazi film efforts are discussed in Mary Williams Walsh, "Hollywood on the Rhine," *Los Angeles Times*, July 16, 1995. Movies made in Babelsberg include the film *The Blue Angel*, directed by Josef von Sternberg and made in 1930 at UFA Studios in Germany. The film *Metropolis* was directed by Fritz Lang in 1927 and released by UFA Studios. The quote is from Walsh, "Hollywood on the Rhine." Goebbels becoming a "patron of the German film": See Lochner, *Goebbels Diary*, 203–204; the entry was written on May 3, 1942. Goebbels's quotes on Italian films: Ibid., 181; the entry was written on April 23, 1942. Goebbels's quotes and views on French films, "be hired by us for German": Ibid., 529; the entries were written on March 5, 1943, and May 15, 1942, respectively.

Riefenstahl's *Triumph of the Will*: The original German film was *Triumph des Willens*, directed by Leni Riefenstahl, produced by Reichspropagandaleitung der NSDAP, Germany, 1935. Quotes from Riefenstahl are in "Leni Riefenstahl," *Holocaust Encyclopedia*, U.S. Holocaust Memorial Museum, www.ushmm.org. Riefenstahl's revisionist account of her film: See Frank P. Tomasulo, "The Mass Psychology of Fascist Cinema: Leni Riefenstahl's *Triumph of the Will*," 104.

The effect of British propaganda films on Goebbels: David Thomson, *The New Biographical Dictionary of Film*, 822. The Lambeth Walk: The Lambeth Walk was from a 1937 musical titled *Me and My Girl*. The name Lambeth comes from a neighborhood and street in London. The original film is available on YouTube at www .youtube.com/watch?v=gYmk3gp3im. Goebbels's plan for an epic propaganda film: Lochner, *Goebbels Diary*, 273; the entry was written on March 4, 1943. See also Moeller, *Film Minister*, 177.

CHAPTER 6. RAISING THE *TITANIC*

The *Titanic* Historical Society provides a comprehensive list of sources and information on the sinking of the infamous ship: See home.earthlink.net/wwwalden /titanic-1943/selpinarticle.html. Films on the *Titanic*: The film *A Night to Remember* was directed by Roy Ward Baker and produced by Rank Organisation, London, England, 1958.

Hitler's interest in ships and the "Strength Through Joy" program: An interesting article is "New Workers' Ship Is Named by Hitler," *New York Times*, March 30, 1938, 8 (1923–current files), search.proquest.com/docview/102655731?accountid=36334. For an overview of Dr. Ley and the Nazis' Strength Through Joy program, see "KdF—Fraft durch Freude: Strength Through Joy," available at Third Reich Books, www.third-reich-books.com/kdf.htm. The theme of the Nazi film on the *Titanic*: "a national disaster" is from Andy Webb, a filmmaker, who is quoted in the documentary *Nazi* Titanic. "expected the *Titanic* movie" is from Friedman Beyer, who is also quoted in *Nazi* Titanic.

Plans for the propaganda film began in 1940 and are discussed in Malte Fieberg, Titanic *(1943): Nazi Germany's Version of the Disaster*, 50.

For an insight history of the Dunkirk evacuation, see Robert Jackson, *Dunkirk: The British Evacuation, 1940*; and Walter Lord, *The Miracle of Dunkirk*. For a helpful history of the Battle of Britain, see Stephen Bungay, *The Most Dangerous Enemy: The Definitive History of the Battle of Britain*. Operation Sea Lion: A website on Operation Sea Lion provides details on Hitler's plans and forces, as well as maps for the possible invasion.

For information on Churchill's "The Few" speech and response to the Battle of Britain, see the Churchill Centre in England at "Their Finest Hour," BBC Archives, June 18, 1940, www.winstonchurchill.org/learn/speeches/122-their-finest-hour. htm. See also "The Few" at the Churchill Centre. Casualties of the battle: Information on the warplanes involved in the battle and casualty counts are in Bungay, *Most Dangerous Enemy*. For information on Britain's preparations and response, see G. Campion, *The Good Fight: The Battle of Britain Propaganda and the Few*. See also Bungay, *Most Dangerous Enemy*.

For a discussion of Goebbels's obsession with British propaganda, see Manvell and Fraenkel, *Dr. Goebbels*. The film *Went the Day Well?* was directed by Alberto Cavalcanti, produced by Michael Balcon at Ealing Studios, England, 1942. The film *In Which We Serve* was directed by Noel Coward and David Lean, produced by Noel Coward at British Lion Films, England, 1942. "Comes to represent": Professor James Chapman of the University of Leicester is quoted in the documentary *Nazi* Titanic. There are some helpful websites that discuss Hollywood's efforts during the war and also list the films and stars. See "Hollywood Goes to War" at the Film Reference site www.filmreference.com/encyclopedia/romar/world-war-ii-hollywood-goes-to-war.html; see also "World War II Movies and Propaganda" at the Hollywood Movie Memories site www.hollywoodmoviememories.com/articles/world-war-ii-movies-propaganda.php. The film *Casablanca* was directed by Michael Curtiz, Warner Brothers Entertainment, Hollywood, 1943.

Chapter 7. The Celebrated Selpin

Selpin's personality: See Brian Hawkins, "The *Titanic*'s Last Victim: In 1942, a German Film Director Put a Uniquely Nazi Take on the Great Ship's Sinking," *National Post* (Canada), April 12, 2012, A14.

The film *Berlin: Die Sinfonie der Grosstadt* was directed by Walter Ruttman and produced by Fox-Europa in Germany, 1928. Selpin's first blockbuster film, *Carl Peters*, was directed by Herbert Selpin and produced by Bavaria Film in Germany, 1941. Goebbels liked Selpin's work, such as in the quote "Selpin was a young," which is from Dr. Rolf Giesen, a film expert, quoted in *Nazi* Titanic. Goebbels's choice of Selpin to direct the propaganda film is also discussed in the film *Nazi* Titanic and in David Gerrie, "See to the Most Important Passengers: The Warped Propaganda Film of *Titanic*," *Daily Mail*, February 25, 2012; and David Gerrie, "Revealed: Warped Nazi Film of *Titanic*," *Main on Sunday* (England), February 26, 2012, 42. A list of Selpin's films and information on each one of them are available at IMDb, www.imdb.com/name/nm0783509/.

Selpin selected Zerlett to rework the script: Jonathan Dawson, "The Film Minister: Goebbels and the Cinema in the Third Reich." A list of Zerlett's movie credits is available at IMDb, www.imdb.com/name/nm/0955076/. About Zerlett: "Walter Zerlett-Olfenius," *Memim Encyclopedia*, memim.com/walter-zerlett-olfenius .html. Descriptions of Zerlett: Friedemann Beyer, *Der Fall Selpin*.

The quotes in the actual film are in *Nazi* Titanic. Analysis of the film: Hawkins, "*Titanic*'s Last Victim," news.nationalpost.com/2012/04/14/brian-hawkins-the -titanics-last-victim/. See also *Nazi* Titanic and Beyer, *Der Fall Selpin*. The German crew member in the film is discussed in Fieberg, Titanic *(1943)*, 51–55.

Selpin's demands: The film's budget is the equivalent of £100 million or $180 million in 2014. See also Dawson, "Film Minister"; and Moeller, *Film Minister*.

Another source on the propaganda film is David Stuart Hull, *Film and the Third Reich: A Study of the German Cinema, 1933–1945.*

CHAPTER 8. A NEW STAR

Problems on the set: See Hawkins, *"Titanic's* Last Victim"; and accounts of Selpin's situation while filming in Beyer, *Der Fall Selpin.* Nazi spies on the movie set: For a lively account of the Gestapo's spies, see the book by former member of the French Resistance Jacques Delarue, *The Gestapo: A History of Horror.* Zerlett accusing Selpin: See *Nazi* Titanic.

CHAPTER 9. THE SINKING OF THE *TITANIC*

The publicity surrounding the film and quotes about it are from Tobis Film-kunst Gmbh, "Press Book No. 5."

John Jacob Astor boasting in the film: Fieberg, Titanic *(1943),* 52. The quotes on the delays in filming and the booklet released by Tobias Studios are also in ibid., 55. "All scum here!": Beyer, *Der Fall Selpin,* 41–42. The film was shot in August and September 1936. Selpin's quote "I know what will happen": Ibid., 132, and was said on July 30, 1942. The quote from the Berlin newspaper is from Fieberg, Titanic *(1943),* 56.

Problems on the set with actors and naval personnel: Ibid., 75–78. The letter from the production manager to Tobis studios: Fritz Maurischat, "Selpin und *Ti-tanic,"* 11. The description of Selpin condemning Zerlett and suspecting his old friend would report him to the Gestapo: Ibid., 18. See also Moeller, *Film Minister.* Hinkle's intervention in Selpin's arrest: Ibid., 169. Maurischat trying to save Selpin: "Walter Zerlett-Olfenius," *Memim Encyclopedia.* Goebbels's quote "I find myself obliged": Moeller, *Film Minister,* 169. The interrogation of Selpin by Goebbels and "Is that correct": Beyer, *Der Fall Selpin,* 137.

Selpin is summoned to Berlin: Hawkins, *"Titanic's* Last Victim." Accounts of Selpin's death: Beyer, *Der Fall Selpin.* "The vast majority of film": *Nazi* Titanic. Selpin's lavish lifestyle and beliefs in the Nazi Party: See Beyer, *Der Fall Selpin.* The discussion of Selpin's extravagant lifestyle while filming the movie is discussed in a letter from SS Sturmbannführer NNSD to Hilleke on October 6, 1942. See file III C3 g PA 14643/36 in SpKa karton 2035 in the State Archives in Munich.

Zerlett's description of Selpin's criticism of German soldiers and sailors is found in the testimony of Walter Zerlett-Olfenius to the Spruchkammer Munich, February 7, 1947. See 2 SpKa Karton 2035 of the State Archives in Munich.

"Near midnight on Friday": *Nazi* Titanic. See also Beyer, *Der Fall Selpin,* 150. Goebbels's letter to Selpin's widow: Hull, *Film and the Third Reich.* See also Beyer, *Der Fall Selpin,* 150. Goebbels ordered Selpin's name removed from the film: Ibid.

The new director, Werner Klinger: Klinger's film credits are available at IMDb, www.imdb.com/name/nm04598011.

Details of Selpin's death and the angry response from the German film industry: Moeller, *Film Minister*, 170. See also Klaus Kreimeier, *Die UFA-Story*, 385; and Joseph Wulf, *Film and Theater in Dritten Reich*, 329. The autopsy by a family doctor and subsequent analysis of Selpin's death (by Dr. Christian Reiter, University of Vienna) come from an interview with Hemma Marlene Prainsack on April 27, 2005. See Prainsack, "How the *Titanic* Sank: Anti-British Propaganda in the National Socialist Movie."

Klinger's film *The Dirty Game* was released in 1965 and produced in France by Oliver A. Unger Productions. It had four directors: Terrence Young, Carlo Lizzani, Christian Jaque, and Werner Klinger. The film *The Terror of Doctor Mabuse* was made in the United States in 1965 by Central Cinema and was made in West Germany in 1962. Klinger's selection by Goebbels and work on the film: *Nazi Titanic*. The use of Selpin's scenes in *A Night to Remember*: This film was directed by Roy Ward Baker, produced by Rank Organisation, London, England, 1958. Discussion on film finally being released around Europe but banned in Germany: See Linda Maria Koldau, *The* Titanic *on Film: Myth versus Truth*, 95–96; and Robert E. Peck, "The Banning of *Titanic*: A Study of British Post-war Film Censorship in Germany."

Chapter 10. The Tide of War Changes

"At this moment": Lochner, *Goebbels Diary*; see June 21, 1941. The Nazi failure in Operation Barbarossa: Details of the campaign are found in Christian Hartmann, *Operation Barbarossa: Nazi Germany's War in the East, 1941–1945*.

Conditions on the German home front: Richard Bessel, *Germany After the First World War*. The situation in Germany by the end of the war: Edward B. Westermann, *Hitler's Police Battalions: Enforcing Racial War in the East*, 191; see also Cathryn Prince, *Death in the Baltic: The World War II Sinking of the* Wilhelm Gustloff, 5. See also Folke Bernadotte, *The Curtain Falls: Last Days of the Third Reich*, 24. The following sources offer a thorough analysis of the situation facing Germany: Jack Morris, *Operation Hannibal*; and Stafford, *Endgame, 1945*. The Siegfried line: See Charles B. MacDonald, *The Siegfried Line Campaign*. Operation Market-Garden: In the two-part Allied operation, "Market" was the air attack, and "Garden" was the ground attack that followed. See www.ww2history.com/key_moments/eastern /operation_bagration. See also "The Battle of the Bulge" at the History Channel website, which contains resources and photos: www.history.com/topics/world -war-ii/battle-of-the-bulge.

Concerns about the Nazis trying to continue the war from Norway: The rumor that the Nazis would make a last redoubt in Norway was spreading among the

Allies. See, for instance, a story in the Sydney newspaper: "Last Nazis May Fight from Norway," *Sydney Morning Herald*, May 4, 1945, 1.

The bombing of Dresden: Debate continues over the legitimacy of this claim and the alleged Allied strategy of terror. See, for example, Hartmut Heyck, "Hold Churchill Accountable for War Excesses," *Ottawa Citizen*, December 1, 2002. Churchill actions are found in his "Memo to His Chiefs of Staff Committee" from March 28, 1945, at the Winston Churchill site www.winstonchurchill.org. Problems in shifting control to fighter command: Max Hastings, *Bomber Command: The Myths and Realities of the Strategic Bombing Offensive, 1939–1945*, 344.

For information on the eastern front collapsing: George Duncan, "Massacres and Atrocities of WWII," www.inet.net.au/rgduncan. Descriptions and quotes on the Soviet atrocities: Christian Graf von Krockow, *Hour of the Women: A Young Mother's Fight to Survive at the Close of World War II*, 83–84. German soldiers' self-inflicted wounds: Michael H. Kater, *Hitler Youth*, 191. For information on Majdanek, there are a website and video from the State Museum of Majdanek in Poland at plus.google.com/108009623560907768178/videos. See also "Majdanek Death Camp," Center for Holocaust and Genocide Studies, University of Minnesota, www.chgs.umn.edu/museum/memorials/majdanek/. The U.S. Holocaust Memorial Museum contains helpful information on Auschwitz: www.ushmm.org /wlc/en/article.php?moduleid=10005189.

Chapter 11. Evacuation

Information on the military factors leading to the evacuation: Mark Weber, "Bergen-Belsen: The Suppressed Story," 806. The "Maginot line": The History Channel has maps, videos, and information on the Maginot line at www.history .com/topics/world-war-ii/maginot-line. Dunkirk: Jackson, *Dunkirk*. See also Lord, *The Miracle of Dunkirk*.

The sailing of the *Wilhelm Gustloff*: Morris, *Operation Hannibal*. See also the article "The Sinking of the M.S. *Wilhelm Gustloff*" on the *Wilhelm Gustloff* website wilhelmgustloff.com/sinking.htm. The murder of Gustloff and Hitler's response: The story was reported in the article "Student Admits to Killing Nazi Thief," *New York Times*, December 10, 1936. Hitler's speech as Gustloff's funeral, "the hate-filled power": Max Domarus, *Hitler: Speeches and Proclamations*, 751. The sinking of the *Gustloff*: See the article "Sinking of the M.S. *Wilhelm Gustloff*."

The sirens and orders for "Everybody off!": Prince, *Death in the Baltic*, 5. Details on the ship being lighted and airing Hitler's speech: Ibid., 116. Details on the sinking of the ship and loss of life: Weber, "Bergen-Belsen"; see also Christopher Dobson, John Miller, and Thomas Payne, *The Cruelest Night: Germany's Dunkirk and the Sinking of the* Wilhelm Gustloff, 67–71, 83, 140–141, and 187–188, discussing the casualty counts. Other helpful sources include Prince, *Death in the*

Baltic, 131–132; and John Ries, "The Little-Known Stories of the *Wilhelm Gustloff*, the *General Steuben* and the *Goya*."

The ship *General von Steuben* is the thirteenth worst maritime disaster in recorded history. Information on Captain Marinesko is found in Prince, *Death in the Baltic*, 102–103. Loss of life on the *Athenia*: See "Greatest Maritime Disasters." Information on Marinesko sinking German ships: There are two informative websites with information on the Soviet submarine fleet of World War II, including the subs in question; see the Russian site "Soviet WW2 Submarines" at wio.ru/fleet /ww2subm.htm and the article "Victories and Losses of Soviet Submarines During WWII," Axis History Forum, forum.axishistory.com/viewtopic.php?t=117516.

Details of the operation to evacuate across the Baltic: Prince, *Death in the Baltic*, 48–49.

Captain Gerdts committing suicide: Wilhelm Lange, Cap Arcona: *Dokumentation*, 61. Official account of Gerdts's death: Ibid., 62. Captain Bertram getting command of the *Cap Arcona*: The event was described in Jacobs and Pool, *100-Year Secret*, 32. See also Schön, *Die* Cap Arcona, 164.

The *Cap Arcona*'s orders to report to Neustadt: See ibid., 128, 158, 162, 166, 168. See also Gunther Schwarberg, *Angriffsziel* Cap Arcona, 39.

Chapter 12. Neuengamme

The construction of Neuengamme: See the article "Neuengamme" at the U.S. Holocaust Memorial Museum website, www.ushmm.org. For a helpful overview of the camps, see Konnilyn Feig, *Hitler's Death Camps*; and Martin Gilbert, *The Holocaust: A History of the Jews in Europe During World War II*. Growth of prisoners at the camp: The information is available through the "Holocaust Education & Archive Research Team" of the Holocaust Research Project, www .holocaustresearchproject.org/othercamps/neuengamme.html. Composition of the prisoner population at the camp: "Neuengamme," U.S. Holocaust Memorial Museum. See also the Jewish Virtual Library article "Neuengamme" and "Holocaust Education & Archive Research Team."

Many of the camp's personnel served at some of the most infamous sites of the Holocaust: Richard Baer was one of the commandants at Auschwitz; Dr. Eduard Wirths functioned as the chief of the medical staff at Auschwitz, Bergen-Belsen, and Dachau concentration camps; several of the camp's SS officers such as Hans Griem, Hans Waldmann, and Freidrich Walter had grisly records while working at Auschwitz; Dr. Bruno Kitt, Dr. Willi Schatz, and Dr. Alfred Trzebinski were physicians at Auschwitz; Dr. Fritz Klein worked as a physician at both Auschwitz and Bergen-Belsen concentration camps; and guards such as Edmund Brauening, Vincenz Schoetti, Willheim Siegmann, and Arnold Strippel also oversaw security at such camps as Auschwitz, Buchenwald, Dachau, and Majdanek. In short,

Neuengamme was staffed by some of the worst of the worst in the camp system. Information on the *kapos*: See Anton Gill, *A Journey Back from Hell: Conversations with Concentration Camp Survivors*, 37.

Work conditions at the camp: See the Jewish Virtual Library article "Neuengamme."

Typhus at the camp: The U.S. Holocaust Museum provides a detailed timeline of Neuengamme from 1938 to 1945, available at www.ushmm.org/wlc/media _cm.php?lang=en&moduleid=10005539&mediaid=2538. A discussion on the children used in the medical tests: See the "Holocaust Education & Archive Research Team." Quotes on the killing of the typhus children: "Neuengamme" at the Jewish Virtual Library. See also Gunther Schwarberg, *The Murders at Bullenhuser Damm: The SS Doctor and the Children*.

Gassing the inmates, "open a couple of harmless": See Shelley Shapiro, ed., *Truth Prevails: Demolishing Holocaust Denial; The End of the Leuchter Report*, 99; the report "The Zyklon B Case: Trial of Bruno Tesch and Two Others," by the United Nations War Crimes Commission, 1947, is available at www.ess.uwe.ac.uk/wcc /zyklonb.htm#dr.%20tesch. For an interesting discussion on the topic, see "The Trial of Wilhelm Bahr and a Gas Chamber at Neuengamme," Axis History Forum, forum.axishistory.com/viewtopic.php?f=6&t=165850&start=0.

CHAPTER 13. A CRUEL RACE

Quotes and information on the plans of Himmler and Goebbels: Peter Padfield, *Himmler: Reichsführer-SS*, 567. For general information on Himmler, see Richard Breitman, *Himmler and the Final Solution: The Architect of Genocide*. Information on Himmler's upbringing: Peter Longerich, *Heinrich Himmler: A Life*. Himmler's rise to power: Padfield, *Himmler: Reichsführer-SS*, 57. See the U.S. Holocaust Memorial Museum files at www.ushmm.org/wlc/en/article.php?moduleID=10007396. Himmler's role in "the Jewish question": See the article "Heinrich Himmler" at the U.S. Holocaust Memorial Museum, www.ushmm.org.

Hitler's decree to liquidate evidence: Lange, Cap Arcona: *Dokumentation*, 107. Himmler's decree "To all Commanders": Ibid., 26. See also Cap Arcona *Case Documentary*. Himmler's ambiguity and plan to save himself: Lange, Cap Arcona: *Dokumentation*, 106–107. Concentration camp commandants meet to decide what to do: See Cap Arcona *Case Documentary*; Lange, Cap Arcona: *Dokumentation*, 25; and Roy Conyers Nesbit, *Failed to Return: Mysteries of the Air, 1939–1945*. Nuremberg Trial of Kaltenbrunner quote "In the middle of April": The operation was given the code name "Cloud A-1"; see the Nizkor Project on the Nuremberg Trials (April 11, 1946) as well as Benjamin Jacobs, "Nizkor Project: A Memoir." Gassing of inmates at Ravensbrück in the final weeks of the war: See Lange, Cap Arcona: *Dokumentation*. Himmler's plan to curry favor with the Allies: Padfield, *Himmler:*

Reichsführer-SS, 582–583; see also Paul Berben, *Dachau, 1933–1945: The Official History*, 184.

Quote on the death marches, "exhaustion, malnutrition, pestilence": Lange, Cap Arcona: *Dokumentation*, 107. Difficulty moving so many prisoners from Neuengamme: See the article "Neuengamme," U.S. Holocaust Memorial Museum. Prisoners from other camps were also heading to Neustadt: Lange, Cap Arcona: *Dokumentation*, 20, 52.

Neustadt was overseen by Gauleiter (governor) Kaufmann: Lange, Cap Arcona: *Dokumentation*, 107. Kaufmann's career: See Helmut Stubbe-da Luz, "Karl Kauffman," 67. The order for the ships to prepare to receive prisoners: Jason Pipes, "The Sinking of the *Cap Arcona*."

Chapter 14. Swedish Savior

Count Bernadotte's work before the war: Bernadotte, *Curtain Falls*, 8–10.

"Nordling had been able": Ibid., 14. Swedish Red Cross agreeing to the plan: Ibid., 18. Count Bernadotte working with Storch: Ibid., 17. "For some time there": Ibid., 17. Goebbels began doubting Hitler: Trevor-Roper, *Diaries of Goebbels*, 231, 232, diary entries written on March 24, 1945, and 214, diary entry written on March 22, 1945.

Bernadotte quote "I had no illusions": Bernadotte, *Curtain Falls*, 21. Meeting with Kaltenbrunner: Ibid., 26. "You are doubtless aware": Ibid., 27. "It seems to me that it": Ibid., 28. "He looked a typical": Ibid., 42. "I don't feel inclined" and "If I were to agree": Ibid., 48. "I told Himmler that": Ibid., 49. "Otherwise it might": Ibid., 59.

Description of Neuengamme as "on par with the Dachau camp": Ibid., 81. Number of prisoners released: Ibid., 83.

"Don't you realize that": Ibid., 87. "Today I can announce" and "The non-Scandinavians": Ibid., 89. "Of course, he was lying": Ibid., 99. The final meeting is discussed in ibid., 101. Release of women at Ravensbrück: Ibid., 102. See also facts from the Swedish Red Cross and government at www.sweden.se/templates/factsheet_4no.198.asp. Truman quote "A German offer of surrender": Information is available at the Harry S Truman Presidential Library and Museum, www.trumanlibrary.org. Total number of prisoners freed: Lange, Cap Arcona: *Dokumentation*, 25. See also the Swedish fact sheet at www.sweden.se/templates/factsheet_4no.198.asp.

Chapter 15. Exodus

Details on the evacuation of Neuengamme: Jacobs and Pool, *100-Year Secret*, 18, 49. The guards shot prisoners during the march: Ibid., 2. Details of the camps evacuated and numbers killed during the evacuation: Major Noel O. Till, "Summary of Events," 10. Rygiel quote "We had absolutely no idea": Cara Brady, "Concentration Camp Mates Reunited," *Morning Star* (Canada), November 11, 2011, 3; see also "Neuengamme," Jewish Virtual Library. The remaining prisoners at Neuengamme were killed: "Neuengamme," U.S. Holocaust Memorial Museum.

Details on the move from Hannover-Stöcken: "Liberation of Hannover-Stocken Concentration Camp, April 1945," oral history, BU 9401 Imperial War Museum, London, www.iwm.org.uk/collections/item/object/205304301. The prisoners were killed in a burning barn: Jacobs and Pool, *100-Year Secret*, 57. The unloading of prisoners at Lübeck, including those who died in the cars: Ibid., 60. See also *Der Fall* Cap Arcona and *History Undercover: The Typhoons' Last Storm*.

"The guards will shoot" and "Before long so many": Jacobs, "Nizkor Project: A Memoir," Chapter 15. Details of the arrival at Buchenwald and Mittelbau-Dora: Ibid. The prisoners' work at Mittelbau-Dora and relocation to the farmhouse: Ibid. "[Master Sergeant], I understand": Ibid.

Details on the arrival of the Red Cross near the end: Ibid., Chapter 16. "The director of the Swedish Red Cross": Ibid., Chapter 17. The quotes in French and conversation between prisoners and the Red Cross: Jacobs and Pool, *100-Year Secret*, 73–74. "Can't you take us?" and "I don't have enough room": Jacobs, "Nizkor Project: A Memoir," Chapter 18. Swedish ships rescuing prisoners: Lange, Cap Arcona: *Dokumentation*, 43–45.

CHAPTER 16. FLOATING CONCENTRATION CAMPS

Description of Neustadt and Lübeck: Lange, Cap Arcona: *Dokumentation*, 52–53. "Some of the seamen": Schwarberg, *Angriffsziel* Cap Arcona, 48. Rumors about the ship's fate: Nesbit, *Failed to Return*, 170.

Germany was running low on spare parts and ships. As such, many military and support ships were rushed back into service. This was the case for the *Cap Arcona* and *Thielbek*. See Cap Arcona *Case Documentary*. "For me it was": Benjamin Jacobs, *The Dentist of Auschwitz*, 192. "There is no way": Schwarberg, *Angriffsziel* Cap Arcona, 49. Kaufmann's meeting with the captains: Lange, Cap Arcona: *Dokumentation*, 64. Details on the ships accepting more prisoners: Jacobs and Pool, *100-Year Secret*, 59. See also Schön, *Die* Cap Arcona, 172. Captain Jacobsen's quote "Starting today": Schwarberg, *Angriffsziel* Cap Arcona, 49.

Kaufmann sending additional Nazis to supervise the loading: Nesbit, *Failed to Return*, 171. Hegener's realization of the situation: Schön, *Die* Cap Arcona, 174. The Nazi Gehrig reporting the problem to Kaufmann: Jacobs and Pool, *100-Year Secret*, 65. "Gehrig had brought": Jacobs, *The Dentist of Auschwitz*, 293. See also Lange, Cap Arcona: *Dokumentation*, 70. The realization that the *Cap Arcona* was now a floating concentration camp: Schwarberg, *Angriffsziel* Cap Arcona, 42, 51.

For general conditions on the ship: Schön, *Die* Cap Arcona, 162; and Lange, Cap Arcona: *Dokumentation*, 39, 75.

Anger among the crew on the *Cap Arcona*: Roy Nesbit, "The *Cap Arcona* Disaster," 289. See also Lange, Cap Arcona: *Dokumentation*, 40; and *Der Fall* Cap Arcona. Pauly's command to Bertram: Schön, *Die* Cap Arcona, 178–179. "I have a wife": Ibid., 180. See also *Der Fall* Cap Arcona. Arrival of SS guards to remove safety devices: Schön, *Die* Cap Arcona, 175. See also Jacobs and Pool, *100-Year Secret*, 68. "They drove us on board": Ibid., 65. See also the series "*Cap Arcona*" in *Stern* magazine; and Stafford, *Endgame, 1945*. Feces, urine, and conditions on the ship: Jacobs, "Nizkor Project: A Memoir," Chapter 17. See also George Martelli, *Agent Extraordinary: The Story of Michel Hollard, DSO, Croix de Guerre*, 273. The SS guards leaving the ship on account of the deplorable conditions: Schön, *Die* Cap Arcona, 177. See also Schwarberg, *Angriffsziel* Cap Arcona, 51; Stafford, *Endgame, 1945*, 294; and "The *Cap Arcona*, the *Thielbek* and the *Athen*." "The dead are removed": Jacobs and Pool, *100-Year Secret*, 67. "My friends" and "Oh God": Martinelli, *Agent Extraordinary*, 274.

The death of Jelis Laskovs aboard the *Cap Arcona* is recorded in the death certificate. Dead bodies being disposed: Schön, *Die* Cap Arcona, 175. See also Jacobs and Pool, *100-Year Secret*, 68. The prisoners organize and attempt to swim ashore: Lange, Cap Arcona: *Dokumentation*, 73–74. Hollard and others are rescued: Martinelli, *Agent Extraordinary*, 276. Captain Bertram meets with Geschonneck: Lange, Cap Arcona: *Dokumentation*, 75, 79.

CHAPTER 17. IN THE BUNKER

Quotes about Hitler and a description of the conditions in Berlin: Trevor-Roper, *Diaries of Goebbels*, 131, entry written on March 13, 1945. See also C. Brian Kelly, *Best Little Stories from World War II: More than 100 True Stories*, 220–223.

Hitler's proclamation "Anyone who proposes": Trevor-Roper, *Diaries of Goebbels*, 346. Goebbels's announcement "The Führer is in Berlin": Stafford, *Endgame, 1945*, 270. Hitler's quote "Ah, if only my generals": Ibid., 270. "He raged like a madman": Angela Lambert, *The Lost Life of Eva Braun*, 446. Göring telegraph to Hitler: David Irving, *Goring: A Biography*, 454. See also Leonard Mosley, *The Reich Marshal: A Biography of Hermann Goering*, 312. Goebbels's quote "Medal-jangling asses": Stafford, *Endgame, 1945*, 212. Hitler's quote "None of this is new": James O'Donnel, *The Bunker*, 131. Göring running for his life: Stafford, *Endgame, 1945*, 213. Hitler's final rage and quote to "Shoot them all!": Hugh Trevor-Roper, *The Last Days of Hitler*, 140–142.

"It's the only chance": Trevor-Roper, *Diaries of Goebbels*, 76, entry written on March 7, 1945. See also 124–134, entry written on March 13, 1945. "Above all I enjoin": Ian Kershaw, *Hitler, 1936–1945: Nemesis*, 810–811. The description of the wedding: Ibid., 80–82.

"For the first time": Lambert, *Lost Life*, 457. "Hold out now": Trevor-Roper, *Diaries of Goebbels*, 349, entry written on April 29, 1945. Goebbels's final letter to his stepson: Ibid., xxxii–xxxiii, entry written on April 17, 1945. Mrs. Goebbels's quote: Ibid., 346–347, entry written on April 28, 1945. Goebbels's quote "We shall go down": Ibid., 347–348, entry written on April 28, 1945.

Proclamation on Hitler's death: Stafford, *Endgame, 1945*, 280. Radio announcement by BBC reporter: "Death of Hitler in the Berlin Chancellery: Radio Announcement Last Night," *Guardian*, May 2, 1945, www.theguardian.com/century/19401949 /story/0,,127801,00.html?redirection=century. The final Nazi resistance: "Neuengamme," Jewish Virtual Library. Goebbels's final propaganda efforts included the film *Kolberg*, directed by Veit Harlan and Wolfgang Liebeneiner, produced by Universum Film AG, Germany, 1945.

CHAPTER 18. OPERATION RAINBOW

Details on the evacuation from Stutthof and quote "They picked out some": Michael Horbach, *Out of the Night*, 255. "The beaches for a good": F. G. Parson, former ADC to General Evelyn Barker, commander of British Army VIII Corps, letter printed in the *Daily Telegraph* (England), March 10, 1983; see also Nesbit, *Failed to Return*, 178. "The prisoners began panicking": *Der Fall* Cap Arcona. "With the first light": Kalafus, "Lovely—Doomed Liner." "The sick and weak": Martin Gilbert, *The Day the War Ended, May 8, 1945: Victory in Europe*, 71.

Conversation from captain to those trying to board the *Cap Arcona*: Jacobs, "Nizkor Project: A Memoir," Chapter 17; Jacobs and Pool, *100-Year Secret*, 37, 51–52. The decisions to move the *Athen* and *Thielbek*: Nesbit, *Failed to Return*, 177. Fuel was loaded onto the *Cap Arcona*: Schön, *Die* Cap Arcona, 207.

Details on Operation Rainbow: Schön, *Die* Cap Arcona, 205. The scuttling of ships at Scapa Flow: See "Scuttling of Scapa Flow," First World War, www.firstworldwar .com/features/scapaflow_scuttling.htm; see also "History: The Fate of the Ships Interned in Scapa Flow in 1918," Historic Scotland, www.scapamap.org/history.php. The scuttling of U-boats in early May: Lange, Cap Arcona: *Dokumentation*, 76.

Accounts of whether the ships in the bay would be sunk: Hal Vaughn, *Doctor to the Resistance: The Heroic True Story of an American Surgeon and His Family in Occupied Paris*, 154–156. For a discussion about Captain Bertram's response: Lange, Cap Arcona: *Dokumentation*, 107. Last-ditch efforts by Hamburg-Süd and Bertram to save the *Cap Arcona*: Ibid., 73. See also Schön, *Die* Cap Arcona, 194.

Surrender negotiations in Neustadt: Ian Traynor, "We Won't Ever Fight Again, Charles Assures Germans," *Guardian* (England), May 4, 1995, 10, search.proquest

.com/docview/294842946?accountid=36634. See also Lange, Cap Arcona: *Doku-mentation*, 22, 94. Major Wolz's surrender: Ibid., 95. For an account of the attack and battles at Neustadt and Baltic, see Chris Thomas, *Typhoon and Tempest Aces of World War 2*; Stafford, *Endgame, 1945*, 296; and Lange, Cap Arcona: *Dokumenta-tion*, 78–79. The prisoners learned of the surrender: Schön, *Die* Cap Arcona, 256. Captain Bertram sends a launch into town: Lange, Cap Arcona: *Dokumentation*, 80, 81, 90. Kaufmann allegedly issues order to sink the ships: Ibid., 78–80. See also Schön, *Die* Cap Arcona, 193.

CHAPTER 19. DEATH FROM ABOVE

Orders to "destroy the concentration": "Operations Records Books of Squad-rons," AIR 25/698, "83 Group Operations Record Book, 4/43–2/46" and 83 Group Operation Order 72, May 3, 1945. For details on the orders, see also Schwarberg, *Angriffsziel* Cap Arcona, 23; and White-Harvey, "Friendly Fires of Hell." "Nazi leaders wanted": Schwarberg, *Angriffsziel* Cap Arcona, 13.

The Nazi plan to flee to Norway and presence of ships in the Baltic: Schön, *Die* Cap Arcona, 210. "Aerial images show": Schwarberg, *Angriffsziel* Cap Arcona, 14. "We were on 'readiness'": Nesbit, *Failed to Return*, 170–178. Count Bernadotte notified the British command: Schwarberg, *Angriffsziel* Cap Arcona, 16. Informa-tion on whether the warnings about prisoners on the ships were transmitted are found in the six-part series *"Cap Arcona"* in *Stern* magazine and at the Cap Ar-cona Museum in Neustadt, Germany, in a pamphlet called Cap Arcona: *Doku-mentation*, written by Wilhelm Lange.

For information on the attack on Rommel, see Pierre Clostermann, *The Big Show*, 194–195.

Weaponry carried by the planes and their specs: Roy Conyers Nesbit, *Coastal Com-mand in Action, 1939–1945*, 149. Information on the Typhoons' battle history: Thomas, *Typhoon and Tempest Aces*, 22. A discussion of the planes and squadrons: Nesbit, *Coastal Command in Action*. The description of the Typhoons and quotes "overheated very quickly" and "The amount of noise": Clostermann, *The Big Show*, 202–205.

The first squadrons to attack: Nesbit, *Failed to Return*, 172–173. Limited air and ground defenses: Lange, Cap Arcona: *Dokumentation*, 108. Long quote and descrip-tion by Saunders: Schwarberg, *Angriffsziel* Cap Arcona, 17, 28. "We flew over": *History Undercover*; see also the six-part series *"Cap Arcona"* in *Stern* magazine. Captain Bertram's efforts to mark his ship: Nesbit, *Failed to Return*, 171; see also Lange, Cap Arcona: *Dokumentation*, 108. Deutschland being hit: Nesbit, *Failed to Return*, 174. Observations of the attack by those at the port: See Cap Arcona *Case Documentary*. Captain Bertram's quote "They must know that" and effort to raise a flag: Schön, *Die* Cap Arcona, 250, 214, 219.

The descriptions of "We couldn't possibly keep it up," "in every bight, in every estuary," and others are from Clostermann, *The Big Show*, 260, 273, 296. The quotes about the damage to the planes are on 296.

Coordinates of the *Cap Arcona*: See Cap Arcona *Case Documentary*. Information on Johnny Baldwin: Thomas, *Typhoon and Tempest Aces*, 75. The attacks on the *Thielbek*: Jacobs and Pool, *100-Year Secret*, 98–99. See also Weber, "Bergen-Belsen." Casualty count on the *Thielbek*: Lange, Cap Arcona: *Dokumentation*, 87–88. "People rushed out of": See the series "*Cap Arcona*" in *Stern* magazine. Mehringer's story is also told in the *Stern* series. The result of the attacks: Lange, Cap Arcona: *Dokumentation*, 88–89.

Chapter 20. Waves

Attack on the *Deutschland*: Jacobs and Pool, *100-Year Secret*, 98–99. Another attack at 6:15: Schön, *Die* Cap Arcona, 209. The eyewitness account of Attenborough is in reel 3 of his oral history.

Descriptions of the ship sinking and the prisoners' plight as well as the quote "At the stairs": Schwarberg, *Angriffsziel* Cap Arcona, 98. Jakubowicz's ordeal: Jacobs, "Nizkor Project: A Memoir," Chapter 17. Suchowiak's ordeal: Stafford, *Endgame, 1945*, 298–299.

Henry Blawnick's eyewitness account is in his oral history interview. The power of 20mm cannons: There are videos on YouTube that demonstrate their power, both contemporary and World War II vintage. They are available at www .youtube.com/watch?v=rnkkfl6-w1o and www.youtube.com/watch?v=8xeem-5jtorm. "We used our cannon": See *History Undercover*. Death of Gehrig: Jacobs and Pool, *100-Year Secret*, 117.

Jukubowicz's ordeal in the water and in town: Ibid., 117. "We can't take anyone" and "It's Berek, the dentist": Jacobs, "Nizkor Project: A Memoir," Chapter 18. Prisoners being taken to a bakery: Ibid., Chapter 19. "I survived Auschwitz": Jacobs and Pool, *100-Year Secret*, 88.

German sailors rescued only soldiers: Ibid., 121. Suchowiak quote "It was clear": "*Cap Arcona*" in the *Stern* magazine series. See also Stafford, *Endgame, 1945*, 299. "I covered myself": Ibid. "You were actually" and final quotes from Rygiel: Cara Brady, "Remembering a Wartime Tragedy," *Morning Star* (Canada), November 11, 2011.

Chapter 21. Final Act

Details on the British arriving at the coast: See Cap Arcona *Case Documentary*. Description and quote about the fighting "In the harbor several": Documents are in the RAF Air Historical Branch collection, *"Cap Arcona"* file. "We discovered that the": "Summary of Events," Report on Investigations: WO 309/501.

The quotes from Colonel H. G. Sheen and the British report are in file GBI/01/CS/000.5–2 of the June 7, 1945, report to the Supreme Headquarters Allied Expeditionary Force, now housed in the Imperial War Museum, London. The quote "But the place will be memorable" is also from Colonel Sheen's report of June 7, 1945.

Details on the attacks on the barges and at the beach: Jacobs and Pool, *100-Year Secret*, 127–128. "The Germans who saw": See *"Cap Arcona,"* the *Stern* magazine series. Suchowiak nearly being shot: Ibid. "After a long time": Ibid. "When we reached": Derek Mills-Roberts, *Clash by Night: A Commando Chronicle*, 203. "We found a hastily": "Summary of Events," Report on Investigations, CO 5 Reece Regiment, WC/B/16 no 2, WCIT. Mills-Roberts clubbing Milch: Jacobs and Pool, *100-Year Secret*, 156. "When I arrived": "Summary of Events," Report on Investigations: WO 309/851.

"Into the square": Jacobs, "Nizkor Project: A Memoir," Chapter 19. British forces providing food and clothing: The information is from a tank commando's note (whose name is not known) in the 23rd Hussars of the British 11th Armoured Division, located in the RAF Air Historical Branch, *"Cap Arcona"* file. German soldiers ordered to dig graves: Stafford, *Endgame, 1945*, 306. "Under instructions not to": Ibid.

The British finally sent boats out to the *Cap Arcona*: Schön, *Die Cap Arcona*, 229. German military did not rescue prisoners from the water: Schwarberg, *Angriffsziel Cap Arcona*, 102. See also Jacobs and Pool, *100-Year Secret*, 123. Wolff rescued prisoners using a tugboat: Lange, *Cap Arcona: Dokumentation*, 93. The ship rolled over, partially exposed in the bay: Kalafus, "Lovely—Doomed Liner." "We were aft" and "I made myself": *"Cap* Arcona," *Stern* magazine series. Additional details on the devastation in the bay: Jacobs, *100-Year Secret*, 148; and Lange, Cap Arcona: *Dokumentation*, 108.

The *Athen*'s prisoners and demise: See Cap Arcona *Case Documentary*. "All aircraft carrying bombs": See "Second World War Combat Reports/Air Ministry Combat Reports," AIR 25/707, the "83 Group Intelligence Summary, 3/45–5/45," May 3 1945. See also Stafford, *Endgame, 1945*, 296. Total sorties flown by the RAF: Lange, Cap Arcona: *Dokumentation*, 86. "In what can only": See "Intelligence Summary," investigation report, No. 266, Second Tactical Air Force, AIR 24/1498, May 3, 1945.

CHAPTER 22. AFTERMATH

Details of the ship exploding: Schön, *Die* Cap Arcona, 264. The ships sinking: White-Harvey, "Friendly Fires of Hell." The last skeleton: Stafford, *Endgame, 1945*, 295. See also *"Cap Arcona, the Thielbek* and the *Athen"*; the 20,000-ton ship sank in minutes at 1830 hours. Divers and dismantling of ships: *Taucher unter Toten*. Divers salvage the remains of victims and their personal effects from the wreckage of the *Cap Arcona* and *Thielbek*: www.ushmm.org/online/film/search/result .php?filmvideo_startdoc=1&filmvideo.

Prisoners dying on the march and at port: Schön, *Die* Cap Arcona, 298. Estimates of casualties: Ibid., 8. The few individuals who survived the tragedy also offer estimates of the death toll on the *Cap Arcona*. Their numbers tend to vary from 4,150 to more than 6,000, with most suggesting that about 5,000 people were lost on the *Cap Arcona* on May 3 alone. Wilhelm Lange (a researcher who studied the incident), Paul Weissman (one of the *Cap Arcona*'s survivors who had been in Neuengamme), and the British units that liberated the town all reported that at least 8,000 people were lost that day. One survivor, Jean Langlet, put the number at around 9,000. However, if one includes the three ships sunk, the attacks at the port and throughout the town, the roughly 1,600 additional prisoners stuck on barges around the harbor, and those who died during the days leading up to May 3 when prisoners at the port and onboard the ships were denied food and water, the count may have been as high as 12,000 to 13,000. Some estimates are given by Lange, Cap Arcona: *Dokumentation*, 96,106; Schön, *Die* Cap Arcona, 289; and Jacobs, "Nizkor Project: A Memoir," Chapter 18. See also "SS *Cap Arcona*," shelf3d. com/i/SS%20Cap%20Arcona, for details on the losses. Bodies washing up: Till, "Summary of Events," 10. See also Schön, *Die* Cap Arcona, 207.

For the casualties at the camp: See "Neuengamme," U.S. Holocaust Memorial Museum. Counts on the prisoners at Neuengamme are also at the Jewish Virtual Library, which estimates similar numbers. Max Pauly's fate: Nesbit, *Failed to Return*, 178. Memorials and exhibits at Hamburg: Klaus Witzeling, "Aus dem Fotoalbum des Unmenschen Witzeling," *Hamburger Abendblatt* (Germany), November 16, 2010.

The survivors' registry, document file EE3486, "Two Lists of Former Neuengamme Inmates Killed in Bombing of Ships *Cap Arcona* and *Thielbek* in the Bay of Lübeck." The names are also listed in "Neuengamme Victims from the Bombing of the *Cap Arcona* and the *Thielbek*." Jakubowicz's story: Jacobs and Pool, *100-Year Secret*. Pivnik's story: Sam Pivnik, *Survivor: Auschwitz, the Death March and My Fight for Freedom*. The Akos story is in the Francis Akos oral history. Rygiel's story and quotes: Brady, "Remembering a Wartime Tragedy." Gerschonneck story: Gaston Kirsche, "Local Shortcuts," *Die Tageszeitung* (Berlin), March 28, 2013, 25; "Deaths Elsewhere," *Sarasota (FL) Herald Tribune*, March 13, 2008, BV12; "German Actor Erwin Geschonneck, 101," *Newsday*, March 13, 2008, A56.

Karl Kaufmann's fate: "Karl Kaufmann biography," FAMPeople, www.fam people.com/cat-karl-kaufmann. Zerlett's fate: Hawkins, "*Titanic*'s Last Victim."

Count Bernadotte's service with the UN and demise: "The Prince of Peace! Count Folke Bernadotte of Wisborg." Truman's support for Israel: Michael J.

Devine, Robert P. Watson, and Robert J. Wolz, eds., *Israel and the Legacy of Harry S. Truman*. Details on Bernadotte's work with displaced-persons camps: Nesbit, *Failed to Return*, 179. The Stern Gang assassination: "Yehoshua Cohen Dies; Linked to '48 Killings," *New York Times*, August 12, 1986, www.nytimes.com/1986/08/12 /obituaries/yehoshua-cohen-dies-linked-to-48-killings.html. Service and commemoration at the end of the war: "Konflikt ums Gedenken," *Die Tageszeitung* (Berlin), November 12, 2008, 24. A good source for the state of affairs at the end of World War II is Gilbert, *Day the War Ended*. Two additional helpful sources on the casualty counts and other facts are the National World War II Memorial in Washington, DC, www.wwiimemorial.com; and "World War II" on the History Channel, www.history.com/topics/world-war-ii.

The wording on the memorial is at the *Cap Arcona* Memorial in Neustadt. "The onus will": Mart-Jan Knoche, "Begegnung am Tatort," *Die Tageszeitung* (Berlin), May 8, 2010; Maja Abu Saman, "65 Jahre Danach—KZ überlebende Kommen Noch Einmal Zurück Nach Neuengamme," *Welt Kompakt* (Berlin), April 28, 2010, 1, 42; Maximillan Probst, "Ich Lebe," *Die Tageszeitung* (Berlin), May 13, 2009, 23.

Appendix I

The ships were not prepared to sail and needed repairs: Lange, Cap Arcona: *Dokumentation*, 102. Written documentation of the decisions at the Baltic: See RAF Operations Record Book, Second Tactical Air Force, AIR 41/68, 243. RAF reports and evidence from the war-crimes tribunals: Michael Armitage, *The Royal Air Force*, 149. The eyewitness account by Henry Blumenfeld is in his oral history interview. The eyewitness account by Harry Cymerint is in his oral history interview. Testimony by Kaufmann and Bassewitz-Behr: Schwarberg, *Angriffsziel* Cap Arcona, 41. Report by Eva Neurath: See cap-arcona.com.

Himmler and Dönitz did not try to escape to Norway, but theories abound: Stafford, *Endgame, 1945*, 295. For the conspiracy theories, see the Axis History Forum at forum.axishistory.com/viewtopic.php?f=38&t=169052. Captain Bertram's official report: Jacobs, "Nizkor Project: A Memoir," Chapter 18.

Appendix II

"The objective of the visit": Nesbit, *Failed to Return*, 173–174. "Although there was ample": Stafford, *Endgame, 1945*, 302. "I attacked a little": Schwarberg, *Angriffsziel* Cap Arcona, 23.

For information on what the RAF pilots knew, see Cap Arcona *Case Documentary*. "Two Hamburg-America ships": Schwarberg, *Angriffsziel* Cap Arcona, 23. "The Intelligence Officer": Till, "Summary of Events." "On the ground": See the report *The RAF in the Bombing Offensive Against Germany*, vol. 6, no. 45, AIR 41/56,

p. 243. See also Lange, Cap Arcona: *Dokumentation*, 103, for reports by the British pilots. The Swedish Red Cross and Dutch Institute of War warnings: Stafford, *Endgame, 1945*, 297. See also the International Tracing Service in Bad Arolsen, which lists Holocaust survivors; and Hans Arnoldsson, *Natt Och Dimma*, 156–165, for war reports. "Ships of all kinds": Stafford, *Endgame, 1945*, 295. "A considerable amount": Schwarberg, *Angriffsziel* Cap Arcona, 40–41. The quotes from David Ince are from his oral history interview. "We were quite": Brady, "Concentration Camp Mates Reunited." "In view of the grievance": de Blonay's grievance was cited in Till, "Summary of Events," 4–5, 15–16.

The British operation in the Baltic: Nesbit, *Failed to Return*, 171–172. See also "*Cap Arcona*," *Stern* magazine series. Stafford, *Endgame, 1945*, 295, also weighs in on the reason for the attack. For information on the conspiracy theories behind the attack, see the Axis History Forum at forum.axishistory.com/viewtopic.php?f=38 &t=169052. The description of air combat including the quote about "risked being roasted alive" is from Clostermann, *The Big Show*, 221. The pilots' describing that "We had a very clear feeling" is on 296.

Don Saunders's discovery: Schwarberg, *Angriffsziel* Cap Arcona, 11. Rumbold's logbook: Ibid., 7–8. "And I'd always": Lesley Roberts, "Let Us Remember: I Was a Witness on Nazi's Beach of Blood but Did Not Know; Veteran Tells How 10,000 Were Killed by Mistake," *Sunday Mail* (England), November 6, 2005, search.proquest .com/docview/328509675?account=36334. The Allied command suppressed word of atrocities: See Stafford, *Endgame, 1945*. "Primary responsibility": Till, "Summary of Events." The "Thirty Year Rule": Nesbit, *Failed to Return*, 174.

BIBLIOGRAPHY

PRIMARY SOURCES

Archives

A. H., Major, DAAG. "Prison Ship *Athen*—Confidential." Main Headquarters, 21st Army Group, June 1945. File Gp/3796/2/A(PS4). Imperial War Museum, London.

Akos, Francis. Papers. U.S. Holocaust Memorial Museum. Permanent collection, 1 folder, accession no. 1990.174, 1944–1951. collections.ushmm.org/search /catalog/irn513251.

"*Cap Arcona*: List of Passengers of the Turbine and Express Steamer." July 4, 1935, voyage. Hamburg-Süd, Germany.

"*Cap Arcona*: Roundtrip to Rio de Janeiro." Cruise information, July 4, 1935, voyage. Hamburg-Süd, Germany.

Cap Arcona Museum of the Municipality Neustadt in Holstein at Kremper Strabe 32, 23730. Neustadt in Holstein. www.stadt-neustadt.de/freizeit_kultur /museum_cap_carcona/.

Captain's logs from the *Cap Arcona*. Each voyage of the ship was recorded. For example, "Last Voyage of Commodore Rolin (46th Trip of the Ship), September 1, 1933–October 6, 1933" and "First Voyage of Captain Niejahr (47th Trip of the Ship), October 20, 1933–November 24, 1933." Documents were accessed through the Office of Corporate Communication, Hamburg-Süd, Hamburg, Germany.

Francuz, Henryk, and Dorota Francuz. Collection. U.S. Holocaust Memorial Museum. Accession no. 2006.387.1, 1939–1945.

Laskovs, Jelis. Death certificate. Reich Registry Office. *Cap Arcona*, April 27, 1945. File KL 38 L43 500 000.

Meier, Christian Heinrich. "Concerning the Drowning of the Neuengamme Camp Inmates Who Were on the Deck of the *Cap Arcona*." Simon Wiesenthal Collection, Center for Jewish Documentation at Yad Vashem, Jerusalem, Israel. See record group M.9; file no. 511.

"Operations Records Books of Squadrons." Public Records Office, Royal Air Force. AIR25/698, "83 Group Operations Record Book, 4/43–2/46" and 83 Group

Operation Order 72, May 3, 1945; AIR27/1169, "197 Squadron Operations Record Book, 10/40–12/46"; AIR27/1170, "198 Squadron Operations Record Book, 12/42–9/45"; AIR27/1548, "263 Squadron Operations."

"Record Book, 10/40–12/46." British National Archives. www.nationalarchives.gov .uk/records/combat-reports-ww2.htm.

"Second World War Combat Reports/Air Ministry Combat Reports." Public Records Office, Royal Air Force. AIR15/474, "Survey of Damaged Shipping in North Germany, 1944–1945"; AIR25/707, "83 Group Intelligence Summary, 3/45–5/45." British National Archives. www.nationalarchives.gov.uk /records/combat-reports-ww2.htm.

Sheen, Colonel H. G. "*Athen* Prison Ship—Confidential." Report of the Forward Headquarters, Office of the Assistant Chief of Staff, Supreme Headquarters Allied Expeditionary Force, June 2, 1945. File GBI/01/CS/000.5–2. Imperial War Museum, London.

"Summary of Events." Report on Investigations: WO 309/501. Col. H. G. Green report, June 2, 1945.

"Summary of Events." Report on Investigations: WO 309/850. In *Operations Record Book*, Second Tactical Air Force, Royal Air Force, May 1–3, 1945. www.raf. mod.uk./history/.

Thousands of Concentration Camp Inmates Met Their Death at Lübeck Bay. Internationaler Suchdienst Arolsen (German archive of materials from the *Cap Arcona* disaster and Neuengamme concentration camp). www.its-arolsen.org/en /research_and_education/historical_background/anniversaries.

Till, Major Noel O. "Summary of Events." War Crimes Witnesses: WO 309/1592 and No. 2 War Crimes Investigation Team, British Army of the Rhine. In *Operations Record Book*, Second Tactical Air Force, Royal Air Force, September 1945. www.raf.mod.uk./history/.

Tobis Filmkunst GmbH. "Press Book No. 5." 1942.

"Two Lists of Former Neuengamme Inmates Killed in Bombing of Ships *Cap Arcona* and *Thielbek* in the Bay of Lübeck." Holocaust Survivors and Victims Resource Center and Database, U.S. Holocaust Memorial Museum, 2001. www .ushmm.org.

"World War I Ended with Treaty of Versailles." America's Story Project, Library of Congress, Washington, DC. www.americaslibrary.gov.

Oral History Interviews

Akos, Francis. Interviewed June 18, 1990, by Linda G. Kuzmack. Accession no. 1990.412.1, RG-50.030*0006. U.S. Holocaust Memorial Museum Collection. collections.ushmm.org/search/catalog/irn504524.

———. USC Shoah Foundation (sfi.usc.edu/). www.youtube.com/watch?v=yyue ceq8kss&list=uum9gtcr9vsm-tsaol9ut5w.

Attenborough, John. Interviewed September 26, 1984, in London. Catalog no. 8303, Imperial War Museum, London. www.iwm.org.uk/collections/item /object/80008101.

Bawnik, Henry. Interviewed in New York. Code 21244 (segment 24). USC Shoah Foundation. vhaonline.usc.edu.

Blumenfeld, Henry. Interviewed in New York. Code 14520 (segment 150). USC Shoah Foundation. vhaonline.usc.edu.

Cymerint, Harry. Interviewed in Michigan. Code 9972 (segment 41). USC Shoah Foundation. vhaonline.usc.edu.

De Strauss, Margot Aberle. Interviewed in Capital Federal, Argentina. Code 36029 (segment 43). USC Shoah Foundation. vhaonline.usc.edu.

Gelb, Jack. Interviewed April 25, 1996, by Sandra Bendayanwith. Collection no. 1999.A.0122, RG-50.477*0685. Bay Area Holocaust Oral History Project, Tauber Holocaust Library of the Jewish Family and Children's Service, San Francisco.

Hirth, Lucien. "My Cross to Bear." Interviewed in Reims, France, February 26, 2005, by the Lycee Clemenceau School. cndp.fr.

Ince, David Henry Gason. Interviewed November 20, 1984, in London. Catalog no. 8651. Imperial War Museum, London. www.iwm.org.uk/collections/items /object/80008447.

Jacobs, Benjamin. "Nizkor Project: A Memoir." 1997. Chapter 15, "The Death March"; Chapter 16, "Dora-Mittelbau"; Chapter 17, "Disaster on the Baltic Sea"; Chapter 18, "Inferno"; and Chapter 19, "Where Do We Go?" www .nizkor.org/features/dentist/.

MacAuslan, John. Interviewed June 18, 1984, in London. Catalog no. 8225. Imperial War Museum, London. www.iwm.org.uk/collections/item/object /80008025.

McQuillin, Terence Charles. Interviewed June 28, 1995, in London. Catalog no. 15540. Imperial War Museum, London. www.iwm.org.uk/collections/item /object/80015074.

Pivnik, Samuel. Interviewed August 15, 1985, in London. Catalog no. 8952. Imperial War Museum, London. www.iwm.org.uk/collections/item/object/800 08744.

SECONDARY SOURCES

Note: Books in German were translated by Kierst Lehman, Selina Keipert, and Stefan Wolf. Articles written in German were translated online through "on-the-fly" machine translation.

Abbott, Kate. "The *Titanic* Discovery." *Time*, September 1, 2010. content.time.com /time/nation/article/0,8599,2015271,00.html.

Armitage, Michael. *The Royal Air Force*. London: Cassell, 1993.

Arnoldsson, Hans. *Natt Och Dimma* (in Swedish). Stockholm: Bonnier, 1945.

Berben, Paul. *Dachau, 1933–1945: The Official History*. London: Norfolk Press, 1975.

Bernadotte, Folke. *The Curtain Falls: Last Days of the Third Reich*. New York: Alfred A. Knopf, 1945.

Bessel, Richard. *Germany After the First World War*. New York: Oxford University Press, 1993.

Beyer, Friedemann. *Der Fall Selpin*. Germany: Verlag/Collection Rolf Heyne, 2011.

Boorstin, Daniel J. *Hidden History: Exploring Our Past*. New York: Vantage Books, 1989.

Breitman, Richard. *Himmler and the Final Solution: The Architect of Genocide*. London: Pimlico, 2004.

Bungay, Stephen. *The Most Dangerous Enemy: The Definitive History of the Battle of Britain*. London: Aurum Press, 2010.

Campion, G. *The Good Fight: The Battle of Britain Propaganda and the Few*. Basingstoke, England: Palgrave Macmillan, 2010.

"Cap Arcona." *Stern* 10–15 (March 3–7, 1983), a six-part series that interviewed the RAF pilots.

"The *Cap Arcona*, the *Thielbek* and the *Athen*." www1.uni-hamburg.de/rz3a035 //arcona.html.

"*Cap Arcona*: When 7K Jews Died in Friendly Fire." *J Space*. www.jspace.com /news/articles/the-cap-arcona-when-7k-jews-died-in-friendly-fire/13881.

The Cap Arcona *Case Documentary*. Directed by Günter Klaucke and Karl Hermann. Produced by Cinetick (coproduced by Norddeutscher Rundfunk). cap-arcona.com.

"*Cap Arcona* Ocean Liner, 1927–1945." www.wrecksite.ed/wreck.aspx?30712.

Clostermann, Pierre. *The Big Show*. 1951 (in French). Reprint, London: Cassell Military Paperbacks, 2004.

Dawson, Jonathan. "The Film Minister: Goebbels and the Cinema in the Third Reich." *Senses of Cinema*, no. 21 (2002). sensesofcinema.com/2002/book-reviews /Goebbels.

Delarue, Jacques. *The Gestapo: A History of Horror*. Translated by Mervyn Savill. New York: Skyhorse, 2008.

Devine, Michael J., Robert P. Watson, and Robert J. Wolz, eds. *Israel and the Legacy of Harry S. Truman*. Kirksville, MO: Truman State University Press, 2008.

Dobson, Christopher, John Miller, and Thomas Payne. *The Cruelest Night: Germany's Dunkirk and the Sinking of the* Wilhelm Gustloff. Boston: Little, Brown, 1979.

Domarus, Max. *Hitler: Speeches and Proclamations*. Vol. 2. Wauconda, IL: Bolchazy-Carducci, 1992.

Der Fall Cap Arcona. Directed by Karl Hermann and Günther Klaucke. Germany: Cinetick, Norddeutscher Rundfunk (CNR), 1995.

Feig, Konnilyn. *Hitler's Death Camps*. New York: Holmes and Meier, 1979.

Fieberg, Malte. Titanic *(1943): Nazi Germany's Version of the Disaster*. Norderstedt, Germany: Books on Demand GmbH, 2012.

Gerhardt, Uta, and Thomas Karlauf. *The Night of Broken Glass: Eyewitness Accounts of Kristallnacht*. Cambridge: Polity, 2012.

Gilbert, Martin. *The Day the War Ended, May 8, 1945: Victory in Europe*. New York: Henry Holt, 1995.

———. *The Holocaust: A History of the Jews in Europe During World War II*. New York: Holt, Rinehart & Winston, 1986.

Gill, Anton. *A Journey Back from Hell: Conversations with Concentration Camp Survivors*. London: Endeavor Press, 2014.

"Greatest Maritime Disasters." International Registry of Sunken Ships. www .shipwreckregistry.com/index6.htm.

Gutman, Israel, ed. *Encyclopedia of the Holocaust*. New York: Macmillan Library Reference, 1990.

Hartmann, Christian. *Operation Barbarossa: Nazi Germany's War in the East, 1941–1945*. New York: Oxford University Press, 2013.

Hastings, Max. *Bomber Command: The Myths and Realities of the Strategic Bombing Offensive, 1939–1945*. New York: Dial Press, 1979.

"Hawker Typhoon and Tempest History." www.military.cz/british/air/war /fighter/tempest/history.htm.

History Undercover: The Typhoons' Last Storm. Directed by Lawrence Bond. New York: History Channel & A&E Television Network, 2000.

Horbach, Michael. *Out of the Night*. Translated from German by N. Watkins. London: Vallentine Mitchell, 1968.

Huchthausen, Peter A. *Shadow Voyage: The Extraordinary Wartime Escape of the Legendary SS* Bremen. New York: Turner, 2008. E-book.

Hull, David Stuart. *Film and the Third Reich: A Study of the German Cinema, 1933–1945*. Berkeley: University of California Press, 1969.

In Which We Serve. Directed by Noel Coward and David Lean. England: British Lion Films, 1942.

Ironlight: History's Greatest Naval Disasters (blog). ironlight.wordpress.com /2010/02/11/sinking-ships/.

Irving, David. *Goring: A Biography*. New York: Macmillan, 1989.

Jackson, Robert. *Dunkirk: The British Evacuation, 1940*. London: Cassell Military Paperbacks, 2001.

Jacobs, Benjamin. *The Dentist of Auschwitz*. Lexington: University Press of Kentucky, 1995.

Jacobs, Benjamin, and Eugene Pool. *The 100-Year Secret: Britain's Hidden World War II Massacre*. Guilford, CT: Lyons Press, 2004.

"Joseph Goebbels." Jewish Virtual Library. www.jewishvirtuallibrary.org/jsource /Holocaust/goebbels.html.

Kalafus, Jim. "The *Cap Arcona*: Gallery of a Lovely—Doomed Liner." *Encyclopedia Titanica*. www.encyclopedia-titanica.org/the-cap-arcona.html.

Kater, Michael H. *Hitler Youth*. Cambridge, MA: Harvard University Press, 2004.

Kelly, C. Brian. *Best Little Stories from World War II: More than 100 True Stories*. Naperville, IL: Cumberland House, 2010.

Kershaw, Ian. *Hitler, 1936–1945: Nemesis*. New York: W. W. Norton, 2000.

Kolberg. Directed by Veit Harlan and Wolfgang Liebeneiner. Germany: Universum Film AG, 1945.

Koldau, Linda Maria. *The* Titanic *on Film: Myth versus Truth*. Jefferson, NC: McFarland, 2012.

Kreimeier, Klaus. *Die UFA-Story*. Munich: Carl Hanser, 1992.

Krockow, Christian Graf von. *Hour of the Women: A Young Mother's Fight to Survive at the Close of World War II*. New York: HarperCollins, 1991.

Lambert, Angela. *The Lost Life of Eva Braun*. London: Century, 2006.

Lange, Wilhelm. Cap Arcona: *Dokumentation*. Stadt Neustadt in Holstein, Germany: Struve's, 1988.

Larsson, Bjorn. "The *Cap Arcona* Maritime Tragedy." www.b-29s-over-korea.com /cap-arcona-maritime-tragedy/.

Ljungström, Henrik. "*Cap Arcona*." www.thegreatoceanliners.com/caparcona2 .html.

Lochner, Louis P., ed. *The Goebbels Diaries, 1942–1943*. New York: Doubleday, 1948.

Longerich, Peter. *Heinrich Himmler: A Life*. New York: Oxford University Press, 2012.

Lord, Walter. *The Miracle of Dunkirk*. Hertfordshire, England: Wordsworth, 1998.

MacDonald, Charles B. *The Siegfried Line Campaign*. Washington, DC: U.S. Army Center of Military History, 1963.

MacLean, French L. *The Camp Men*. Atglen, PA: Schiffer Military History, 1999.

Manvell, Roger, and Heinrich Fraenkel. *Dr. Goebbels: His Life and Death*. New York: Skyhorse, 2010.

Martelli, George. *Agent Extraordinary: The Story of Michel Hollard, DSO, Croix de Guerre*. London: Collins, 1969.

Maurischat, Fritz. "Selpin und *Titanic*." *Filmkundliche Mitteilungen des Deutsches Instituts für Filmkunde*, nos. 2–3 (1970): 228.

Mills-Roberts, Derek. *Clash by Night: A Commando Chronicle*. London: W. Kimber, 1956.

Moeller, Felix. *The Film Minister: Goebbels and the Cinema in the Third Reich*. Fellbach, Germany: Axel Menges, 2001.

Morales, Rafael Marino. "The *Cap Arcona*: The Glamour, the Holocaust." *Temas Generales* (October 2011).

Morris, Jack. *Operation Hannibal*. N.p.: Amazon Digital Services, 2013. E-book.

Mosley, Leonard. *The Reich Marshal: A Biography of Hermann Goering*. London: Weidenfeld and Nicolson, 1974.

Nazi Titanic. Directed by Oscar Chan. New York: History Channel, 2012.

Nesbit, Roy. "*Cap Arcona*: Atrocity or Accident?" *Aeroplane Monthly* (June 1984).

———. "The *Cap Arcona* Disaster." *Aeroplane Monthly* (June 1984).

———. *Coastal Command in Action, 1939–1945*. Phoenix Mill, Gloucestershire: Budding Books, 2000.

———. *Failed to Return: Mysteries of the Air, 1939–1945*. London: Patrick Stephens, 1988.

"Neuengamme." Jewish Virtual Library. www.jewishvirtuallibrary.org/jsource /holocaust/neuengamme.html.

"Neuengamme Victims from the Bombing of the *Cap Arcona* and the *Thielbek*." Jewish Gen. www.jewishgen.org/databases/holocaust/0116_neuengamme. html.

A Night to Remember. Directed by Roy Ward Baker. London: Rank Organisation, 1958.

O'Donnel, James P. *The Bunker*. New York: Da Capo Press, 1978.

Othfors, Daniel, and Henrik Ljongström. "Ship Histories." www.thegreatocean liners.com.

Padfield, Peter. *Dönitz, the Last Führer: Portrait of a Nazi War Leader*. New York: Harper & Row, 1984.

———. *Himmler: Reichsführer-SS*. New York: Henry Holt, 1990.

Peck, Robert E. "The Banning of *Titanic*: A Study of British Post-war Film Censorship in Germany." *Historical Journal of Film, Radio and Television* 20 (2000): 427–453.

———. "Misinformation, Missing Information, and Conjecture: *Titanic* and the Historiography of Third Reich Cinema." *Media History* 6 (2000): 59–73.

Persico, Joseph F. *Roosevelt's Secret War: FDR and World War II Espionage*. New York: Random House, 2001.

Pipes, Jason. "The Sinking of the *Cap Arcona*." *Feldgrau*. www.feldgrau.com/articles .php?id=79.

Pivnik, Sam. *Survivor: Auschwitz, the Death March and My Fight for Freedom*. London: Hodder & Stoughton, 2012.

Prainsack, Hemma Marlene. "How the *Titanic* Sank: Anti-British Propaganda in the National Socialist Movie." PhD diss., University of Vienna, 2013.

Prince, Cathryn. *Death in the Baltic: The World War II Sinking of the* Wilhelm Gustloff. Hampshire, England: Palgrave Macmillan, 2013.

"The Prince of Peace! Count Folke Bernadotte of Wisborg." The Esoteric Curiosa (blog). thesotericcuriosa.globspot.com/2010/10/prince-of-peace-count-folke -bernadotte.html.

Ries, John. "The Little-Known Stories of the *Wilhelm Gustloff*, the *General Steuben* and the *Goya*." *Institute for Historical Review*. ironlight.wordpress.com /2010/02/11/sinking-ships/.

Schön, Heinze. *Die* Cap Arcona—*Katastrophe: Eine Dokumentation Nach Augenzeugen—Berichten*. Stuttgart, Germany: Motorbuch Verlag, 1989.

Schwarberg, Gunther. *Angriffsziel* Cap Arcona. Göttingen, Germany: Steidl Verlag, 1998.

———. *The Murders at Bullenhuser Damm: The SS Doctor and the Children*. Bloomington: Indiana University Press, 1984.

Shapiro, Shelley, ed. *Truth Prevails: Demolishing Holocaust Denial; The End of the Leuchter Report*. New York: Beate Klarsfeld Foundation, 1990.

Sheer Luck: A Holocaust Survival Story. Produced by Justin Weinrich. Visual Center—Online Film Database of Yad Vashem, 2010. Item ID: 10006066.

Shirer, William L. *Berlin Diary: The Journal of a Foreign Correspondent, 1934–1941*. Baltimore: Johns Hopkins University Press, 2002.

Stafford, David. *Endgame, 1945: The Missing Final Chapter of World War II*. New York: Little, Brown, 2007.

Stubbe-da Luz, Helmut. "Karl Kauffman." In *Hamburg Lexikon*, edited by Franklin Koplitzsch and Daniel Tilgner. 3rd ed. Hamburg: Ellert & Richter, 2005.

Taucher unter Toten. Steven Spielberg Film and Video Archive (RG-60.4671; film ID: 2851; event date: 1946; segment at 2:27:52). U.S. Holocaust Memorial Museum. www.ushmm.org/online/film/search/result.php?filmvideo_startdoc=1 &filmvideo.

Thomas, Chris. *Typhoon and Tempest Aces of World War 2*. Botley, Oxford: Osprey, 1999.

Thomson, David. *The New Biographical Dictionary of Film*. 5th ed. New York: Alfred A. Knopf, 2010.

Titanic (1943 original film). Kino Video licensed from Transit Films, Friedrich-Wilhelm Murnau Stiftung, Germany, 2004.

Tomasulo, Frank P. "The Mass Psychology of Fascist Cinema: Leni Riefenstahl's *Triumph of the Will*." In *Documenting the Documentary: Close Readings of Documentary Film and Video*, edited by Barry Keith and Jeannette Sloniowski. 2nd ed. Detroit: Wayne State University Press, 2013.

Trevor-Roper, Hugh, ed. *The Diaries of Joseph Goebbels: Final Entries, 1945*. New York: G. P. Putnam's Sons, 1978.

———. *The Last Days of Hitler*. Chicago: University of Chicago Press, 1992.

Vaughn, Hal. *Doctor to the Resistance: The Heroic True Story of an American Surgeon and His Family in Occupied Paris*. Sterling, VA: Potomac Books, formerly Brassey's, 2004.

Wagner, Jirka. "Hawker Typhoon and Tempest History." *British WWII Fighters*. www.military.cz/british/air/war/fighter/tempest/history.htm.

Walker, Alastair. *Four Thousand Lives Lost: The Inquiries of Lord Mersey into the Sinking of the* Titanic, *the* Empress of Ireland, *the* Falaba *and the* Lusitania. Stroud, Gloucestershire: History Press, 2012.

Weber, Mark. "The 1945 Sinkings of the *Cap Arcona* and the *Thielbek*." *Institute for Historical Review* 19, no. 4 (2000). www.ihr.org/jhr/v19/v19n4p-2_weber.html.

———. "Bergen-Belsen: The Suppressed Story." *Journal of Historical Review* (May–June 1995).

Went the Day Well? Directed by Alberto Cavalcanti. England: Ealing Studios, 1942.

Westermann, Edward B. *Hitler's Police Battalions: Enforcing Racial War in the East*. Lawrence: University Press of Kansas, 2005.

Wistrich, Robert S. "Joseph Goebbels." In *Who's Who in Nazi Germany*. New York: Routledge, 1997.

Wolfer, Joachim. Cap Arcona: *Biographie eines Schiffes; Geschichte einer Reederei*. Hamburg: Koehler, 1977.

Wulf, Joseph. *Film and Theater in Dritten Reich*. Franfurt: Ullstein, 1966.

Zentner, C., and F. Bedürftig, eds. *The Encyclopedia of the Third Reich*. New York: Da Capo Press, 1997.

INDEX

940.542135 WATSON

Watson, Robert P.
The Nazi Titanic

SOF

R4002591683

SOUTH FULTON BRANCH
Atlanta-Fulton Public Library